W9-BXX-917

The
GREAT COMEBACK

The

GREAT COMEBACK

HOW ABRAHAM LINCOLN

BEAT THE ODDS TO WIN THE 1860

REPUBLICAN NOMINATION

GARY ECELBARGER

THOMAS DUNNE BOOKS

ST. MARTIN'S PRESS ❧ NEW YORK

THOMAS DUNNE BOOKS.
An imprint of St. Martin's Press.

www.thomasdunnebooks.com
www.stmartins.com

Design by Maggie Goodman

Library of Congress Cataloging-in-Publication Data

Ecelbarger, Gary L., 1962–
    The great comeback : how Abraham Lincoln beat the odds to win the 1860 Republican
nomination / Gary Ecelbarger.
        p. cm.
    Includes bibliographical references and index.
    ISBN-13: 978-0-312-37413-6 (alk. paper)
    ISBN-10: 0-312-37413-5 (alk. paper)
    1. Lincoln, Abraham, 1809–1865—Political career before 1861.   2. Presidents—United
States—Election—1860.   3. Political campaigns—United States—History—19th century.
4. United States—Politics and government—1857–1861.   5. Republican Party (U.S.:
1854–).   6. Presidential candidates—United States—Biography.   7. Presidents—United
States—Biography.   I. Title.
    E457.4.E28 2008
    973.7092—dc22   2008020649

First Edition: September 2008

10   9   8   7   6   5   4   3   2   1

To my children:

Daniel, Matthew, and Amber

Dare to Dream

CONTENTS

ACKNOWLEDGMENTS

I am indebted to Ed Knappman of New England Publishing Associates for representing this work, and for his astute suggestions to tailor my ideas to a period of time that yields this dramatic story. His faithful dedication to my Lincoln interest will always be appreciated.

I thank those at Thomas Dunne Books/St. Martin's Press for their efforts on my behalf. I am particularly grateful to my editors, Rob Kirkpatrick, for guiding this work to completion; Mark Laflaur, for giving this book a top-notch home; and Lorrie McCann, for her assistance in collating all the necessary ingredients that yielded this book. I am also grateful to Adam Goldberger, the copy editor who so skillfully polished the manuscript by correcting my foibles of punctuation, grammar, and style.

All of the archivists at the libraries and museums I have visited have proven instrumental for this project. In particular, the staff at the Abraham Lincoln Presidential Library have provided invaluable assistance to me during my visits to their departments. Special thanks to Jan Perone and Debbie Ross for guiding me through the library's newspapers; to Debbie Hamm, Glenna Schroeder-Lein, and Cheryl Schnirring for the attention they devoted to me in the manuscript department; and to Roberta Fairburn and Jim Helm for providing rare photographs of some of Lincoln's associates. I am equally indebted to Jane Gastineau, the collections manager at the Lincoln Museum in Fort Wayne, Indiana, for her swift and thorough effort to locate and reproduce the Lincoln images specific to the period covered in this book.

The road to Lincoln's nomination passed through Bloomington, Illinois, where several dedicated "Lincolnites" live today. They are not only some of the most knowledgeable people about Lincoln's career in the state, but are also among the kindest and friendliest people I have ever met. Special thanks are extended Marcia Young, Mark Plummer, Guy Fraker, Danny Leifel, Ed Carroll, and Stewart Winger for treating me to a wonderful experience during my visit to the town in June 2007, and especially to Bob Lenz for organizing the event and for his guidance and patience in handling my Lincoln queries. Fred Wollrab earns my eternal gratitude for guiding me on a tour of the exact location of the scene described in the opening of this book.

I thank my friends Scott Patchan and Rod Gainer for reading portions of my manuscript and offering suggestions to improve it. I am also grateful to David Mowry of Cincinnati, who pinpointed the location of Lincoln's 1859 Cincinnati speech for me during my visit there.

Most important, I wish to acknowledge my wife, Carolyn Ecelbarger, for her patience and support. Her understanding of the necessities of researching and writing history, and the sacrifices she made in order for me to craft and publish this book, are responsible for the completion of this work. I not only love and respect her, I am eternally grateful to her.

The

GREAT COMEBACK

INTRODUCTION

BLOOMINGTON, ILLINOIS: DECEMBER 1858

Abraham Lincoln stepped out of the courthouse and into a biting prairie wind that raced across the town square, a slap in the face to remind him how close he had come to living a dream. Lincoln had to swallow the jagged fact that he was serving a life sentence on the Eighth Judicial Circuit of Illinois, a prisoner of his profession who would rather be somewhere else and doing something else. Two months shy of his fiftieth birthday, Lincoln had just completed his twenty-second year as a circuit-riding attorney. Over that time he had made more than fifty trips to Bloomington, a town he knew as well as any in Illinois save for his home of Springfield. He enjoyed the town; he had many friends here. But he had prepared, hoped, and expected to give up the circuit and enter a national phase of his career—in essence, a new life. Now, based on what had transpired over the previous autumn, Lincoln well knew that he would frequent Bloomington again and again, year after year, and perhaps for the rest of his life.[1]

If Lincoln took the time to size up his year, he would have deemed it more bitter than sweet. He was still smarting over the 1858 Senate campaign, one in which he stood toe-to-toe with "the Little Giant"— Stephen A. Douglas—for seven debates. As a result of that campaign more Republican votes were tallied than Democratic ones in the November elections in the state. But U.S. senators were not elected directly by the vote of the people, as were U.S. representatives. The Founding Fathers had determined that Senate elections would be an example of a "republican democracy"; that is, the voting public directly elected state legislators, who would in turn vote for the U.S. senator. Despite the Republican majority in the popular vote in Illinois in November 1858, more assemblymen were elected from the Democratic Party than from the Republican Party. (The votes were closer in districts where Douglas-supporting legislators prevailed, and there were more holdover Democratic state senators not up for reelection.) So unless a huge surprise was in the offing, in the first week of January the General Assembly was destined to officially award Stephen A. Douglas his third six-year term as United States senator from the state of Illinois.

Lincoln had worked hard to stay stoic and upbeat in the face of his inevitable defeat—his second in four years as a U.S. Senate candidate. "The fight must go on" was his rally cry. "Let no one falter," Lincoln had urged a supporter after the November election; "we shall [have] fun again." Lincoln later claimed he developed this positive attitude while walking home that rainy night in November after learning the disheartening election returns that showed the Democrats maintained control of the legislature. "The path had been worn hog-backed and was slippery," recalled Lincoln. "My foot slipped from under me, knocking the other one out of the way; but I recovered myself & lit square: and I said to myself, *'It's a slip and not a fall.'*"[2]

But Lincoln had indeed fallen in the month that had passed since encouraging Republican Party loyalists. Witnesses testified that even in crowded rooms Lincoln somehow looked alone, "as if he had lost all his friends." He would not conceal his melancholy; when asked the reason for his sadness, he responded by linking his Senate defeat with his approaching fiftieth birthday, an age that reflected most of a man's productive life in the nineteenth century.[3]

One of Lincoln's Bloomington friends, Jesse Fell, was passing along the south side of the town square at the same time Lincoln exited the courthouse. "I espied the tall form of Mr. Lincoln emerging from the courthouse door," recalled Fell decades later. "I stopped until he came across the street." The two exchanged friendly greetings, and Fell likely saw his comrade in this usual state of dejection. Few men could pick Lincoln up from these depths. Jesse Fell, however, was one capable of grand successes. Fell and Lincoln had been friends and political allies for a quarter of a century, since their earliest days together in the state legislature when it met in Vandalia in the mid-1830s. Fell had founded Bloomington's Republican newspaper, the *Pantagraph*; had been so steeped in Republican politics as to be recognized as a "founding father" of the state party in Illinois; and was an original supporter of Lincoln for the Senate seat in 1858.

Lincoln's gloominess likely steered Fell to act in his friend's favor. He escorted Lincoln to his brother's law office, where they could discuss a matter Fell deemed deeply important. Having traveled extensively in all the eastern states except Maine, as well as in Indiana, Michigan, and Ohio, Fell assured Lincoln that he felt the pulse of the voters in those states. He saw firsthand how Lincoln had risen from obscurity in those states to national name recognition as a result of the press coverage of his debates with Senator Douglas. "I have a decided impression," declared Fell to Lincoln, "that if your popular history and efforts on the slavery question can be sufficiently brought before the people, you can be made a formidable, if not a successful, candidate for the Presidency."

This likely was not the first time Lincoln had heard this through a confidant; nor was it the first time his performance against Douglas had people consider him presidential timber. Newspapers in Illinois and Ohio tied Lincoln's name with the presidency; others as far away as Reading, Pennsylvania, confirmed Fell's appraisal of Lincoln as a first-class statesman for his debate performance, implying that he was qualified to handle the highest political office in the land.

But Fell's blockbuster of an idea failed to shake the blues from his friend. "Oh Fell, what's the use of talking of me for the presidency," Lincoln responded, noting that New York senator William H. Seward and Ohio governor Salmon P. Chase were powerhouses and better-known representatives of the Republican Party. Fell claimed that these supposed giants were in fact flawed candidates, with past proclamations and current positions that painted them as radicals. Fell maintained that both of these front-runners could be upset by a rising star like Lincoln, whose consistent, middle-ground politics appeared attractive to a general electorate, in contrast to the extreme views of Seward, Chase, Senator Simon Cameron of Pennsylvania, and other nationally prominent Republicans. All Fell needed from Lincoln was for him to prepare an autobiographical sketch that Fell could circulate in his native state of Pennsylvania and elsewhere, "and thus help in manufacturing sentiment in your favor."[4]

Lincoln refused to bite; in fact, his melancholy deepened after he was asked to provide the story of his life and career. Lincoln needed only to compare his story to that of the early presidential front-runners in the Republican Party to depress him further. His career was a story of forward and reverse steps. According to his friend and junior law partner, William Herndon, Lincoln first dreamed of destiny in 1840. Back then he was an active and rising Whig, running state party functions and events during the presidential campaign in Illinois. He honed his skills as a debater—several times matching skills against a young Stephen A. Douglas. Lincoln's political star shone brightly during the campaign to elect William Henry Harrison as the first Whig to occupy the White House. By the end of the campaign, Lincoln was known statewide and was even mentioned as a gubernatorial candidate.

But all of Lincoln's gains made in 1840 seemed to disappear during the winter of 1840–41. His political philosophy at the time collapsed with the state's financial health. He was completing his fourth consecutive term in the Illinois General Assembly, but he and his fellow Whigs were blamed for causing the state's financial crisis, by overextending monetary resources for internal improvements. Lincoln also broke his engagement with Mary Todd that winter, believing he was in love with another woman, a teenager named Matilda Edwards, who infatuated the thirty-one-year-old Lincoln although she never reciprocated his crush on her. His mental and physical health drastically declined, and several months were necessary for him to make a full recovery. He subsequently rekindled his relationship with Miss Todd and married her in 1842. His social stability perhaps helped his political recovery. Lincoln ascended the political ranks enough to win election to the U.S. House of Representatives in 1846.

He served one term, an unfortunate term for him due to his opposition to the United States' involvement in the war with Mexico. For calling upon a resolution to identify the spot where Mexico invaded U.S. soil, Lincoln was castigated for opposing President James K. Polk, a successful president and commander in chief during a popular war. Lincoln returned to Illinois with the unsavory moniker "Spotty Lincoln." It stuck to him like a barnacle. Lincoln believed his political career was over and had settled his mind to live the rest of his life as a circuit-riding attorney. "When Lincoln returned home from Congress in 1849, he was a politically dead and buried man," insisted Billy Herndon.[5]

Lincoln experienced a political resurrection five years later in 1854. Senator Douglas rammed through Congress the Kansas-Nebraska Act, a law that repealed the Missouri Compromise of 1820 and opened territories and future states west of the Mississippi River to slavery, reversing a thirty-five-year-old ban in the northern segments of the Louisiana Purchase. Douglas predicted that the Kansas-Nebraska Act would cause a "hell of a storm." It certainly did. It fractionated political parties into pro- and anti-Nebraska segments, eventually driving the Whig Party into extinction. But the death of the Whigs led to the birth of the Republican Party, a fusion of "anti-Nebraska" Whigs, Democrats, and other smaller political factions.

Lincoln became the most vocal spokesman of the new party even before it assumed its new name. As an anti-Nebraska Whig, Lincoln returned to the stump in the autumn of 1854, debating Douglas and delivering his biggest speech ever, a well-researched and impeccably delivered stemwinder opposing Douglas and his bill. His speech was so successful, and Lincoln was so pleased with the reaction to it, that he became convinced he was a viable U.S. Senate candidate after anti-Nebraska assemblymen surprisingly won the majority of statewide elections in 1854. On the first ballot Lincoln fell five votes short of winning the February 1855 election in the Eighteenth General Assembly. Unable to pick up votes ten ballots later, he conceded his loss by shifting his support to anti-Nebraska Democrat Lyman Trumbull (who became a Republican later in the 1850s).

Despite the election defeat, Lincoln was back in politics to stay, embracing the new Republican Party. Briefly talked up as a vice-presidential candidate in 1856, Lincoln made his greatest mark in 1858 by challenging Douglas for the Senate. The election and incumbency of predominantly pro-Douglas legislators in November had sealed Lincoln's fate, scheduled to be official on January 5, 1859. Although he was considered a strong Republican, Lincoln could hardly look at that political career—one controversial term in the House of Representatives and two failed attempts at the U.S. Senate—and deem worth summarizing in a biographical sketch for Jesse Fell to circulate. By contrast, William Henry Seward in New York, Salmon P. Chase of Ohio, and Simon Cameron of Pennsylvania were all successful political figures with national stature. Lincoln's biography could not compete with theirs. On top of that, Seward had the backing of Thurlow Weed, the head of New York's and the nation's most formidable political machine, while Chase was backed by powerful Republicans in Ohio, as was Senator Cameron by Pennsylvania Republicans. It was no surprise that these prominent Republicans hailed from the three states that would contribute the most delegates at the national convention that would nominate the party's candidate in the spring of 1860.

Lincoln could hardly consider himself an attractive candidate during the waning days of 1858. He was a self-taught attorney, less-than-happily married, with three surviving children. Lincoln considered his father so insignificant that he had decided not to travel to attend the old man's funeral back in the winter of 1851. (Indeed, his father died without ever seeing his daughter-in-law and grandchildren, despite living within two days' ride of them for the last twenty years of his life.) Lincoln's mother had died when he was eight years old; throughout his adult life Lincoln believed she was a product of an illegitimate union, a scandal that could never be refuted. His humble upbringing in Kentucky and Indiana was politically attractive, especially to the antiaristocratic segments of society, but Lincoln was about to enter his thirtieth year as a resident of Illinois. Neither his profession nor his political history had convinced him that he could turn his handicapped childhood and unremarkable adulthood into a great American story for Fell to market outside of Illinois.

Fell's enthusiasm about the 1860 presidential election failed to lift Lincoln from his dark mood. Lincoln turned to him and explained, "Fell, I admit the force of much that you say, and admit that I am ambitious, and would like to be President." He then shot down Fell's suggestion by claiming that "there is no such good luck for me as the Presidency." As for marketing his biography, Lincoln declined again: "There is nothing in my early history that would interest you or anybody else." He curtly ended the conversation with his friend, bade him a good night, wrapped himself in a shawl to shield his clean-shaven face and upper body from the brutal winter winds, exited the building, and walked away.[6]

"And thus ended, for the time being, my pet scheme of helping to make Lincoln President," said Jesse Fell in recounting the December evening encounter. But he refused to let Lincoln have the last word that night. As Lincoln's six-foot-four-inch, shawl-wrapped frame disappeared in the darkness, Fell shouted out to him that this was not the last of it. Although Lincoln must have heard him as he walked toward his hotel, he ignored his friend. As far as he was concerned, this *was* the last of it. The General Assembly vote on January 5 would pound the nails into the Lincoln-for-President coffin and turn away even Jesse Fell, seemingly the only pallbearer to carry that coffin.

Little did Lincoln realize that what he thought would be the upcoming day of his political death, January 5, would also spur his resurrection, and imbue him with determination and passion to buttress his ever-glowing ambition to counter every argument he placed in front of Jesse Fell. It would set the stage for a dazzling political comeback, an unprecedented sixteen-and-a-half-month surge that carried Lincoln from the depths of despair to the exhilaration of claiming his party's most cherished prize.

One

RECOVERY

EARLY WEDNESDAY AFTERNOON, January 5, 1859, one
hundred members of the Twenty-first General Assembly of Illinois
made official what Abraham Lincoln as well as nearly everyone in the state
of Illinois had for two months deemed inevitable: the reelection of Stephen
A. Douglas to his third consecutive term in the U.S. Senate. Springfield
spectators—mostly Douglas Democrats—crammed the gallery and the
lobby of the House of Representatives in the twenty-year-old domed capitol building where the assemblymen completed the U.S. Senate election by
a strict party-line vote. Douglas received fifty-four votes from state senators
and representatives, while Lincoln garnered forty-six out of the one hundred cast.

The onlookers reacted to the fait accompli as if the result had been sus-
penseful. "The result was announced at half-past two o'clock P. M., and the
Douglasites went crazy soon afterwards," complained a vastly outnum-
bered Lincoln supporter, who claimed the Democrats "made enough
noise generally to give a nervous man a severe headache." The galleries
above the hall shook with the boisterous acclaim by the Douglas supporters, relieved that the hard-fought campaign of the previous summer and
autumn had produced the result expected from the November election.[1]

Charles Lanphier, the editor of Springfield's Democrat-biased newspaper, the *Illinois State Register*, witnessed the uninhibited joy displayed upon the announcement, a reaction that spilled out the doors and onto the streets surrounding the state capitol. He took in the House speaker's inability to maintain order, the processions, the banners, the waving handkerchiefs, and even the firing of a small cannon rolled into the town square for the occasion. Lanphier immediately sent a telegram to Senator Douglas, who was traveling to Washington. "Glory to God and the Sucker Democracy, Douglas 54, Lincoln 41," crowed Lanphier in his message (the term "Sucker" was a nickname for Illinoisans). Although he shortchanged Lincoln by five votes in his wired tally, Lanphier accurately gauged the reaction to it: "Announcement followed by shouts of immense crowd present. Town wild with excitement. Democrats firing salute. . . . Guns, music and whisky rampant."[2]

Not surprised, but pleased and relieved at the message transmitted to him, Senator Douglas wired a short response from Baltimore back to Lanphier: "Let the voice of the people rule." The editor of the city's rival paper, the Republican-biased *Illinois State Journal*, spewed bitterness at the irony of the senator's response, given that pro-Lincoln legislators had received more votes from the people of Illinois than had those who supported Douglas, based on the November election totals. "If he were to allow any such thing as this," wrote the editor in reference to Douglas and his telegram, "he would not have been re-elected. The voice of the people of Illinois is against him. He is a minority Senator." Equally bitter, the *Chicago Press and Tribune* seethed, "Mr. D. can now finish his wanderings, take his seat and uncork his vials of wrath."[3]

Archibald Williams, a Springfield judge and a staunch Republican, had heard quite enough of the celebratory voices of the Democrats at the state capitol. He took it upon himself to notify the loser of what had just taken place. Walking westward from the building, he crossed to the northwestern side of the town square. Williams beelined to the LINCOLN & HERNDON sign swinging on its rusting hinges over the 100 block of Fifth Street. He walked up the narrow stairway behind the sign, traversed an equally narrow hallway above John Irwin's store, and entered the Lincoln-Herndon Law Office. There Williams found the senior partner of the firm sitting and writing alone at one of the two tables forming a sloppy T at the center of the unkempt room.[4]

Lincoln worked alone this day, trying to treat this as a normal Wednesday of legal business. He had been to the capitol earlier, getting a request granted by the Illinois Supreme Court for an extension to a case before that august body. After leaving the court chambers on the lower floor, Lincoln left the statehouse rather than ascend the spiral staircase to the bicameral legislature on the second floor. He removed himself from witnessing the painful vote destined to go against him and instead returned to the confines of his office. This was the end point of his routine six-block walk from his house. Lincoln neglected the ugly effects of a mild winter on the town square this day, but newsmen did not. "Look at the dark, dismal, life-endangering, unfathomable profundity of mud," wailed an Ohio reporter assigned to Springfield to cover the proceedings of the legislature. "An Arkansas swamp must be attractive in comparison."[5]

After enduring a hectic two-season campaign in 1858, Lincoln had dedicated himself to his law work, in part to offset the financial difficulties of the Senate campaign. Indeed, this very day he was in the midst of winning nearly $1,400 for two clients for whom he filed cases for the preceding year. No one needed to tell him that Douglas was elected, for even though the office was in the back—well west of the street—with his two windows overlooking a vacant side alley instead of the public square, Lincoln could hardly ignore the reverberations of the booming cannon and the cacophonous band on the streets of the square delivering that message loud and clear. The appearance of Judge Williams at the doorway would trigger Lincoln's first reaction to Douglas's election.[6]

"Well," declared Williams, "the Democrats are making a great noise over their victory."

Lincoln responded, "Yes, Archie, Douglas has taken the trick, but the game is not played out."[7]

Once again he put on a facade to conceal his misery at what had transpired. He yearned to be a senator, but with Douglas safe for six more years and the other seat occupied by Lyman Trumbull, a friend who shared Lincoln's views on opposing the spread of slavery into the territories of the United States, Lincoln saw his chances to earn the seat during the prime of his life as remote at best. He was resolved to support Trumbull and Republican candidates in future races dedicated to prevent slavery's spread, but the appearance was deceiving. Lincoln was indeed an ambitious man; toiling behind the scenes was not in his nature.

Within perhaps an hour of Williams's brief meeting with Lincoln, another fellow attorney burst into the law office. Henry C. Whitney expected to commiserate with Billy Herndon, Lincoln's junior law partner, but was surprised to find Lincoln working this day without any sign of Herndon. Like Archie Williams, Whitney was fed up with how unabashedly "the unterrified Democracy proceeded to paint the town very red." Whitney had abruptly excused himself from a contentious meeting of Republicans in the immediate wake of the legislative vote, disgusted at how quickly party operatives blamed Lincoln for their defeat to the gloaters of Springfield. Whitney recalled, "I found Lincoln entirely alone—entirely idle—gloomy as midnight, and evidently, brooding over his ill-fortune." Spending more time with Lincoln that evening, Whitney was struck by his bitterness. "I expect everyone to desert me," predicted Lincoln, perhaps in response to hearing about the verbal defections in the aftermath of the vote in the legislature.[8]

As if triggered by the vote in the General Assembly, the weather in central Illinois changed abruptly in the wake of the election. Snow began to fall later that day and continued unabated for the next forty hours, throughout all of Thursday, producing the first genuine winter's day in Springfield for the season. Although the blanket of white covered the hideous mud, the rutted roads froze solid, making it impossible to travel by sleigh. Temperatures dipped and then hovered close to single-digit readings, leaving residents longing for the mild early-January climate they had enjoyed in the prairie land to launch the new year.[9]

The inclement weather failed to hamper the business of politics in the center of Illinois. On that snowy night of January 6, Lincoln joined a contingent of fellow Republicans for an informal strategy meeting at the state capitol. Apart from his house on the northeast corner of Eighth and Jackson streets and the law office, Lincoln spent more time in the statehouse than in any other building in Springfield. Since its completion in the winter of 1840–41, Lincoln had routinely handled cases in the supreme court office, studied in the state library, delivered stirring speeches in the Hall of the House of Representatives, and visited Assembly members during breaks in their wintertime legislative sessions.

This particular Thursday night Lincoln and his Republican allies descended to the lower floor of the capitol building, to the library room. Perhaps as many as a dozen men of like political mind gathered amid the collection of books housed in the room to discuss informally Republican plans for the coming year and the following—particularly the grand election year of 1860. The prominent lawyers and judges of the region, including John M. Palmer, Leonard Swett, Jesse Fell, and Ozias M. Hatch, met with their old friend Lincoln to analyze Senator Trumbull's reelection bid as well as the 1860 presidential prospects of western Republican candidates.

One of Lincoln's oldest friends, Judge David Davis, sat with him that night in the library. The Davis-Lincoln friendship had begun shortly after Davis moved from New England to Illinois in the mid-1830s. Both men became twenty-year fixtures of the Eighth Judicial Circuit, Davis the judge and Lincoln the lawyer traveling together from town to town, sharing abominable meals and abysmal lodgings, and enjoying the bond strengthened by two decades of companionship, a bond that never interfered with the unbiased dispersal of duties of the judge and attorney in the same courthouse trial. On occasion, Davis even had Lincoln preside over cases when he could not be available to judge them.

They were professionals, but not immune from acting like children. Leonard Swett, also in the library that night, would fondly tell anyone asking about Lincoln of the first time he met his lanky friend. It was during an evening several years before in the prairie town of Danville, one of the county-seat stops on the circuit. Informed at a lodging site that Lincoln could be found upstairs visiting Davis, Swett sheepishly climbed the stairs to the esteemed judge's room and knocked on the door. Two voices on the other side told him in unison to enter. Swett opened the door to behold a spectacle he would never forget: Lincoln and Davis "engaged in a lively battle with pillows, tossing them at each other's heads." After the rotund judge (Davis weighed over three hundred pounds) and the towering figure battling him completed their pillow fight, the latter—decked out in an immense saffron yellow nightshirt, with the largest feet Swett had ever seen protruding from below the garment—crossed the room and announced, "My name is Lincoln," as he shook Swett's hand. "I will not say he reminded me of Satan," confessed Swett of his first encounter with Lincoln, "but he certainly was the ungodliest figure I had ever seen."[10]

So the strategy meeting of January 6 was not simply one among professionals and politicians; it was among a group of old friends who knew
one another well enough to converse freely and informally as they shared
their thoughts. John M. Palmer started the discussion by pointing out the
huge punch the Republican Party had taken in 1858, not only from Douglas's victory but from the defection of Horace Greeley into the Douglas
camp. Greeley was the editor of the *New York Tribune*, the most prominent
Republican newspaper in the country. His shift to Douglas spoke volumes
of the Little Giant's political acumen and bode ill for Republicans across
the country and in the library room that night. That the four-year-old
party might disintegrate in 1859 was evidence of the long climb Republicans had to make in order to oust Democrats in the 1860 elections. Yet,
despite this devastating blow, all in the room shared the desire to maintain
the party and fight for its principles.[11]

The talk then turned to the presidency. Probably because of Lincoln's
reaction to his suggestion back in December, Jesse Fell apparently never
pressed the issue of Lincoln as a potential nominee for the Illinois bigwigs
to back. He and Lincoln generally remained silent through this part of the
evening's meeting. Ozias Hatch, the Illinois secretary of state, also remained mum on Lincoln that evening although Hatch's correspondents
had begun to clamor, "Cant we make him President or vice."[12]

The night was a watershed moment for Abraham Lincoln, not just for
what was said but for what was not said at the meeting. After listening to
the men drone on about the strengths and weaknesses of each name put
forward, Lincoln was vexed that the most obvious name—*his*—had yet to
enter into the conversation. Perhaps this was purposeful, given that the
discussion transpired in the wake of the Senate defeat, merely one day after the official vote; or (as Lincoln may have gleaned from his conversation
with Henry Whitney twenty-four hours earlier) the men in the library
may never have considered Lincoln—now a two-time Senate loser—as a
viable presidential candidate.

Lincoln stewed as his associates dragged out the meeting without mentioning his name, particularly because these men more than any other
should have considered him as the nominee to favor, even though Lincoln
had not publicly announced it. It was hardly a new concept. The *Olney
Times* had already placed "Lincoln for President" on its masthead that

month, and several other papers had strongly hinted at his candidacy. Lincoln must have been particularly disappointed in Davis, not knowing that the judge was harboring ten-year-old ill feelings toward Lincoln because he would not openly support Davis in his bid for circuit judge of the district in 1848 (his opponent was a distant family member of Mrs. Lincoln). Two decades later Davis had still not forgiven him, complaining to Billy Herndon that Lincoln lacked the manhood to override his wife's wishes to support a friend who had done so many favors for him.[13]

According to a colleague, Lincoln's decades-long bond of friendship with Davis had begun to weaken by the late 1850s because Lincoln did not view Davis under an eternally flattering light. "I don't think Lincoln held Davis very close to his heart," opined Whitney, who believed Lincoln thought Davis "too loquacious—too vain—too vacillating in his friendships." If the assessment was accurate, then Davis's personality ran counter to Lincoln's, which Davis claimed lacked emotion or spontaneity. Whatever mind game was being played out that night in the library, Lincoln seethed at the lack of regard and respect he felt he deserved. Not able to tolerate it any longer, Lincoln spoke up. "Why don't you run me?" he blurted. "I can be nominated, I can be elected, and I can run the Government."[14]

Lincoln's declaration caught them all by surprise. "We all looked at him and saw that he was not joking," Judge Davis recalled. Someone followed up on Lincoln's suggestion and declared, "We are going to bring out Abraham Lincoln as a candidate for President." Others discussed him as a vice-presidential candidate—a position for which Lincoln had no desire. According to Whitney (who did not mention Lincoln's earlier outburst), Lincoln rose and began to speak, but everyone coerced him to keep quiet, for all had been said that was needed. No consensus was reached, nor was Lincoln expecting one. A year and a half away from the national convention, Lincoln merely wished his friends and allies to include him in the mix. His blunt outburst must have pleased Jesse Fell, who could now take satisfaction in encouraging Lincoln to reach higher than he had ever wished to reach before. The Republicans adjourned their meeting that night without conclusion but finally considered seriously the proclamation made by Lincoln. Completely satisfied with the outcome, Lincoln remarked as the group began to disperse, "I am real glad we have had this little talk; I feel much better for it."[15]

Unburdening himself, Lincoln also worked himself free from his dark mood. Reporter Henry Villard saw this the next afternoon when he visited Lincoln. Villard had first met Lincoln the previous October during the Senate campaign. Writing for a pro-Democrat German newspaper at the time, Villard was left with a less-than-flattering first impression of Lincoln, a man he thought was unsophisticated. But he warmed to his subject, particularly to his folksy charm. Once during the 1858 campaign, Lincoln told Villard that his wife expected him to win the Senate seat as a stepping-stone to the presidency. Not exhibiting the same ambition as his wife at the time, Lincoln exclaimed to Villard, "Just think of such a sucker as me as President!"[16]

Villard may not have been in Illinois long enough to understand Lincoln's use of the word "sucker." Nor, apparently, did Villard remind Lincoln of the conversation when he met him again in January 1859. Reporting on activities of the Illinois legislature, his first assignment for the *Cincinnati Daily Commercial*, Villard called upon Lincoln two days after the official defeat and half a day after the Republican meeting in the capitol. "He is just as full of fun now than he ever was," observed the reporter, pleased to see Lincoln "possessed of that never failing remedy against the embittering influences of disappointment and defeat—good humor." When he asked Lincoln for his reaction to the reelection of Senator Douglas, Lincoln entertained Villard by comparing it to the response of a Kentucky boy who got his finger squeezed: "[I am] too big to cry, and too badly hurt to laugh."[17]

The "good humor" remained with Lincoln throughout the month. He found time apart from his heavy docket of work in the U.S. courts for festive events. During the last week of January he attended a banquet commemorating the one hundredth anniversary of the birth of one of his favorite poets, Robert Burns. Lincoln participated in the heavy toasting with the other attendees of the centennial celebration. He did not discuss his presidential plans at this or any other public event. Notwithstanding his self-effacing statement to Henry Villard in 1858, Lincoln did indeed consider himself presidential material. This was consistent with his overpowering ambition, a trait appreciated by very few of his contemporaries. Billy Herndon understood Lincoln's ambition better than anyone. He insisted that any man who was led to believe that Lincoln passively waited for others to achieve for him "has a very erroneous knowledge of Lincoln. He was always calculating, and always planning ahead. His ambition was a little engine that knew no rest."[18]

Lincoln revealed his hand in the January 6 meeting, but for the rest of 1859 he hid his cards. He told Archie Williams, "The game is not played out," but he decided his best chance was by the tactics of surprise and momentum. In the meantime, he realized he had to stay in the game for the next year and a half, underestimated by the politicos and the press as he sought to increase his visibility and relevance both in Illinois and throughout the Northern states. Above all, Lincoln needed to vie for the presidency without appearing to do so. Herndon maintained that Lincoln was a master of hiding his desires: "He had his burning and his consuming ambition, but he kept his secrets and opened not."[19]

Perhaps Mary Lincoln burned with more ambition for "Old Abe" than he did himself. Whereas Lincoln had viewed membership in the U.S. Senate as the pinnacle of his political life, Mary Lincoln had considered it a rung on the ladder to the presidency. Since January 6, Abraham Lincoln was on record with his presidential intentions, a plan he likely revealed to his wife, if only to lift her spirits and plant in her mind the notion that he needed not to be a senator before they resided in the White House.

One week after the Burns celebration, Mary Lincoln had recovered enough from her husband's Senate defeat to host a large party at the Lincoln home. This February 2 event was a festive one, like the previous public gathering at the house on the northeast corner of Eighth and Jackson streets. No one at the party remarked about anything Mary Lincoln had said or done that night. Based upon gossip generated from previous activities at the Lincoln home, the absence of opinions on Mary Lincoln that night meant that the party ran without incident.[20]

Whether deserved or not, Mary Lincoln had provided an incredible amount of grist for the local rumor mill ever since she moved to Springfield at the end of 1839 as twenty-one-year-old Mary Todd. Lincoln had courted her during her first winter in the new state capital, vying for her attention against other potential suitors (including Stephen A. Douglas). A sometimes stormy, hot-and-cold relationship was consummated three years later when they were married in November 1842. Their first child, Robert Todd Lincoln, was born exactly nine months after their wedding night. Robert was accompanied by three younger brothers (Edward died in 1850). Mary's four known pregnancies over the first eleven years of marriage—the span of her childbearing years—bore evidence that behind closed doors Abraham and Mary Lincoln shared a passion for each other that was typical of any husband and wife in their era.

When those doors opened, however, the Lincolns were often viewed as a less than happily married couple. A smattering of Springfielders insisted that Mary Lincoln was an unreasonable and unstable wife who frequently scolded her passive husband and sometimes physically abused and threatened him with fists, a broom, and even a table knife. (One person asserted that this began when they were newlyweds, with an enraged Mary throwing hot coffee in Lincoln's face at a breakfast table occupied by gasping diners.) Her temper became legendary (Billy Herndon called her "the female wildcat of the age"). Judge David Davis concluded that Lincoln was happiest while away from home when he traveled on the judicial circuit. Insisting that Lincoln oftentimes remained on the road over weekends while most lawyers had returned to their families, Davis surmised, "It seems to me that L. was not domestically happy."[21]

But Lincoln never confessed to his friend that he was unhappy in his marriage, nor did he tell Billy Herndon or anyone else within his inner circle of confidants. He rarely registered a complaint about Mary throughout sixteen wedded years. He was more analytical than artistic (although poetry was one of his passions); therefore, Lincoln would never be known as a romantic, or ever viewed as a loving husband. Despite his and his wife's personal shortcomings, if Lincoln was not happy with his domestic life, he appeared to be satisfied with it—Mary's erratic moments notwithstanding.

It appears the greatest source of Lincoln's domestic satisfaction was his children, particularly his two youngest sons, who became his constant companions in Springfield throughout the latter half of the 1850s. Thomas—called "Tad" by his parents—was five years old in the winter of 1859, and William ("Willie") had just turned eight. Their dad, who celebrated his fiftieth birthday on February 12, was old enough to be their grandfather and doted on them like one. A common sight along the paved portions of Springfield was of Lincoln pulling a little red wagon with both boys sitting in it for the ride. "He was the most indulgent parent I ever knew," concluded Joe Gillespie, a fellow lawyer and friend of Lincoln's since the 1830s.[22]

Gillespie was not guilty of uttering an overstatement. Willie and Tad had developed an unflattering reputation as brats, in large part due to Lincoln's lax discipline. "His children litterally ran over him," Gillespie observed, "and he was powerless to withstand their importunities." Lincoln's associates automatically gauged the boys' behavior differently than that of other boys their age. One of Lincoln's friends revealed to his wife his relief after spending time with Willie and Tad, commenting to her that "the children have been reasonably good considering what they are."[23]

Other associates of Lincoln never regarded the two boys as "reasonably good." Much to the dismay of Billy Herndon, on occasional Sundays Lincoln would pull his little wagonload right up to the law office and bring the boys upstairs to run wild while he and Herndon wrote out legal papers. "The children—spoilt ones to be sure—would tear up the office," recalled Herndon, who would seethe as Lincoln let them "scatter the books, smash up pens, spill the ink, and piss all over the floor." Deciding not to intervene with his partner's parenting, Herndon held his tongue, but he admitted how much he wanted "to wring their little necks." He claimed that Lincoln was entirely charmed by their antics; Herndon maintained, "Had they shit in Lincoln's hat and rubbed it on his boots, he would have laughed and thought it smart."[24]

In the winter of 1859 Lincoln may have been blind to the escapades of his children, but he was well attuned to political activities that ran counter to his own ambitions. Near the close of the legislative session of the Twenty-first General Assembly, the Republicans of the Illinois House and Senate held a legislative caucus. Their purpose: to plan how to get Lincoln on the national ticket for the 1860 election. But the prevailing attitude of the members was that Lincoln could not carry the top of the ticket; he was not presidential timber in their collective mind. They felt the most feasible approach to get an Illinois man on the ticket was to push Republican leaders to secure Lincoln's nomination as vice president, a more comfortable place as a strong Western balance for an Eastern presidential nominee like Senator Seward. Perhaps none of these assemblymen had sat in the capitol's library room that cold night in January when Lincoln had blurted out his presidential desires. Few of them understood how repulsed Lincoln would be by the vice presidency.

One legislator sitting in the caucus who shared Lincoln's mind-set in the matter was Norman B. Judd. As chairman of the Republican State Central Committee and associated with the widely circulated party organ, the *Chicago Press and Tribune*, Judd was one of the most influential Republicans in the state. Like many members of the fledgling Republican Party, Judd began his political career as a Democrat until the Kansas-Nebraska Act of 1854 disillusioned him. He lived in Chicago but after fourteen consecutive years in the state senate was also a mainstay of Springfield.

As one of the most experienced legislators in Illinois history, Judd had earned a reputation as "the shrewdest politician" in the state. He knew how to work a room, relying on sound experience and a winning demeanor. He impressed associates as "a wonderfully indefatigable and genial man," known for the glitter in his eyes and the lighted cigar between his lips. Considered more a partisan than a statesman, Judd was oftentimes able to conceal his own ambitions; a friend considered him "sly, cat-like and mysterious." The forty-four-year-old New York native had his sights set on the governorship of Illinois in the winter of 1859, a seat to be decided upon in the election of 1860. "Judd ought to be Governor," asserted a Republican in the west-central portion of Illinois; "he has worked hard for our party and is a good man."[25]

There appear to have been as many Judd detractors within Illinois Republican ranks as there were supporters. Judd's alliances, politics, and ambitions sometimes caused more friction within his party than with the opposition, a problem tracing back to the U.S. Senate election of February 1855. Back then, before the Republican Party existed in name, in Illinois, Judd had voted for Lyman Trumbull (a fellow anti-Nebraska Democrat) and not his Whig friend Abraham Lincoln, earning the enmity of other members of Lincoln's circle. Mary Lincoln disliked him. Billy Herndon never trusted him; neither did David Davis. Their distaste for Judd heightened after Lincoln's 1858 defeat, when Judd was made the scapegoat for mismanaging their man's campaign. Lincoln's own trust in Judd remained solid in the face of both Senate defeats, a fact that enhanced the jealous desires of Lincoln's friends to drive a wedge between the two.[26]

In the winter of 1859 Judd appeared oblivious of the growing animus against him, and was more concerned with improving Lincoln's long-shot chances in 1860. Rumors would persist until his death that Judd never

took Lincoln seriously as a presidential candidate, but his actions beginning in the aftermath of Lincoln's loss to Douglas suggest otherwise. A
rock-solid Lincoln devotee, Judd appeared to be the only ally that winter,
aside from Jesse Fell, looking to hoist Lincoln onto the political mountaintop and not the ledge below it. Judd grew increasingly disgusted at the
February caucus in the capitol as each Republican legislator took his turn
to speak in support of promoting Lincoln for the vice presidency. "When
it came my turn to give my views," remembered Judd seventeen years
later, "I strongly opposed this action, saying the proper and only thing to
do was to claim the Presidency for him and nothing less." To Judd's dismay, the caucus dissolved with the near-unanimous intention of getting
Lincoln on the second slot of the national ticket.[27]

It was likely Judd who notified Lincoln about the action of the Republican assemblymen. Within a few days of the meeting, Lincoln entered
the house of representatives—the scene of so many big events in his professional life, from his rousing "Springfield" speech in October 1854 to the
more famous and controversial "House Divided" speech of June 1858—
on the west side of the second floor of the capitol. Another big event occurred in the senate chambers on February 3 when a chimney fire broke
out in the northeast corner and threatened to destroy the entire building.
Although firefighters quickly extinguished the threat, the scars were present along the eastern side of the statehouse for the remainder of the session.[28]

Lincoln could not have missed the sight and smell of the smoke damage the day he visited the General Assembly. The house members had apparently taken a break from their late-winter session, allowing Lincoln to
converse with Republican Elijah M. Haines, a Chicago legislator representing Cook County. Small talk eventually worked its way to the caucus
decision. Lincoln clumsily tied in his cloaked desire with an anecdote.
Haines claimed that Lincoln "answered by a story which I do not clearly
recall, but the application of which was that he scarcely considered himself a big enough man for President, while the Vice-Presidency was
scarcely big enough office for one who aspired to a seat in the Senate of
the United States."[29]

Most noteworthy in Lincoln's discussion with Haines was not his disdain
for the vice presidency, but his disingenuous claim that the presidency was

too big an office for his skills. Lincoln had purposely sold himself short; but his declared lack of qualification for the presidency did equal an admission of a lack of interest. Still, the mantra he uttered on January 6—"I can be nominated, I can be elected, and I can run the Government"—negated his feigned lack of fitness for the job. Aware that he was a long-shot candidate, a name near the end of a lengthy list of prominent Republicans claiming national appeal, Lincoln must have calculated there would be little risk in personally trying to start a groundswell. If this failed, as appeared likely in the first half of 1859, he would at least lift his prominence in the wake of the defeat to Douglas, and perhaps this would keep him viable to run against Douglas again for the coveted Senate seat in 1864.

Lincoln had decided that he needed to generate interest in promoting his name at the top of the ticket and not in the second slot. The only way Lincoln could get full-hearted support from Republican leaders was for them to see an elevated interest from the populace in him. This could be achieved only by a response to Lincoln's words and deeds. Thus, Lincoln's strategy was to keep his name viable through public presentation and behind-the-scenes activism.

He learned a lesson from his past about how detrimental it was to disappear from the political scene—particularly after a huge defeat. Ten years earlier, Lincoln had returned from Washington politically dead after his controversial term in the U.S. House of Representatives, and he had acted that way. His political speeches waned to oblivion over the next three years, producing a two-year gap in public addresses between 1852 and 1854. After he was defeated for the U.S. Senate back in 1855, Lincoln did not drop out of politics as he had in the early part of the decade, but he spent most of the year away from the stump, forcing another rebirth as a Republican in 1856.

Working in Lincoln's favor was the "good humor" noted by reporter Henry Villard, a positive sense of his self-worth that was reinforced by the uplifting words of old friends. One of them, Dr. Anson G. Henry, had been a confidant and supporter of Lincoln since the latter's early days in Springfield. Henry was now removed to Oregon Territory, but he and Lincoln continued their bond of friendship through letters. "You have not 'sunk out of sight' as you seem to anticipate, [nor] will you be forgotten," Henry assured Lincoln that winter. The physician went on to predict that the loftiest heights would be achieved by his lofty friend: "The people—the great & glorious People, will bear you on their memories untill the time comes for putting you in possession of their House at Washington, which they are bound to do in their own good time."[30]

Those warm assurances helped keep Lincoln from suffering the winter blues in the wake of his defeat to Douglas. He also refreshed himself by taking a hiatus from politics, a break Lincoln deemed safe for a few weeks in the early months of 1859. Lincoln traveled to Jacksonville, a town thirty miles southeast of Springfield, to deliver a speech entitled "Discoveries and Inventions," a retooled lyceum speech first presented in April 1858. On its face, the lecture reads as an uninspiring chronicle of the history of worldwide innovations, comparing the established product of "Old Fogy" and the attempts of "Young America" to alter and improve it.[31]

The lecture departed from his political speeches—perhaps. Lincoln may have crafted this speech to convey a subtle political message. His description of Young America ("Some think him conceited and arrogant; but has he not reason to entertain a rather extensive opinion of himself?") matched Stephen A. Douglas too strongly perhaps to be a coincidence, while his characterization of Old Fogy appears consistent with the institutions established by the Founding Fathers; therefore, the struggle between Young America and Old Fogy was, in essence, the same struggle between Douglas and the Constitution that Lincoln had preached about in the debates of 1858. If that indeed was the intent (Lincoln never revealed that it was) then he was too clever for his own good, for no one recognized the speech for anything other than how it appeared on its face.[32]

Lincoln delivered the speech three times in ten days: in Jacksonville on February 11, in Decatur on February 13, and then again in Springfield on February 20. He received polite praise from the newspapers, confirmed by hearty applause by his audiences. This, however, failed to squelch criticism of the lecture by Lincoln's friends and associates. "Part of the lecture was humorous; a very small part of it actually witty; and the rest of it so commonplace that it was a genuine mortification to his friends," claimed one opinionated friend. Billy Herndon absolutely hated the speech. After he listened to Lincoln deliver it, Herndon's disappointment stuck with him for three decades. "It was a lifeless thing, a dull dead thing," he complained in 1891. "It fell on the ears of the audience a cold flat thing. There was no life, imagination, or fancy in it, no spirit and no life. The whole thing was a kind of farce and injured Mr. L.'s reputation as a man of sense among his friends and enemies."[33]

Herndon exaggerated the negative fallout from the speech. Notwithstanding the criticisms, the speech was popular enough to fuel multiple requests for Lincoln to perform in Galesburg and Rock Island. Lincoln necessarily declined due to pending Eighth Judicial Circuit duties which would coincide with the dates requested for him to speak outside that district. He was able to slip in the three presentations between the fall and spring seasons of court duties.

The legislature completed its business and emptied out of Springfield late in February. Lincoln also departed town, riding the rails to Chicago. The city experienced a population explosion in the 1850s. It was already a big city at the start of the decade with close to 30,000 people housed within its borders. Nine years later, Lincoln entered a metropolis of 100,000 citizens. Chicago was easily the largest city in Illinois, and seemingly overnight its population skyrocketed to make it the ninth-largest city in America. Chicago's pull over the rest of the state was a source of contention with the middle and lower counties of Illinois; after all, the state population approached 1.7 million—the fourth most populous state in the country—and Chicago represented a mere 6 percent of that total. But Illinois's vast area, particularly from north to south, scattered the citizens into clusters that could not compete with the size of Chicago, which exceeded the next largest city (Peoria's 14,000 inhabitants) by sevenfold in a state whose northernmost latitudinal line was shared with the border of Massachusetts and Maine, while its southernmost city, Cairo, was on a line equal to the border of Virginia and North Carolina.

Political influence flowed from the six-figure population of Chicago. Whereas many Illinois towns published a daily or weekly Republican-oriented paper, Chicago boasted three with impressive distribution throughout the state. When Lincoln served his last term in the Illinois General Assembly in 1841, only four legislators represented Cook County out of a body of 138 in both houses. The Twenty-first General Assembly, which had adjourned the day before Lincoln's trip northward, sat only five Cook County representatives, but the entire body was streamlined to a hundred members. It was certain that once the official U.S. Census of 1860 caught up with the population boom of Chicago, the representation was destined to increase. The region was noteworthy for favoring aboli- tion, a view contrary to that of the central counties and antithetical to the pro-Douglas region of the southernmost counties.

Lincoln had been a frequent visitor to Chicago since 1854. Circuit- court duties, meetings with politicos, and speeches were his prime motiva- tions for the 185-mile trek, a trip reduced from several days to several hours with the completion of the St. Louis, Alton & Chicago Railroad. He de- veloped a cadre of friends to visit whenever he could. One of his most gratifying visits was with Norman Judd, whose elegant home on Forty- seventh Street offered Lincoln a stirring view of Lake Michigan from the piazza. Ada Judd, Norman's wife, was a favorite hostess and conversational- ist for Lincoln. (It was on the Judds' piazza on a moonlit night in 1857 that Lincoln may have developed the concept of his "Discoveries and Inven- tions" lecture.) The Judd home bustled with children (including a baby boy), adult family members, and Irish servants. Lincoln enjoyed visiting the Judds, not only for the lakefront view and the hospitality of Mrs. Judd, but also because of his friendship with his campaign manager of 1858.[34]

To the dismay of several of Lincoln's associates, his faith in Judd's ex- perience and his trust in Judd's loyalty did not waver as a result of the los- ing campaign. His correspondences with Judd, although business related, still exuded warmth and sincerity—a testament to the camaraderie strengthened by fighting a huge political battle together. Shortly after the November election, when Judd wrote Lincoln, "If you feel as blue as I have since the election I do not blame you," Lincoln immediately re- sponded, "You are feeling badly. *'And this too shall pass away.'* Never fear." Lincoln prodded his depressed comrade to continue the fight against Douglas and the Democrats, and his entreaties served as the antidote to Judd's blues. "I am glad you are in such fine spirits," responded Judd. "I am for continuing the fight. . . . I have some sand in my gizzard yet."[35]

Lincoln and Judd had begun to employ an easygoing banter in their correspondence. Lincoln exaggerated his humbly understated style, a de- vice he seemed to use preferentially with Judd. In a letter written *after* the November elections, Lincoln declared, "Doubtless you have suspected for some time that I entertain a personal wish for a term in the US Senate; and had the suspicion taken the shape of a direct charge, I think I could not have truthfully denied it. But let the past as nothing be." Judd reciprocated by employing a favorite nongrammatical phrase: "Things is working."[36]

Judd and Lincoln teamed up for another event on March 1 in Chicago, this one with happier results. Judd was the first of the two to enter a boisterous Republican headquarters in Mechanics Institute Hall. The party had won a tremendous victory in ward elections throughout the city, creating a very festive mood that evening as returns came in, each one read aloud by Chairman Judd. So ecstatic was the crowd that the messenger delivering the news of the Republican victory in the Seventh Ward was literally passed over the heads of the crowd to the front, where he announced the victory amid intense cheers.[37]

That night in Chicago Lincoln delivered his first overtly political speech since the 1858 senatorial campaign. Enough time had passed from the debates with Douglas for Lincoln to take a fresh approach and craft a new address, the core of which he planned to present as often as he could during the year. He had worked on the speech during the winter lull, most likely in January and early February. Lincoln entered the frenzied hall at nine P.M. "He was received with an uproar of enthusiasm," noted a witness, and tumultuous cheers followed him to the podium. After congratulating the Republican crowd on its hard-fought victory, Lincoln declared, "I am exceedingly happy to meet you under such cheering auspices on this occasion—the first on which I have appeared before an audience since the campaign of last year."[38]

Promising the crowd a brief discourse, Lincoln entered the first phase of his presentation by acknowledging and thanking his supporters. Although he was not saddled with self-consciousness, Lincoln's body language bespoke a strange combination of confidence and awkwardness. He leaned forward as he spoke, as if on an incline toward his audience. He began his speeches with his arms tucked behind his back, the knuckles of the left hand nestled into the palm of the right. When he began to speak, his voice was shrill and unpleasant; he squeaked and piped as he attempted to raise the decibel level of his speech. As Lincoln warmed up, however, either he squeaked less or the audience grew more accustomed to the odd pitch. His hands were now in front of him, fingers interlocked with one thumb tracing the outline of the other. Lincoln used his body much more infrequently than most speakers. His hands sometimes just hung at his sides, but when he chose to gesticulate for emphasis, he did so favoring his right hand, usually by pointing his long, bony forefinger while his thumb rested atop his folded middle finger. He rarely sawed or beat the air with his hand, preferring instead to jerk his head about for emphasis.[39]

What Lincoln emphasized most in this Chicago speech, both with his voice and with his body, was clarifying those positions espoused in the late campaign that drew the most criticism from his own party. In particular he focused on his middle-ground position on slavery, a stance that had angered the abolition wing of the party, including the clergy in Chicago. Lincoln had gone out of his way to distance himself from the abolitionists in 1858. During a debate speech in Charleston in Coles County five months earlier, he had left the impression that he was against black citizenship, and in other debates and speeches he had repeatedly supported upholding the Fugitive-Slave Law—requiring Northerners to return runaway slaves to their Southern owners—as constitutional and binding. This position had led the New England abolitionist Wendell Phillips to deride Lincoln as "the slave hound of Illinois."[40]

Lincoln would not change his position, particularly if he was considering running for president, for shifting his views into line with the abolitionists' was political suicide. But the fledgling Republican Party must be strong and united if it had any chance to improve upon the results of the 1856 election. To do this Lincoln must emphasize a statesmanlike position; he had to reiterate his hatred of slavery, his mission to prevent its spread, and his desire to see it dissolve to extinction once it was contained. Knowing that he had repeated this aspect of his policy time and time again, Lincoln focused on the intraparty disagreement with him. He was determined to present himself as a principled pragmatist rather than a radical.

He told his audience that the disagreements between the abolitionists and him were really minor when looked upon in a grand scope. Rather than accentuate their policy differences regarding the Negro's future in America, insisted Lincoln, Republicans should focus their efforts where they agreed the most—in resisting the extension of slavery into the territorial regions of the country. "I say this," continued Lincoln, "for the purpose of suggesting that we consider whether it would not be better and wiser, so long as we all agree that this matter of slavery is a moral, political, and social wrong, and ought to be treated as a wrong, not to let anything minor or subsidiary to that main principle and purpose make us fail to cooperate."[41]

He also took a preemptive strike at the movement within the Republican Party to support Senator Douglas as their presidential candidate. Douglas had been the strongest and best-known advocate of popular sovereignty, the doctrine under which slavery in the territories was to be determined by the settlers of the region. The U.S. Supreme Court's *Dred Scott v. Sanford* decision of 1857 appeared to obliterate Douglas's position, for it asserted not only that all blacks (free and slave) were not U.S. citizens and therefore were inferior to whites in America, but that slavery was permitted throughout the territories. Douglas countered that the doctrine of popular sovereignty could not be trumped either by the executive, the legislative, or the judicial branch of the federal government. He had gone on record in the Freeport debate to nullify this portion of the landmark decision when he declared "slavery cannot exist a day or an hour anywhere, unless it is supported by local police regulations."

Douglas's Freeport Doctrine appeased and pleased many Republicans, as did his earlier opposition to President James Buchanan's support of Kansas Territory's proslavery Lecompton Constitution. Douglas's positions grabbed the support of *New York Tribune* editor Horace Greeley, who had promoted Douglas as a fusion candidate for senator, since his positions were deemed tolerable for Northeastern Republicans. Back in December Lincoln had predicted that Douglas's positions would prove so intolerable to hard-line Democrats that they would reject him in the future Democratic National Convention, scheduled to be held in the spring of 1860 in Charleston, South Carolina. What concerned Lincoln was Douglas's innate and opportunistic skill at reading tea leaves. Lincoln worried that if the Democratic leaders at that convention would "push a Slave code upon him, as a test, he will bolt at once, turn upon us, as in the case of Lecompton, and claim that all Northern men shall make common cause in electing him President as the best means of breaking down the Slave power." Lincoln feared that this would dupe the Republicans into electing him president.[42]

Lincoln was irked by the swelling support for Douglas within his party;

it had been evident before, during, and after the senatorial campaign. So, in Chicago on March 1, Lincoln crafted a counterargument to this consideration. "I have believed," declared Lincoln, "that in the Republican situation in Illinois, if we, the Republicans of this State, had made Judge Douglas our candidate for the Senate of the United States last year and had elected him, there would to-day be no Republican party in the Union." Lincoln said of the Republicans who were preparing to line up behind Douglas, "They do not absorb him; he absorbs them." He claimed Douglas had no moral convictions about the institution of slavery; to him it was "simply a question of dollars and cents." Supporting Douglas was equivalent to abandoning principles, lectured Lincoln, and thus would be a death knell to a party that owed its very existence to its moral principles.

Within the Douglas discussion, Lincoln incorporated the final point of his speech—a reiteration of the Republican fight against the spread of slavery. Here Lincoln took pains to warn his audience that the Supreme Court and Douglas would not only squash the dream of seeing slavery contained and dwindle to extinction, but would create the possibility of seeing slavery extend into the North with a subsequent Supreme Court ruling that would nullify any antislavery doctrines existing within Northern states (much as the original *Dred Scott* decision did with the Missouri Compromise of 1820):

> *Suppose it is true that the Almighty has drawn a line across this continent, on the south side of which part of the people will hold the rest as slaves; that the Almighty ordered this; that it is right, unchangeably right, that men ought there to be held as slaves, and that their fellow men will always have the right to hold them as slaves. I ask you, this once admitted, how can you believe that it is not right for us, or for them coming here, to hold slaves on this other side of the line? Once we come to acknowledge that it is right, that it is the law of the Eternal Being, for slavery to exist on one side of that line, have we any sure ground to object to slaves being held on the other side? Once admit the position that a man rightfully holds another as property on one side of the line, and you must, when it suits his convenience to come to the other side, admit that he has the same right to hold his property there. Once admit Judge Douglas's proposition and we must all finally give way.*[43]

The first trial balloon with the second *Dred Scott* theory had been launched late in the senatorial campaign by Lincoln. But in Chicago he was simplifying the argument by taking the first *Dred Scott* decision and Douglas's support of popular sovereignty (a butchered form of it that Lincoln always derided as "squatter sovereignty") to their logical conclusions. After planting this scenario in the collective mind of his audience, Lincoln highlighted the absurdity of Douglas as a Republican candidate for president in 1860: "Our only serious danger is that we shall be led upon this ground of Judge Douglas, on the delusive assumption that it is a good way of whipping our opponents, when in fact, it is a way that leads straight to final surrender."

An hour had elapsed since Lincoln stepped up to the platform. He closed his address by rallying the Republican crowd to adhere to their principles and not be swayed by either the Douglas faction or abolitionist critics—"Allow nothing to turn you to the right or to the left"—while urging them to speak out united on this cause.[44]

Lusty cheers immediately followed Lincoln's closing words. The performance and its response did not go unnoticed by the opposition. The *Chicago Herald*, one of the city's Democratic papers, had adopted a new nickname for the Democrats' political rivals—Blacks (reduced from "Black Republicans"). "The Blacks made a great blow last night at Mechanics Institute," the *Herald* derisively reported, "and were assisted by 'Old Abe' and several other equally distinguished rampant Abolitionists."[45]

As caustic as it was, the *Herald*'s report devoted more ink to Lincoln's performance than did any of the three Republican newspapers in the city combined. The *Chicago Press and Tribune* never reported on the speech even though it sent its gifted shorthand reporter, Robert R. Hitt, there to record the speech. Lincoln's middle-ground position apparently concerned Joseph Medill, the paper's coeditor and a strong advocate for the repeal of the Fugitive-Slave Law, enough to ignore Lincoln's presence in Chicago that night. Lincoln's painstaking attempt to dismiss Douglas as a candidate was not popular with influential Douglas advocates in the party, which may have added more weight to the decision to table the speech rather than print even a brief report of it. The other two Republican papers of the city also leaned stronger toward the position of radicals rather than toward Lincoln's moderate one, clearly not agreeing with the *Herald*'s characterization of Lincoln as a "rampant Abolitionist." Their issues also avoided any mention of Lincoln speaking in Chicago on March 1, 1859.[46]

Lincoln's maintenance of his principled pragmatism is exactly what made the Chicago speech important. It demonstrated the strength of his convictions in the face of overwhelming pressure to modify his views. Lincoln chose instead to clarify them, arguing that his course was true and unambiguous and represented the model to which all Republicans could rally. A strong and united Republican Party, particularly in Illinois, would only improve Lincoln's chances to attain the mountaintop. To serve that end, Lincoln dedicated himself to strengthening his party both state- and nationwide. Armed with a new speech that squarely placed him between the extreme wings of his party—the pro-Douglas and abolitionist factions—Lincoln was prepared to be the hardworking statesman, one who helped to reap the ultimate reward for his labors from an appreciative populace who would recognize that his views best reflected theirs.

Nowhere in the speech did Lincoln's presidential ambitions come to light, continuing the tactic he had devised in January. But to continue to conceal his ultimate desire required him to be less than truthful. When Thomas Drummond, the judge of the U.S. District Court in Chicago, broached the subject of the presidency with Lincoln during his visit there, Lincoln brushed away the suggestion with a response that was as consistent as it was disingenuous: "I hope they will select some abler man than myself."[47]

While declaring this, Lincoln looked forward to proving that *he* was indeed the ablest man for the job.

Two

DIVIDED HOUSE

TWO DAYS AFTER his Chicago speech, Abraham Lincoln rode the rails back to Springfield with no immediate plan to build upon the momentum generated by the new speech. He shunned the lecture circuit in the spring of 1859 due to his responsibilities on the judicial circuit. His practice flourished and his caseload remained heavy. Lincoln was flattered with requests to present more "Discoveries and Inventions" lectures in Illinois towns, but he humbly turned down most of them. Chances are that he had lost some enthusiasm for the speech, denigrating it as "a sort of lecture," but he was dismayed to discover that the populace was even less enthusiastic than he. He suffered the humiliation of canceling an early-spring lecture for lack of interest. A college student was in the audience that night. "I paid a quarter and went in early to get a seat," he wrote his father. "It was a beautiful evening, and the lecture had been well advertised but for some reason not explained, only about 40 persons were present, and Old Abe would not speak to such a small crowd, so they paid us back our quarters at the door."[1]

Although he allowed several months to pass without delivering a political speech, Lincoln did remain politically active. He could not afford the post-defeat hibernation he had chosen after the Senate election of 1855; too much was at stake in 1859. Lincoln dabbled in local politics in the first weeks of the spring by agreeing to take part in a Springfield convention for nominating Republican municipal officers and in a mass meeting for selecting an alderman.[2]

The most important benefit Lincoln attempted to contribute to his own political cause was the publication of his debates with Stephen A. Douglas. Motivated by his adaptability and performance, and knowing how Douglas stuck to his text in nearly every debate, Lincoln sought to display those speeches in print to a nationwide audience. The origination of the idea for publication came from a Tazewell County supporter who wished to organize clippings of Lincoln and Douglas speeches from the *Chicago Press and Tribune*. Overcome by a desire for objectivity, Lincoln responded to the query by suggesting that Douglas's newspaper clippings be taken from the *Chicago Times*, a Democratic paper Douglas had helped to create five years earlier. The supporter's plan was to have the speeches published by September, "for I hope to succeed in 1860." Lincoln, of course, hoped for the same outcome, but the project stalled due to his publisher's limited finances.[3]

Lincoln's words did receive a national audience during the spring of 1859 in the form of a letter. He had received an invitation from a Boston committee headed by Henry L. Pierce, a Boston manufacturer (and future mayor), to attend an April 13 festival to honor the 116th anniversary of the birth of Thomas Jefferson, "the father of the 'ordinance of 1787,' and the apostle of State Rights." Lincoln contemplated making the trip, but declined a week before the event in a several-page letter apparently crafted to be read at the event. In his letter, Lincoln claimed that Republicans were Jefferson's true descendants and pointed out the irony that Democrats, notwithstanding their claim to be the disciples of Jefferson, "have nearly ceased to breathe his name everywhere." He took the Democrats to task for claiming that the Republicans were actually descended from John Adams's Federalists (an unflattering comparison in the mid-1800s) and so could have no claim on Jeffersonian principles. Lincoln likened this assertion to two intoxicated men fighting each other while still wearing their coats. Although the brawl produced no clear-cut winner, each man "fought himself *out* of his own coat, and *into* that of the other." That was the quandary of the Democrats' claim that they upheld Jeffersonian ideals, while the Republicans adhered to Federalist ideology: "They have performed the same feat as the two drunken men."

Lincoln castigated Democrats—calling them the "so called democracy"—for elitism and derided them as the champions of oppression and despotism over the Jeffersonian principles of free government. "This is a world of compensation," argued Lincoln; "and he who would be no slave, must consent to have no slave. Those who deny freedom to others, deserve it not for themselves; and, under a just God, can not long retain it."[4]

Lincoln clearly intended the letter to be read at the celebration, which it was, but he must have been astounded at how well his words carried across the country. Pro-Republican newspapers in at least five states published Lincoln's letter in total or in excerpt. It was positive and unexpected publicity, press coverage that not only kept his name alive within and outside of Illinois, but also succeeded in treating him as presidential timber a full year before the Republican National Convention was likely to convene. Nathan M. Knapp, a prominent Scott County Republican, read the letter in a newspaper and immediately rated Lincoln as "the most available candidate for unadulterated Republicans." Knapp wrote Ozias M. Hatch to rave about Lincoln's letter and to stack him up against the other likely nomination candidates. "God made him the biggest man in the lot," he declared. "There is more of old '76 Republicanism, enlarged in his speeches of last summer and in his said letter, than any of them have got. . . . Don't be surprised at any result in reference to him."[5]

Whether or not Hatch relayed the positive effect of his published letter, Lincoln must have been pleased to see his words carry as well as they did. But at the same time, he must have lamented the lost opportunity to make a public appearance in the Northeast. In order to become a viable candidate in 1860, Lincoln well understood that he had to be visible in the East and the West.

Lincoln trained to Bloomington in April, the time of year when the town's name should have been literal, but not so for the spring of 1859. An out-of-town newspaper prematurely reported that plum and peach trees were blooming in the town, but Lincoln was not greeted by the perfumed fragrance and inviting colors of the fruit blossoms when he exited the depot. Instead he could see wood smoke drifting from the chimneys and townsmen still donning their winter overcoats. Despite this, all indications suggest that Lincoln had successfully shaken off the winter blues that had clung to him during his last stay in Bloomington in December. As was his routine, he registered at the Pike House, his preferred hotel. The *Bloomington Pantagraph* also followed its routine of announcing his arrival, calling Lincoln "The Tall Sucker" in its local news headline for the visit.[6]

Lincoln again teamed up with Norman Judd, who was in Bloomington to chair a meeting of the Republican State Central Committee. Judd continued to show that glitter in his eye, and he likely still chomped a cigar, but he was beset with problems in his role as chairman of the committee, both at the state and national levels. Through his conversation with him, Lincoln realized that the party's ill health could impair their campaigns for the statehouse, the retention of Lyman Trumbull's U.S. Senate seat, and the nominee for president in 1860.

The 1858 senatorial campaign had weakened the Republican Party in Illinois, and not only because Lincoln lost to Douglas. The party had fallen into four-figure debt. Judd performed yeoman's service to rectify the problem by donating $1,300 and soliciting others to make contributions and to contact others to do the same. (He even convinced Lincoln to contribute $500 late in 1858, even though Judd owed him $3,000.) Judd's efforts and the sacrifices of Lincoln and other Republicans in Illinois kept the party solvent throughout those financially strapped months after the election.[7]

The Republican Party's financial troubles masked an even greater problem in Illinois in 1859. Its most prominent members were tearing each other apart. The most frequent target was Judd, who announced his plans to run for the governor's seat in 1860. Judd's ambition, although not a secret to most high-ranking Republicans, provided his most strident detractors with the ammunition necessary to fault Judd for Republican failures.

Unfortunately for Judd, his most ardent critic was also one of the most powerful and passionate politicians in Chicago: John Wentworth, known as "Long John" for his six-foot-five-inch frame, a height that made him one of a select few politicos in Illinois taller than Abraham Lincoln. Weighing more than three hundred pounds, Wentworth lived as large as he looked. His over-the-top lifestyle was rumored to include a pint-per-day whiskey habit, and his passion for food may have included more than thirty items for one meal. Wentworth even wrote "big"; his characteristic scrawl seemed to announce a contest to fill a page of his correspondence with the fewest number of words.

Wentworth, like Judd, hailed from the East and was a former Democrat who had converted to the Republican cause in the wake of the Kansas-Nebraska Act. Talked up as a Senate candidate himself, Wentworth had served five terms in the U.S. House of Representatives and had been the first Republican mayor of Chicago, from 1857 to 1858. He and Judd shared a fondness for Lincoln—which may have been the greatest source of hard feelings between the two. That Judd remained in Lincoln's inner circle, while Wentworth wallowed on the outside looking in, was a fact too uncomfortable for "Long John" to stand.

As the owner and managing editor of the *Chicago Democrat*, a Republican newspaper with daily and weekly issues, Wentworth had power and wanted more if it. Deepening his disdain for Judd was the latter's affiliation with the *Chicago Press and Tribune*, the chief rival to Wentworth's newspaper. Backlash against Wentworth's strong-arm tactics, particularly while he was the mayor, hurt him financially. While the *Press and Tribune* thrived, Wentworth's paper, regarded as the official newspaper of Chicago in 1858, was on a pace to lose eight thousand dollars in 1859.[8]

Wentworth was wounded and limping; his animal instincts took over, and he fought back by crafting a series of editorials and reports in the *Democrat* to denigrate his rivals. His favorite target was Judd, who was frequently stung by Long John's editorial barbs in the spring of 1859. The situation spun out of control, climaxed by Wentworth's impromptu appearance at a Republican mass meeting in Chicago on April 2. Ostentatious as ever, Wentworth swaggered toward the platform with a bagpiper trailing him while playing "Yankee Doodle." Wentworth then lit into Judd and other associates of what he called the "*Pressed Tribune*" in a harangue that consumed an hour and a half. Judd immediately followed with a heated response, calling Long John "a most corrupt liar and knave." In a private letter, Charles Wilson, the editor of the *Chicago Journal*, wrote that Judd and Wentworth "flailed each other" that night and worried how their public feud was hurting the party. War had begun within the Republican ranks.[9]

No doubt Lincoln heard all about it five days later when he and Judd got together in Bloomington. As a subscriber and frequent reader of the Chicago papers, Lincoln was well apprised of Wentworth's antics even before Judd bent his ear about them. Wentworth was clearly a loose cannon, but Lincoln also recognized him as an important cog in the Republican machine of Illinois, particularly in regards to garnering the ethnic vote in Chicago. Moreover, Wentworth's opinions attracted at least one in Lincoln's inner circle. David Davis had become a disciple of Long John's anti-Judd philosophy. Davis confidentially forwarded to Lincoln excerpts of a letter Wentworth wrote him attributing Lincoln's Senate loss to the Republican State Central Committee's mismanagement of his campaign. Wentworth maintained that too many people on the committee made Lincoln secondary to their true motive: to enhance Judd's run for the Illinois statehouse in 1860. Wentworth's opinion reinforced the same one brewing within Judge Davis. "I agree with him religiously," Davis confided to Lincoln.[10]

Judd learned all too painfully that Wentworth could be vicious if one rubbed him the wrong way. He sought solace from Long John's cutting editorials and public-meeting antics by opening up about the problem to anyone who would listen. He even wrote Governor William Bissell about Wentworth's relentless attacks. "Poor Judd takes things quite too much at heart," the governor relayed to Ozias Hatch after receiving Judd's complaints in the mail. Bissell believed Wentworth's influence in the state was vastly overrated and suggested that Judd should, "as the boys say, keep a stiff upper lip." He at least empathized with Judd about Wentworth's domineering image. "What a vexing devil is W.!" exclaimed Bissell of Wentworth. "He can unquestionably annoy one beyond endurance."[11]

Fortunately for Lincoln, he remained in Long John's good graces. Ozias M. Hatch and Jesse Dubois, however, did not, with Wentworth making their lives more uncomfortable. Lincoln did not follow Wentworth's line concerning Hatch, the secretary of state, and "Uncle Jesse" Dubois, the state auditor. Both men held statewide responsibilities that could only benefit Lincoln politically. He genuinely liked both men, as he did Leonard Swett and Richard Yates, two other politicians whom Wentworth abhorred. But the latter pair also disliked each other and shared a common dislike for Norman Judd. Both Yates and Swett also eyed the governorship in 1860 and considered each other a rival as well as Judd.[12]

Given all of these conflicting ambitions and animosities, Lincoln made no attempt to do the impossible and form a team out of these embittered yet prominent Illinois politicians. But because they all shared Lincoln as a common friend, they independently aided him in their respective regions and by their responsibilities in the state. This allowed Lincoln to reap the benefits of their collective expertise and skills without attempting to make them get along with one another. Most important to Lincoln was to make sure that they did not tear one another apart.

Lincoln's hands-off approach did not satisfy Norman Judd, who preferred someone to intervene on his behalf to stop Wentworth's personal attacks against him. Judd was vexed at how influential the undisciplined editor remained with prominent Republicans in the state. Studying every issue of the *Chicago Democrat* he could get his hands on, Judd questioned Long John's conviction and loyalty after reading his accolades of Missourian Edward Bates and Kentuckian John Bell as potential presidential candidates for the Republican Party—despite the fact that neither of these politicians was a member of the party. Judd accused Wentworth of "whoring after Strange Gods, men who have never had any affinities or connection the Republican Party."[13]

Judd let his problems with Wentworth drop by the time the Republican State Central Committee convened in Bloomington on April 7. The meeting was composed of some of the same personnel who had met informally in the statehouse library back in January, the momentous day when Lincoln declared his desire for the presidency. The committee had the power and backing to promote Lincoln's candidacy openly, but chose not to. This was likely a decision based on Lincoln's request. One of his most innate political skills was his impeccable sense of timing. The spring of 1859 was no time to whirl up a Lincoln boom, for it would generate a year of national scrutiny and diminishing momentum that would certainly hamper his chances a year later at the national convention.

Although the minutes of the meeting have not survived, the decision of this body was revealed in the memoirs of Gustave Koerner, one of the most prominent Germans in Illinois. Koerner was not present in Bloomington but was told shortly afterward about the plans concerning Lincoln's candidacy. "Upon consultation with some of the members of the Republican State Central Committee and other leading Republicans, it was agreed that the best policy for the party in our state was to keep Lincoln in the background for the present, or at least not to push his claim to any extent," Koerner recalled. This strategy not only prevented a premature boom for Lincoln but allowed the front-runners to weaken under their meddling managers. According to Koerner, the committee forecast that the handlers of Seward, Chase, and Cameron "would fight against each other, and necessarily damage the candidates they upheld." By concealing Lincoln's candidacy until "the proper time," the Republicans of Illinois could help shield him from the fighting expected among the camps of the front-runners and ultimately present him "with no embittered enemies."[14]

The strategy to run Lincoln appears to have had no detractors within the committee, primarily because it did not force any commitment upon its members this early in 1859. For Judd—still recuperating financially from the arduous U.S. Senate campaign—this strategy also freed the committee to concentrate on more pressing matters. His major topic for the committee meeting was national party unity, recently jeopardized by the Republican-dominated legislature of Massachusetts. The Bay Staters moved against the 1856 Republican national platform by submitting an amendment to the state constitution that prohibited naturalized immigrants from voting until they resided in Massachusetts for two years. This doctrine placated the old Know Nothing element of the party, a controversial nativist wing that had fused with the Old Whigs and Anti-Nebraska Democrats to form the Republicans a few years earlier.

This action touched off a nationwide political furor with Republicans sensitive to the fodder it provided Democrats for 1859 and 1860 elections because of the harmful effects it would have in states with large foreign populations. The Germans were particularly sensitive to the measure, with the most radical newspaper editors advising their readers to punish Republicans by voting for Democrats in the upcoming elections. Germans were the largest and fastest-growing population in Illinois; their population quadrupled within the Prairie State during the 1850s to swell their ranks above 130,000. On average, one out of every thirteen residents of Illinois was a German. Although not strictly devoted to any political party as the Irish were to the Democrats, the Germans were considered more friendly to Republican views because of their strong antislavery sentiments, but the Know Nothing element of the party—an anti-immigrant fringe—prevented Germans from becoming rock-solid Republican voters.

The Massachusetts amendment seemed to confirm German suspicions about the influence of the radical elements of the Republican Party. Norman

Judd was deeply concerned about the upheaval it caused in Illinois; German papers seized upon the implications and threatened to bolt from the Republican ranks and form a new party, while German clubs met in Illinois towns to denounce the state party for their silence on the matter.[15]

Although he was not one of the eleven members of the Republican State Central Committee, Lincoln agreed to a special request from Judd to prepare a series of resolutions to condemn the Massachusetts legislature for the act. Lincoln was disappointed in the shortsightedness of the Massachusetts Republicans, who "should have looked beyond their noses; and then they could not have failed to see that tilting against foreigners would ruin us in the whole North-West." Lincoln drafted and read off the resolutions in a conference of committee members and other prominent Republicans present in Bloomington, including Senator Trumbull. As damaging as the amendment would be to his reelection bid in 1860, Trumbull spoke out against Lincoln's resolutions, preferring to use the condemnation against the Democrats rather than against their own party. Apparently others agreed, and the resolutions were not adopted.[16]

This left Judd toothless, but he made the best of it. Soon afterward German clubs throughout Illinois complained to him about the lack of action by the state Republican Party against the measure. Judd responded by crafting a letter with two false claims: He feigned that the committee had not met about it, and he proposed to speak for the committee members in denouncing it as "an act of tyranny and oppression that should be rebuked by the Republicans throughout the Union." Although it was tainted with white lies, Judd made sure his response was published by the *Press and Tribune*, and it was subsequently excerpted by other papers.[17]

Although his resolutions never came to light, Lincoln's wording was apparently more muted than Judd's. Shortly after he returned to Springfield he corresponded with Theodore Canisius, the editor of the city's German newspaper, the *Illinois Staats-Anzeiger*, who queried Lincoln about his opinion on the Massachusetts amendment. Lincoln the lawyer responded in carefully selected verbiage. "Massachusetts is a sovereign and independent state; and it is no privilege of mine to scold her for what she does," he explained. He went on to proclaim that although he had no right to denounce it for Massachusetts, he did indeed oppose it in Illinois or any other state. "Understanding the spirit of our institutions to aim at the *elevation* of men, I am opposed to whatever tends to *degrade* them," he proclaimed.[18]

Lincoln's letter of response, like Judd's, was published in newspapers across Illinois, in both German and English. This in itself did not guarantee that Springfield's German press was placated. Canisius had suffered financial difficulties, and his demands had caused much grief for the Republican Party throughout 1858. Judd likened Canisius to a leech; he warned Lincoln, "He sucked more blood from you at Springfield and from the [Committee] than the whole establishment was worth." Lincoln took an extraordinary step to assure German support for the Republican Party. He closed a deal to purchase the *Illinois Staats-Anzeiger* that spring. He worded the contract to specify that Canisius maintained the autonomy to edit and publish the paper, but if he printed anything in opposition to the Republican Party, Lincoln had the option of personally taking over the press. Lincoln then set out to market his new German Republican paper by sending out copies to state Republicans and asking them to get him subscribers.[19]

Statesmanship, statewide exposure, and national attention combined to heighten Lincoln in the minds of Republican editors across Illinois. Thomas J. Pickett and C. W. Waite, the joint owners of the *Rock Island Register*, recognized this more than anyone in the spring of 1859, and—dissatisfied with the sparse official endorsements of Lincoln for president—they sought to create their own Lincoln boom in Illinois, one they hoped would spread across the North. Pickett notified Lincoln of his plan to contact editors throughout the state urging them to endorse him simultaneously for the presidency.[20]

Lincoln squelched the idea. He was not nearly as naive as the editors to think that a significant number of Illinois newspaper editors supported him for the presidency; at best there existed a movement to consider him as vice president. None of the Chicago papers leaned in his direction; neither did the Springfield ones. A premature attempt at mass endorsement not only would fail, and miserably so, but would also injure his opportunities to garner support in 1860, as the election drew closer and endorsements carried more weight. Nor did Lincoln wish to publicize his desire for the presidency a full year before the national convention for the nomination was to be held, an ambition most would glean by reading these pronouncements. The synchronized newspaper endorsements across the state would fly in the face of the strategy adopted by the Republican State Central Committee to hide Lincoln from the scrutinizing eyes of the managers of the front-running national candidates. Consistent in his approach to the matter, Lincoln disingenuously informed the editor, "I must, in candor, say I do not think myself fit for the Presidency. I certainly am flattered, and gratified, that some partial friends think of me in that connection; but I really think it best for our cause that no concerted effort, such as you suggest, should be made."[21]

Although he had quelled a premature attempt to produce a Lincoln boom, the importance of solid backing within his home state did not escape Abraham Lincoln. As he conducted his legal business in the courts and his political business outside the courts throughout the Eighth Judicial Circuit, Lincoln did not fail to meet with newspaper editors or to hobnob with the most prominent members of each county seat he traveled to. In Champaign, Lincoln made time between court sessions to visit the office of the *Central Illinois Gazette*. There he found the editor, Dr. John W. Scroggs, and the two chewed the fat about presidential prospects in 1860. Scroggs offered up Lincoln as a candidate, a gesture that Lincoln humbly brushed away. Still, Lincoln's effort to meet Scroggs paid dividends. The newsman brought Lincoln's name up in the next issue of his paper and proceeded to rave about the visit to his readers two weeks later. "Few men can make an hour pass more agreeably," he claimed of Lincoln.[22]

Lincoln found nothing agreeable about the Republican newspaper in Clinton. The *Central Transcript*, an influence in the center of the state, ran a provocative editorial. Without naming him, the paper piled upon Judd, blaming Lincoln's defeat on "the course pursued by these Northerners in putting none but the most ultra men on the track as candidates for the most important State and federal offices—men who boast of stealing negroes and violating the laws of the land." The paper dropped Judge Davis's name as an acceptable candidate and insisted that the central and southern parts of the state would choose the governor, completing its charge against the Chicago area.

Lincoln received the paper and responded immediately. Fearing a regional war within the Republican ranks of Illinois, he took the paper to task on its claim, emphasizing that no Chicago politician had been a candidate for state or national office in the election cycles of 1856 and 1858, and in fact had thrown their support to candidates from the central and southern parts of the state. "I shall heartily support for Governor whoever shall be nominated by a Republican State convention . . . ," insisted Lincoln. "But is not the fling you make at our Northern bretheren [*sic*] both unjust to them, and dangerous to our cause?" Lincoln's angst spilled over in the letter, a rare communication with an editor explicitly instructed not to publish it. "I plead . . . my great anxiety that we shall have great harmony and not discord," he preached in closing; "have candidates by agreement and not by force;—*help* one another instead of trying to *hurt* one another."[23]

In his quest for party unity Lincoln preached moderation and adherence to federal and state constitutions. He had demonstrated his consistency in his muted response to the Massachusetts amendment. The moderate stance was tested again by Republican initiatives outside Illinois. Ohio Republicans crafted a platform which included a plank that turned Lincoln's head—a demand to repeal the national Fugitive-Slave Law. This controversial plank startled Lincoln to immediate action. Originally established in 1793 and clarified again as part of the Compromise of 1850, the Fugitive-Slave Law had been one of the most divisive edicts between North and South, particularly after Harriett Beecher Stowe's *Uncle Tom's Cabin* became an instant bestseller when it was published in 1852. Lincoln abhorred this law, he confessed to a friend in 1855, for it forced him to "bite my lip and keep quiet" as escaped slaves were legally "hunted down, and caught, and carried back to their stripes, and unrewarded toils." The Ohio Republicans now forced him to act in defense of this law.[24]

He wrote to Governor Salmon P. Chase to discuss the matter. Just as the Massachusetts amendment appealed to a radical wing of the Republican Party, so did the Ohio plank. The Fugitive-Slave Law was a rally cry for the abolitionist element of the party, but Lincoln saw it as a guaranteed right established in Article IV, Section 2 of the U.S. Constitution and subsequently protected by the 1793 and 1850 statutes. Any attempt by Republicans to repeal the law in such a politically charged environment would be too radical to win over votes of the moderates. Knowing that Chase favored the plank (a position that hindered his appeal as the future presidential nominee of the party), Lincoln's pique consumed him. He did not mince words to argue against it. "This is already damaging us here," Lincoln bluntly reported to

Chase; "I have no doubt that if that plank be even *introduced* into the next Republican National convention, it will explode it." Hoping that Chase would be able to remove the plank, Lincoln assured him that "the cause of Republicanism is hopeless in Illinois, if it be in any way made responsible for that plank."[25]

Chase's response did not satisfy Lincoln. The governor reminded him that bold measures were necessary for the sake of principle, as Lincoln himself had argued in his controversial "House Divided" speech. Chase treated the 1850 Fugitive-Slave Law as "unnecessarily harsh & severe" and suggested that many considered it unconstitutional because it did not provide for a trial by jury and could not be legally legislated by Congress. (Here Chase ignored the three-month-old Supreme Court decision *Ableman v. Booth*, which upheld the law against a constitutional challenge.) Moreover, Chase considered it "next to worthless" and impractical. "I shall be very glad to have your views," closed Chase's letter to Lincoln.[26]

One week later Lincoln raced through the door Chase had opened for him. "You say you would be glad to have my views," Lincoln began, and he followed with a presentation of those views. Well aware that the constitutionality of the law was debatable (the document never used the word "slave"), Lincoln pointed out to Chase that the U.S. Constitution clearly stated that the fugitives "shall be delivered up" without specifying who should do it (the clarifying 1850 statute put that responsibility on U.S. marshals). He went on to illustrate that the Articles of Confederation had implied that these types of laws depended on the states for their execution. Lincoln had no desire to debate the Constitution with Chase but wanted to focus on the effect of state party decisions on the national level. Lincoln repeated that any attempt to add this measure to the national platform would throw the national convention into chaos and destroy the Republican Party. "Having turned your attention to the point, I wish to do no more," coldly concluded Lincoln.[27]

Governor Chase was able to read between the lines and chose not to respond to Lincoln. The Fugitive-Slave Law, however, would continue to hound the party. Unlike the isolated attitudes of nativists, Lincoln knew that the repeal of the Fugitive-Slave Law was welcomed by thousands of abolition adherents in Illinois, particularly in Chicago. Evidence for this was in Chase's mail, in the same pile as Lincoln's letters. Republican

Joseph Medill, the co-owner and editor of the *Chicago Press and Tribune*, had been a Chase supporter since 1855, when he had run a newspaper in Cleveland. Although more aligned with Illinois politics in 1859, Medill had been exchanging letters with Chase from April to June, crafting a months-long plan to promote Chase as an attractive Western candidate and a sound alternative to Senator Seward. Medill pointed out a chief reason for favoring Chase, one that boded ill for Abraham Lincoln: "Your platform pleases our people most hugely."[28]

Salmon P. Chase was not the only recipient of Lincoln's efforts to quell eruptions within the national Republican ranks. Lincoln also corresponded with Nathan Sargent, an Old Whig who knew Lincoln from their stint in Congress together in the 1840s. Sargent had suggested that the upcoming national convention include a plank in the platform that called for opposing the opening of the slave trade and "eternal opposition to the rotten democracy." Lincoln read the tea leaves of such a partisan statement ("rotten democracy" was a pejorative for the Democratic Party) and calculated its implications for the election of 1860.

Friends warned Lincoln to respond to Sargent "with a proper degree of caution" to keep him on his side, for "such a pen as he wields is worth something to any public man." Lincoln shunned caution and instead chose to reprimand Sargent. Lincoln bluntly reminded him that the Republican Party consisted of thousands of former Democrats who had united with them due to their opposition to the spread of slavery. Since Sargent's caustic plank insulted these Democrats and did nothing to restrict the spread of slavery within the country, Lincoln predicted it would drop Republican voters in Illinois from an estimated 125,000 in 1858 to fewer than 50,000 in 1860.[29]

Reopening the slave trade had become an issue of great concern throughout the North, but Lincoln preferred to address it by comparing it to the spread of slavery into the territories. His pessimistic streak ran directly through the slave-trade issue; Lincoln determined that the argument for the territorial spread of slavery—established by law with the Kansas-Nebraska Act of 1854 and protected by the *Dred Scott* decision of 1857—could be the same argument to import slaves again into the United States. He illustrated his conclusion with the following point: "Try a thousand years for a sound reason why congress shall not hinder the people of

Kansas from having slaves, and when you have found it, it will be an equally good one why congress should not hinder the people of Georgia from importing slaves from Africa."[30]

Lincoln's correspondences clearly demonstrate a preemptive effort to prevent a brittle party from shattering under the weight of inner conflicts. He railed against the shortsightedness of Republicans, like those in Massachusetts and Ohio, who clung to popular local issues without regard for the damage they created outside their localities. "What is desirable," preached Lincoln, "is that in every local convocation of Republicans, a point should be made to avoid everything which will distract republicans elsewhere." His letters also suggest that the populace would be swayed more by issues than by party loyalty. Anti-Nebraska Democrats, both those who did and those who did not call themselves "Republicans," would unite within the Republican Party if it stood on a platform of unity rather than strident opposition. This was the issue Lincoln sought to exploit in the year leading up to the national convention. He was doing so as a party statesman, one who did not appear to be running for a political office. "I do not deny that there are as good men in the South as the North," Lincoln explained in the early summer of 1859, "and I guess we will elect one of them if he will allow us to do so on Republican ground." He purposely neglected to add the condition that he would support this if *he* could not be the nominee.[31]

Discussing politics through the mails remained a favorite activity for Lincoln. He became a frequent sounding board for Samuel Galloway, a Columbus, Ohio, lawyer and former member of the U.S. House of Representatives. "We cannot have Salmon P. Chase, or any man representing his ultra ideas as our Candidate in 1860," professed Galloway as he laid out the Republican field for the presidency. Galloway informed Lincoln that his name, along with those of Senators Trumbull and William P. Fessenden, had been suggested with increased frequency. "I would cheerfully adopt any one of you but I am candid to say you are my choice," he proclaimed.[32]

Remaining true to his strategy, Lincoln continued to publicly downplay his political ambition as 1859 passed its midpoint. This was becoming more difficult, as his name was linked to the White House again and again. Lincoln responded to Galloway by offering his opinion while cloaking his ambition. He agreed with Galloway that Chase "may not be the most suitable as a candidate for the Presidency." But he must have surprised Galloway with an assessment of himself that he had used previously: "I must say I do not think myself fit for the Presidency." The self-effacement was even more disingenuous than it had been the first time he used it.[33]

Lucrative cases kept Lincoln locked in to his circuit duties throughout the spring, forcing him to decline invitations to spread his message in Minnesota and Kansas Territory, as well as within Illinois. Summertime freed up Lincoln considerably, at least enough to accept speaking invitations, even on short notice. Early in July, he passed through the town of Lincoln, the seat of Logan County and the only municipality to bear his name during his lifetime. Riding in his newly refurbished carriage, sparkling with a fresh coat of paint and adorned with new silk curtains, he rode out to Atlanta, a town nestled in the northeastern corner of that county, forty miles north of his home in Springfield.[34]

Lincoln arrived in time for Atlanta's daylong Independence Day rally, a festive event complete with brass band, glee club, prayers, speeches, and ice cream. He listened to addresses delivered by James H. Matheny, his friend of twenty years, and Sylvester Strong, a War of 1812 veteran who called upon Lincoln to step up and speak to the crowd. Lincoln complied with the wishes of the attendees and delivered a few remarks. Immediately after this Strong presented Lincoln with a walking cane. This presentation was considered the highlight of the day. Made from South American orange-wood, the cane was adorned with small silver plates across its length, each one imprinted with Lincoln's first initial and each letter of his surname. That night a round of toasts was offered up by the dignitaries and invited guests. "Speeches at large were made by Gen. Matheny and Hon. A. Lincoln," reported the local newspaper. "Matheny quoted the poets and Lincoln talked about eating."[35]

Lincoln's involvement in the Logan County event was hardly earth-shattering, but it showcased the appreciation held for Lincoln by people like old Mr. Strong, who had known Lincoln for more than a quarter of a century. Equally noteworthy were Lincoln's Fourth of July speeches— brief as they were—the first public presentation he had delivered in four months, but totally devoid of politics. Although several offers reached him to deliver political addresses in and out of Illinois, Lincoln agreed to none of them for the bulk of the summer of 1859.

He left his schedule open to award himself time to travel and relax, likely keeping a promise he had made to his wife. He took his family to Chicago for a few days in July; they relaxed at the Tremont House with the families of Jesse Dubois and Stephen Logan (a former law partner). Three weeks later Lincoln left his family back in Springfield. Accompanied by Ozias M. Hatch, he rode the rails westward to St. Joseph, Missouri, picked up a steamer there, and plied the Missouri River upstream. Late in the afternoon of August 12, Lincoln and Hatch disembarked at Council Bluffs, Iowa, the westernmost destination of Lincoln's entire life.[36]

The traveling venture afforded Lincoln the opportunity to inspect seventeen lots plus ten additional acres offered as security of a quit claim deed from Norman B. Judd, who owed Lincoln three thousand dollars— a residual of the lasting debt of the Republican Party in Illinois. They arrived too late to view the lands, so Lincoln and Hatch rode the stage to the Pacific House, the finest establishment of the town.[37]

Lincoln's celebrity attracted many well-wishers who greeted him at the Pacific House. The remainder of his Friday was spent at the home of Thomas Officer, a former Springfield friend who gave Lincoln an impromptu reception that evening. Officer invited the public to attend, and anyone looking for him could easily pick out Lincoln's tall form in the corner of the parlor swapping stories and jokes with acquaintances old and new. It was likely here where Lincoln was called upon to address the townspeople of Council Bluffs on the issues of the day. Too flattered to refuse, Lincoln agreed to do so the following night.

Lincoln spent a leisurely Saturday in Council Bluffs on a tour offered by another former Springfielder, W. H. M. Pusey. This day Lincoln viewed the collateral offered by Judd, and also was escorted to the most scenic part of town. It was called "the Outlook," the edge of the Missouri River bluff that was home to Fairview Cemetery. But the graveyard's name was understated, for the view here was more than fair—it was spectacular. One of the townspeople claimed, "They could see up and down the Missouri river for perhaps thirty miles . . . could see the Nebraska hills sloping eastward to the river." It was on this spot where the men talked about the future of a transcontinental railroad. Lincoln was apprised of the efforts of Council Bluffs to make itself the terminus of a ribbon of iron from the Pacific Coast. Lincoln confidently announced, "Not one, but many roads will center here some day." As Lincoln looked westward into Nebraska Territory, he may have reflected on how the formation of that territory by the Kansas-Nebraska Act of 1854 had set in motion his return to politics after a years-long hiatus.[38]

The overriding issue of the Kansas-Nebraska Act, extension of slavery into the territories, was the issue that Lincoln brought to the public several hours later. That night, true to form, Lincoln entered a packed Concert Hall, and at 7:30 P.M. and he began to speak. The *Bugle*, the Democratic paper of Council Bluffs, was forced to admit, "He was listened to with much attention, for his Waterloo defeat by Douglas has magnified him into quite a lion here."

What the Iowa crowd heard was Lincoln working through the issues dividing his party, much of which he had covered in his past six months of correspondences. He apparently repeated a portion of the same themes addressed in his Chicago speech of March 1, reiterating the importance of adhering to constitutional rights by not opposing the Fugitive-Slave Law. As he had stressed in his letter to Nathan Sargent, he opposed Republicans who proposed an us-versus-them approach to relations with the Southern states. He also repeated his willingness to nominate a Southerner at the convention, provided he espoused the conservative principles Lincoln had been addressing.

An audience member was impressed by the "able, attractive, and convincing" speech. He recalled, "His manner of presenting his argument was very simple, his points so clear and well defined that it was easy for anyone to comprehend it." The Republican-biased paper, the *Nonpareil*—to the surprise of no one—lauded Lincoln as "a man of great intellectual power" and "a close and sound reasoner." Even the Democratic editor of the *Bugle* offered grudging praise for Lincoln in his report of the speech. Acknowledging that Lincoln strove to strike the middle ground, the editor determined, "His speech was in the character of an exhortation to the Republican Party, but was in reality as good a speech as could have been made for the interest of the Democracy."[39]

That Lincoln could garner a positive review from a paper antithetical to his views bears testimony to the charm of the speaker and the nonconfrontational tone of his message in an era of bellicose rhetoric. Two days after the presentation, Lincoln returned to Springfield, stopping again at

St. Joseph to pick up the train. Again, his celebrity status was perhaps greater than he realized, as several citizens called upon him at his hotel. Advantaged with a keen political sense, Lincoln made a point to visit with the editor of the *St. Joseph Journal* before he boarded his train, for no other possible reason than to make himself known. The visit had the desired effect. The pleased editor described Lincoln in the subsequent issue: "In personal appearance, he looks like any other 'six-foot' Kentuckian, and is very affable in manners."[40]

Nine days after embarking upon his trip to Iowa, Lincoln stepped back into his home on Thursday, August 18. He opened a stack of mail and found more offers of speaking engagements, in Minnesota and Wisconsin. Aware of a huge murder trial scheduled to commence in Sangamon Circuit Court at the end of the month, Lincoln was forced again to decline.[41]

As satisfied as he must have been with his performance in the two major addresses he had delivered thus far in 1859 (Chicago and Council Bluffs), he would have been equally displeased at the lack of attention his speeches received. The Chicago speech garnered no press at all, and the Iowa speech was covered only in western Iowa papers. Lincoln left Council Bluffs before the subsequent issue of the weekly papers rolled off the presses; he would have been pained to learn that the Democratic paper offered more attention to his speech than did the Republican one.

The sparse coverage all but guaranteed that his address would not be excerpted and recirculated in other papers. No better evidence for this exists than letters Lincoln received from Iowa Republicans asking him to travel to Iowa to deliver a speech—clearly ignorant of the fact that he had already been there and done that. This legless reporting may have been a small reason for Lincoln to turn down other out-of-state offers.

Lincoln needed widespread coverage to change public opinion about him, an unwanted side effect of the publicity he had earned from the 1858 Senate campaign. The most memorable line of any of Lincoln's speeches from the 1830s through the summer of 1859 was from his one-year-old "House Divided" speech, delivered in Springfield to accept the Republican nomination for the Senate. "A house divided against itself cannot stand," said Lincoln in June 1858; "I believe this government cannot endure permanently half slave and half free." Stephen A. Douglas hung these words on Lincoln like a chain of leaden balls throughout the summer and fall of 1858, painting Lincoln as an abolitionist. Before long Lincoln's speech was taken out of context as a premonition of a civil war, although the third and fourth sentences of the "House Divided" excerpt suggest otherwise: "I do not expect the Union to be dissolved—I do not expect the house to fall—but I do expect it will cease to be divided. It will become all one thing, or all the other."[42]

One year later Lincoln's "House Divided" speech remained controversial and threatened to crumble the foundation he had worked so hard to build in his 1859 comeback. He was not alone, for Senator Seward, the Republican front-runner, suffered a similar blemish from a speech delivered in Rochester in October 1858. Reviewing the clash of the free-labor culture of the North and the slave-labor culture of the South, Seward explained, "It is an irrepressible conflict between opposing and enduring forces, and it means that the United States must and will, sooner or later, become either entirely a slaveholding nation, or entirely a free-labor nation." The lines were similar to Lincoln's analogy, and both speeches would forever be known by their provocative terms: "house divided" and "irrepressible conflict."[43]

Both men suffered from the provocative words even though neither was predicting bloodshed to settle the issue. But that is the way they were viewed in the summer of 1859. Letters continued to pour into newspapers, using those 1858 speeches—and by extension the authors of the speeches—as evidence of the radical turn of the Republican Party. Lincoln's and Seward's words were so well known that a letter writer to an upstate New York newspaper needed only to mention their names to castigate the Republican Party's positions. "To adopt Seward and Lincoln's principles that there must be an eternal war between the free and slave States, they would not yet have the courage, as it would involve the safety of the Union," claimed the correspondent about the Republican Party, "and on that issue they dare not go even before their own fanatical followers."[44]

To be seen as too "fanatical" for a political party to support was usually the death knell for any candidate wishing to claim the majority of the nation's votes in the Electoral College. That Seward was stung but was still surviving the ill use of his inflammatory words testified to his strength as the recognized front-runner for the Republican nomination of 1860. For

Lincoln, a long-shot candidate, the misperception of him as so radical as to *advocate* civil war was clearly more detrimental, for he needed to dispel those myths in his quest to become the middle-ground, safe, alternative candidate of the Republican Party. Perhaps he felt he had made some headway through the first three seasons of 1859 to ensconce himself in the mainstream, but the claim of the letter writer in New York State indicated how far he still had to go.

Lincoln's "House Divided" speech was his and his alone, and he had to endure withering criticisms of it not only from the opposition but from his own Republican supporters in Illinois. Norman Judd told Lincoln that if he had seen those lines before Lincoln delivered them, he would have cut them out of the text. Other intimates were just as critical. Leonard Swett joined several other friends of Lincoln for a dinner during the summer of 1859 at which the subject of the "House Divided" speech was brought up. "We all insisted it was a great mistake," recalled Swett six years later, "but [Lincoln] justified himself and finally said, 'Well Gentlemen, you may think that the Speech was a mistake, but I never have believed it was, and you will see the day when you will consider it was the wisest thing I ever said.'" Lincoln's stubborn pronouncement was one no one at the dinner party consented to at that time.[45]

His court schedule was filling up in the fall, providing Lincoln with few opportunities to travel great distances to speak. Despite this he had made great strides since the Senate loss to reestablish himself as a party spokesman with a clear, consistent, and forthright message. Above all he was still "Honest Abe," the politician to trust, even though he had been less than trustworthy about his ultimate ambitions. The Lincoln boom had made such a small groundswell that no one paying attention to it would have noticed it. That is the way Lincoln preferred it, for the present.

The next step in his slow push to the nomination was to become more visible outside the state. He needed to generate public support from non-Illinoisans, he needed to reverse the radical tag placed upon him, and he needed his words to gain traction. For this reason, the missed opportunities—from the Jefferson birthday event in Massachusetts to the political events in Kansas, Minnesota, and Iowa—were woefully regretted.

Most lamentable was deciding against speaking at the Republican convention in Kansas Territory in the middle of May. Horace Greeley, the renowned reporter of the *New York Tribune*, was there in the midst of a much ballyhooed overland journey to the Pacific Coast, a trip whose chronicle he published the following year. Greeley and Lincoln had met briefly in Bloomington late in December, when Greeley happened to be giving a speech there while Lincoln was in town for court duties. One month removed from his Senate defeat to Douglas—whom Greeley had supported in his typical maverick style—Lincoln was still smarting enough to snub Greeley when he invited Lincoln to visit him at his Bloomington hotel. Greeley was a man who would never forget such a slight.[46]

Kansas would have afforded Lincoln the perfect opportunity to make amends with Greeley, whose influence in the Republican Party was as strong as any individual's in the late 1850s. Greeley addressed the convention in a speech published in several newspapers. If Lincoln saw the reprinted text he would have rejoiced and winced at the same time when he read Greeley's line: "The able and gallant Lincoln of Illinois, whom we had hoped to meet and hear today . . ." How beneficial it would have been for Lincoln to be there, not only to receive widespread coverage but to do so from a former critic of his positions in the 1858 campaign![47]

As August faded to September, no more offers had come in and the convention was less than ten months away. Lincoln needed a big break in his favor or this darkest of dark horses would never leave the gate.

Three

CHASE'S BACKYARD

POLITICS WAS EVERYTHING in Illinois, even during the hazy late-summer weeks of 1859, an "off year" for the state with few elections of interest coming up in November. Not only was Springfield considered the geographic center of the state, but as the state capital, it was the political heart of the state. Politics permeated the pages of the three daily papers of the city, including the *Independent*. Politics was a business; it was entertainment; and for many, it was their religion.

For these reasons, any diversion from the fatiguing inundation of politics in Springfield was treated with zeal. The last days of August and the first two of September offered one of the most popular diversions for the region—a murder trial. Back in the middle of July, Peachy Quinn Harrison and Greek Crafton, two boyhood friends now in their early twenties, got in a heated argument in a drugstore in Pleasant Plains, a sleepy village fifteen miles northwest of Springfield. The verbal warfare between the two grew more contentious, and before his brother could intervene to stop it, Crafton lay mortally wounded with an abdominal knife wound. He died two days later. Harrison was subsequently arrested and escorted to jail.[1]

The father of the accused hired the team of Lincoln, Stephen T. Logan (Lincoln's law partner prior to William Herndon), and Shelby Cullom to defend his son. Two weeks after Lincoln's return from Iowa, the trial commenced in Sangamon Circuit Court, removed from the Eighth Judicial Circuit in 1857 and, therefore, no longer part of Judge David Davis's jurisdiction. Judge E. Y. Rice presided, with a team of three, including John M. Palmer, set to prosecute on behalf of the state. *The People of Illinois v. Peachy Quinn Harrison* became the most celebrated event in central Illinois that September. Every paper in Springfield as well as smaller presses outside the town covered the trial. Robert R. Hitt, the gifted shorthand reporter for the *Chicago Press and Tribune*, came down to Springfield to record the proceedings for the press. Based on the publicity generated by the preliminaries at the courthouse, the circuit-court trial was certain to attract widespread attention. The grand jury indictment itself drew huge crowds with, according to the newspapers, "many being attracted there to hear the able arguments of the counsel in the case."[2]

The four-day murder trial began on Wednesday, August 31, with the selection of a jury consisting of ten farmers, an engineer, and a carpenter. This was an inauspicious start to what was easily Lincoln's most interesting case of 1859 and one of the most noteworthy ones of his career. It turned out to be the only Lincoln case with a transcript (nearly one hundred pages long) that survived for posterity. It also set a legal precedent—albeit an uncomfortable one—on the second day, when one of the twelve jurors asked for information from one of the witnesses and received a lengthy response, with absolutely no objection from either team of attorneys, all of whom had no concerns about the impropriety of this type of exchange.

Above all, the trial became embedded in Lincoln lore due to Lincoln's behavior in the court. Lincoln and Logan's defense conceded that Peachy Harrison did indeed cause Crafton's death but argued that the stabbing was justified, since Crafton had threatened Harrison on several occasions prior to and including the day he was mortally wounded. On the second day of the trial, when Lincoln tried to introduce this evidence through a witness, the prosecution protested on the grounds that even if true, it did not prove that Harrison was made aware of Crafton's threat. Judge Rice sustained the objection, leaving an opening for the defense to reintroduce it once it could prove that the threat had reached its client. Despite the open-ended decision, Lincoln was incensed at the judge's ruling, the court transcript revealing that "there was now a good deal of feeling excited on the subject at the moment." But he swallowed his anger and continued his defense.

Lincoln's ire peaked when he called up his main witness that Thursday afternoon. The venerable Peter Cartwright, a famous circuit-riding preacher who had run unsuccessfully against Lincoln for Congress in 1846, took the stand to testify for the defense. He was Harrison's grandfather, and he claimed—in his role as God's servant—to have visited Crafton on his deathbed. Lincoln knew that Crafton had given Cartwright a statement that benefited his client, but when he asked the minister to reveal that statement for the jury, John Palmer swiftly objected again for the prosecution, insisting that the deathbed confession was inadmissible. Common sense dictated that it should be omitted. Regardless of his standing as a man of the cloth, the grandfather of the accused claiming that he was the sole witness to an exonerating deathbed confession from the man his grandson had mortally wounded rendered Cartwright's testimony problematic. Without mentioning the nepotistic problem, Judge Rice sided with Palmer. He ruled that the jury could not hear the testimony and that the court would adjourn for the day with Cartwright returning to testify to Crafton's deathbed statement to him on Friday morning—before the jury reconvened.[3]

The judge's ruling lifted Lincoln from his chair. Protesting that he "had never heard of such law," Lincoln denounced Rice's decision in the courtroom, closing in upon but not crossing the fine line of a contempt-of-court charge. "He roared like a lion suddenly aroused from his lair," claimed the court crier, "and said and did more in ten minutes than I ever heard him say or saw him do before in an hour." Herndon was present as an observer and sat stunned as his senior partner became "so angry that he looked like Lucifer in an uncontrollable rage." Judge Rice brushed off Lincoln's fury, promised his ruling in the morning, and adjourned the case for the day.[4]

During the break in the trial Lincoln discussed the case with Herndon. Convinced that the judge, a Democrat, had ruled against him because of a political rivalry, Lincoln prepared to take up the argument again. He studied case law that night and, armed with a stack of books, marched back into the courtroom on Friday morning. The judge decided to adhere to his earlier rulings to not allow the testimony to be admitted and to excuse the jury while he heard Cartwright's statement. Hitt underlined three words in his transcript to underscore what happened next: "Defendant's counsel excepted." Lincoln peppered the judge with facts and inquiries concerning his rulings. "Lincoln was mad, vexed, and indignant," recalled Herndon. "When a great big man of mind and body gets mad he is mad all over, terrible, furious, eloquent, etc." Judge Rice withered under Lincoln's pressure and—after hearing Cartwright's testimony alone—reversed his decision, which allowed the deathbed statement to be heard by the jury.[5]

After the jurors took their seats, Lincoln queried Cartwright about what Crafton had said to him. Cartwright responded that while he held his hand during the last moments of the victim's life, Crafton told him, "I have brought it upon myself, and I forgive Quinn." The defense obtained a second victory in the wake of Cartwright's explosive testimony when Judge Rice—over the persistent objections of John M. Palmer—allowed witness testimony of Crafton's threats against Harrison in the days prior to the stabbing to be heard by the jury. "The Court was actually badgered by Lincoln into its final decision. . . . Palmer couldn't stop Lincoln's force and eloquence," claimed Herndon of the judge's decisions. The sweltering heat eventually closed the eventful trial day when the other two members of Lincoln's defense team fainted in succession while attempting to present closing arguments.[6]

Brimming with confidence at his ability to force two reversals by Judge Rice, Lincoln carried the momentum with him into court the following morning for his closing argument in the defense of Harrison. The crowd remained large this Saturday; those unable to cram into the courtroom hung around outside, gathering at the doors or climbing to the windows to hear Lincoln's defense speech. He did not disappoint. After discussing the evidence from both sides, Lincoln reminded the court that the dead victim was a student of his, and yet he sympathized with the families of both Crafton and his defendant, Peachy Harrison, whom he portrayed as completely innocent of murderous intent.[7]

He played on the sympathies of the jury with great effect. According to the memories of a witness in the room, "Burst after burst of eloquence followed, until not an eye could be seen without a glistening telltale standing at the portal of the soul, having been enticed there from the niche of sorrowful affection to witness the earnest gesture and listen to the burning, soul-stirring eloquence of Abraham Lincoln." Maximizing the effect of Peter Cartwright's testimony, Lincoln closed his two-hour argument by imploring the court to practice the same forgiving spirit exhibited by the victim to the defendant. That afternoon the verdict came in: "not guilty." It was perhaps Lincoln's most powerful performance in the courtroom. "It was a proud day for Lincoln," insisted Billy Herndon; "Lincoln was a grand man, an imposing figure that day, I assure you."[8]

The winning attorney had no time to bask in the victory. A huge political opportunity arrived on his doorstep in the form of a stamped letter. William T. Bascom, the secretary of Ohio's Republican State Central Committee, sent Lincoln a plea. Informing him that Douglas was making speeches in Ohio, Bascom stated, "Now, we desire to head off the little gentleman, and in behalf of the Rep. State Cent. Com I invite you to visit our State to make a few speeches, say 3 or 4, at such prominent points as we may select." The very next day, a similar plea came from Peter Zinn, another member of Ohio's Republican State Central Committee, requesting Lincoln's appearance in Cincinnati.[9]

Although Lincoln had turned down several out-of-state offers, he could hardly resist these. The requested dates coincided with a break in Lincoln's legal schedule. Speaking in Ohio gave him the opportunity to broaden his appeal, a benefit made more timely with the Republican National Convention likely commencing in less than a year. The offer was expenses paid, certainly a big plus considering Lincoln's poor financial health earlier in the year.

Perhaps the most important factor enticing Lincoln was the opportunity to oppose Stephen A. Douglas. The Ohio events, however, were not at all like the Senate campaign in Illinois one year earlier. Lincoln would speak in the same towns as Douglas but several days after Douglas's appearance. Although popular sovereignty was still the central debating issue, Douglas raised the stakes with a heady move meant for both self-promotion and credibility. He published a nineteen-page article in the September issue of *Harper's New Monthly Magazine*, one of the largest circulating monthly periodicals nationwide. Entitled "Popular Sovereignty in the Territories," Douglas's article painstakingly answered the questions posed by his critics regarding the issue. He went so far as to claim that his position of allowing or disallowing slavery to extend into the territories by the majority vote of its citizens was the intent of the Founding Fathers. The article forced Lincoln to modify his speech to counter Douglas's claims.[10]

Lincoln informed Bascom and Zinn on September 6 that he would speak in Columbus and Cincinnati. The Columbus speech was scheduled to be delivered on September 16, a few days after Douglas stopped there, and Cincinnati would be addressed the following evening. With no lengthy cases to clog up his time before then, Lincoln took the opportunity to prepare his speeches. He studied Douglas's lengthy article and wrote detailed notes to counter what he considered Douglas's most objectionable claims. He incorporated these additions into the framework of the speech he had prepared months earlier, the one he had planned to present in May at the Republican convention in Kansas Territory before bowing out due to his work schedule. During this preparation, Lincoln received a panicked letter from Norman Judd, overreacting to a report put out by the Democrats' organ, the *Chicago Times*, that Douglas was about to make a speech in Chicago. "If that is attempted Rome will howl," ranted Judd, who insisted that Lincoln drop everything at once to squelch the political threat: "Now you must come up without fail—and that will bluff them if they are so trickey [*sic*]."[11]

Lincoln declined to make the trip and yet he could not fault Judd for the hypersensitive reaction to Douglas's presence. It showed how far Douglas had burrowed under the skin of Illinois Republicans. Lincoln was not immune to these chiggers. Although he understood that Douglas would probably win the Democrats' nomination at their national convention in Charleston in the spring of 1860, Lincoln was haunted by the scenario of Douglas bolting the convention in opposition to the slave code that Southern Democrats would force him to adopt, thus leading him into the arms of a conciliatory Republican Party that had warmed to his anti-Buchanan position. Lincoln feared that Douglas's version of popular sovereignty—one that he claimed back in Freeport in 1858 could supersede the Supreme Court's *Dred Scott* decision regarding slavery in the territories—was acceptable to Republicans nationwide.[12]

Lincoln's notes have survived for posterity; they offer a peek into what he would say in Ohio. "The Republican cause can not live by Douglas's position," averred Lincoln. The chief problem confronting Lincoln was the widespread approval of popular sovereignty. As long and tortured as

Douglas's article was, the piece received national circulation, both in *Harper's* and in newspapers republishing it. The senator was undoubtedly the best-known politician in the land. While Douglas was speaking in Ohio to support Ohio Democrats in their October statewide election, his article and early-September Ohio tour unofficially initiated his national campaign for the presidency. More distressing to Lincoln and the Republicans was the Little Giant's strategy, one spelled out in the article. Douglas was firmly positioning himself between the political extremes with the claim that popular sovereignty had been supported by the Founding Fathers, by intent if not by the written law. That his article and Ohio speeches were receiving nationwide coverage showed Douglas's unprecedented influence and popularity. In the seventy years of the nation's political history, no presidential candidate had received such extensive billing fourteen months before the election than had Stephen A. Douglas in September 1859. This is what fed into Lincoln's paranoia over the possibility that Douglas could receive the Republican nomination if Democrat extremists barred him from the Democratic helm.[13]

Lincoln planned to neutralize the Democrats with a strong but safe presentation, one that accomplished the same effect as an invective-filled stump speech but this time with the facts trumping the style. Ohio politics necessitated this, for the American Party (an organization transformed from the Know Nothings) was still a significant force in Cincinnati and elsewhere. In an effort not to alienate this faction and to improve their chances to overthrow the Democrats in the statewide October elections, Republicans in Cincinnati wisely adopted the term "Opposition Party" to encompass the ideals of all factions opposed to the Democrats. Future president Rutherford B. Hayes, the Republican city solicitor of Cincinnati in September 1859, anticipated Lincoln's arrival in Columbus. He notified Ohio's secretary of state that the esteemed visitor should be warned about giving a partisan Republican speech when he got to Cincinnati. "We go by the name of 'Opposition Party,' and injury might be done if party names and party doctrines were used by Mr. Lincoln in a way to displease the American element of our organization," advised Hayes on September 14. Hayes surmised that the American Party adherents had sympathized with Lincoln in the 1858 campaign against Douglas, and he expected that even though they would not adopt all of his views, Lincoln should still "make a fine impression here."[14]

Lincoln used the term "Opposition Party" in his pretrip letters to Cincinnati, but it is unclear if he ever received Hayes's pointed advice. In fact, he was advised to do just the opposite of what Hayes recommended in a letter from an unexpected source. Joseph Medill, an avowed Chase supporter, reminded Lincoln that he had been raised in Ohio prior to taking his editor's position with the *Chicago Press and Tribune*. Medill informed Lincoln that unlike Illinois, Ohio was a homogeneous state in regards to its politics, but he did consider Cincinnati "nearly as radical as Chicago" and reminded Lincoln about the repeal of the Fugitive-Slave Law plank in the Ohio Republican platform. Medill suggested a partisan speech over a statesmanlike address, claiming that the Buckeyes relished hard-hitting firebrands. "Go in boldly," declared Medill, "strike straight from the shoulder,—hit below the belt as well as above, and kick like thunder."[15]

Lincoln's steady and growing popularity was bound to climb more than ever in Ohio, for these speeches were destined to be reported as the sequel to the 1858 debates with Douglas even though the combatants would not be performing in the same event. The *Chicago Press and Tribune* even sent stenographer Robert R. Hitt to the Buckeye State to feed the newspaper an account of Lincoln's speeches. Editor Medill inadvertently confirmed that Lincoln's clandestine strategy to win the Republican nomination was running smoothly when he advised him, "As you are not a candidate you can talk out as boldly as you please."[16]

With Mary and one of his young sons at his side, Lincoln rode the rails eastward to Columbus, arriving at Ohio's capital and Salmon Chase's hometown late on Friday morning, September 16. The Lincolns stepped into the depot, where he was greeted by—no one. As much as the Ohio Republican State Central Committee wanted Lincoln to speak in Columbus, none of its members made an effort to make their special guest feel that way. With no escort to guide them, the Lincolns made their way to the Neil House, where members of the Young Men's Republican Club eventually found him. Lincoln delivered a speech that afternoon to a crowd of fewer than a thousand gathered on the eastern terrace of the capitol building (the disappointing numbers were attributed to competition from a large agricultural fair held at the same time). Conspicuously absent that Friday was the top Republican of Columbus and the entire state, Salmon P. Chase. The Buckeye governor was out of town this day. One of the two Republican newspaper editors, John Greiner of the *Columbus Gazette*, made no effort to welcome Lincoln. The fact that Greiner was a Chase supporter lent credence to the notion that Lincoln was being snubbed by the Chase men for his critical response to Chase's views on the Fugitive-Slave Law back in June.[17]

Lincoln delivered a much shorter speech a few hours later at city hall to the Young Men's Republican Club. Again, the crowd was small, and Lincoln was there in part to introduce another Republican speaker. The *Ohio State Journal*, the chief Republican paper of Columbus, failed to make a record of Lincoln's evening speech but did reproduce his afternoon speech the following morning in its daily issue. Despite the smallness of the crowd that actually heard his remarks, the speech was so popular in print form that the *Journal* felt compelled to run it two more times in the triweekly and weekly editions.[18]

Lincoln did not stay in Columbus long enough to soak up all the printed critiques of his speech. After sitting for a daguerreotype on Saturday morning (a photographic likeness that has been lost to history), he, Mary, and his son stepped back on the train, this time heading west to Dayton, where they disembarked at Union Station. Lincoln had to transfer in Dayton to go to Cincinnati. He'd originally had no plans to speak in Dayton, but apparently he changed his mind in Columbus and confirmed this in a Friday-evening telegram. The Republicans in Dayton were relieved at the change of plans. Douglas had spoken in town to great Democratic fanfare one week earlier; now his words would be challenged by the man who had debated him more frequently and effectively than any other.[19]

With a population of twenty thousand, Dayton was bigger than Columbus and the third-largest city in Ohio. Like Columbus, Dayton had two Republican newspapers, the *Gazette* and the *Journal*; both announced Lincoln's pending courthouse speech that Saturday in their morning editions. Unlike in Columbus, the Lincolns were greeted by Dayton's dignitaries, including Robert C. Schenck, a former Whig congressman who had served with Lincoln in the U.S. House of Representatives in the 1840s. The escorts delivered Lincoln to the Valentine Winters mansion, a wealthy banker's home adorned with a huge flag draped across the stone pillars of the front porch for this occasion. Under that enormous flag, Lincoln addressed the crowd gathered on the street in front of him. His brief speech roused the well-wishers to hearty cheers.[20]

After a short visit with the Winters family, the Lincolns were led to the finest hotel of the town, the Phillips House, where again Lincoln briefly addressed a gathering crowd. After this, he was found sitting at a table in the hotel, where he exchanged jokes and anecdotes with Schenck and two or three other Republican bigwigs. Shortly after noon Lincoln took a stroll with the dignitaries to kill some time before his scheduled speech.

The spare time finally died at 1:30 P.M., when a crowd numbering in the hundreds congregated in front of Dayton's courthouse. The citizens stood on the steps and on the walkway in front of the courthouse, facing east toward the street, where a speaker's box was set up for Lincoln. He stepped onto the makeshift platform and spoke for less than two hours, delivering an extended excerpt of what he planned to deliver in Cincinnati that night. Although the Democratic paper of Dayton dismissed Lincoln's arguments as "a net work of fallacies, and false assumptions throughout," the Republican faithful, footsore from standing in place on such a hard and uncomfortable surface, deemed themselves fortunate to hear him that day. A Dayton attorney had low expectations of this event but was so moved by Lincoln's performance as to confess in his diary, "His speech was a perfect surprise to everyone—a close, logical argument without anecdote or illustration and yet so clear and so intensely interesting that although the audience stood upon the Courthouse steps and the pavement, not one person left until he closed." No one was more impressed than former Whig congressman Robert Schenck. Based on the speech he heard in Dayton that afternoon, Schenck was convinced that Abraham Lincoln should be a candidate for president of the United States.[21]

Within minutes of his completing his Dayton address, Lincoln and his family stepped back on the train and headed sixty miles southward through the autumn-tinged Miami River valley to Cincinnati. A planned but brief stop occurred at the town of Hamilton, where a crowd gathered at the railroad station to hear Lincoln speak from the rear platform of the train. The crowd cheered when Lincoln stepped out on the platform; then they laughed when the diminutive John A. Gurley, the U.S. representative from Cincinnati who was traveling with Lincoln from Dayton, came out and stood next to the towering speaker. Lincoln's timing and sense of humor took over immediately. Pointing to himself, he declared, "My friends, this is the long of it," and then placing his hand on top of Gurley's head, he finished the sentence: "and this is the short of it." Capturing his appreciative crowd, Lincoln followed up with a brief speech commending the beauty of the region before delving into Douglas, Kansas, and slavery.[22]

Applause at the close of the speech competed with the sound of the screeching locomotive as it steamed onward to Cincinnati. This was a return trip for Lincoln, for he had traveled to the Queen City on a business trip back in March 1855. The past experience conjured up awful memories for Lincoln. Snubbed by prominent lawyers and judges during the previous visit to partake in a celebrated trial, Lincoln had departed the city with an injured pride and harboring doubts about his abilities as a lawyer. He had vowed that the first visit would be his last, assuring his hostess in 1855, "I never expect to be in Cincinnati again. I have nothing against the city, but things have so happened here as to make it undesirable for me ever to return here."[23]

Four and a half years later, on September 17, 1859, Lincoln defied his earlier expectation as he stepped onto the depot platform in Cincinnati at seven P.M. The bad memories of 1855 dissipated with the overwhelming reception he received the moment he came into view. Hundreds of citizens thronged to the depot to greet him. A large formal committee escorted the Lincolns to the city's best hotel, the Burnet House, where a second committee took over to whisk Lincoln away to an open carriage that would transport him to the Fifth Street Market Place, the site of Lincoln's well-advertised speech.

Lincoln's ride to his speech could not have been more exhilarating. Brass bands blared bouncy renditions and cannons fired their booming announcements of Lincoln's arrival. His carriage was paraded down to Fifth Street, preceded by a mounted escort and bookended by a German militia brigade while others joined the march bearing blazing torches. Upon Lincoln's arrival bonfires and fireworks lit up the marketplace, where a crowd well in excess of three thousand filled the area, drawn there by the heavily advertised event and a perfect mid-September evening of seventy degrees. The country's seventh most populous city, Cincinnati could also boast ten daily newspapers and dozens of weekly and triweekly publications. Representatives from several of these newspapers and from papers in other towns in Ohio and Illinois mingled with the crowd, prepared to report on Lincoln's themes, exact words, and style. Lincoln entered a brick house, appeared on the balcony above his audience, and—with torches assisting the moon to illuminate the speaker on this September evening—began his speech.[24]

What he said in Cincinnati on Saturday night included most of his address the previous day in Columbus and encompassed his teasers at Dayton and Hamilton several hours earlier. It expanded upon the ideals first introduced in his speeches of 1854, when he returned to politics, and later developed in the campaign of 1858. It highlighted the arguments presented in Chicago in March and likely incorporated themes he had presented in Iowa one month earlier, the same themes he had initially prepared in the winter of 1859 to present at the Kansas convention.

But Cincinnati still became the scene of a new address, one that showcased Lincoln as a studied politician who prepared a logical counterargument to the ideals presented in Douglas's rambling September piece in *Harper's New Monthly Magazine*. What made the speech different from what he had presented at Columbus was not its content but the method he chose to express his arguments to his audience. This was a product of planning before he left Illinois and an assessment of what he felt were the strongest and weakest points of his Columbus speech.

Lincoln did not have access to Douglas's September 9 speech in Cincinnati, but he displayed no concern over this, for he knew from his history of debating the Little Giant that Douglas was a rigid orator, one who had stuck to the same text throughout the 1858 campaign. Therefore, Lincoln could easily have considered the *Harper's New Monthly Magazine* article as the true template of Douglas's speech and the only item he needed to study to prepare an appropriate response. It is also apparent that he was able to get a copy of Douglas's Columbus speech to affirm what he had already prepared.[25]

Unlike Douglas, Lincoln modified his speeches based on his feel for the audience, the location of the speech, access to current literature to incorporate into his speech, and the time allotted to deliver the address. In Columbus, Lincoln had begun his speech by reading to his audience an excerpt from the Democratic paper of the city that had attempted to damage Lincoln by claiming that he favored Negro suffrage. Lincoln took pains to counter the claim with a long-winded response in which he resorted to reading tedious excerpts of previous speeches. The time spent responding to this charge shows Lincoln as a presidential candidate (albeit unannounced), more sensitive to what was said about him than to what he would say about the issues.

Lincoln opened with a similar theme in Cincinnati, but he chose a different tack. Gone were the stale recitations of previous speech passages and newspaper excerpts. Instead, Lincoln waited for the applause to wane, then immediately tackled Douglas's criticism of his "House Divided" speech as a frank statement of Lincoln's support of abolition. After repeating the controversial sentences of that speech, Lincoln explained, "I declared then, and I now re-declare, that I have . . . little inclination to . . . interfere with the institution of Slavery where it now exists . . . as I believe we have no power to do so."

He acknowledged that Douglas had successfully linked the "House Divided" speech with Seward's "irrepressible conflict." (An audience member, perhaps having heard Douglas the week before, shouted that Douglas claimed Seward's controversial two words were "original with Lincoln"). Lincoln informed the crowd that abolitionist Pennsylvania congressman John Hickman had since said something similar with no objection from Douglas. Why? Because, Lincoln reasoned, Douglas did not want to alienate a politician who might still support him. "That is the difference!" Lincoln declared. "It is not unpatriotic to hold that opinion if a man is a Douglas man." Lincoln then informed the Cincinnati crowd that he, Seward, and Hickman were all preceded by *Richmond Enquirer* editor Roger A. Pryor in 1856, who predicted that the country would become all slave instead of all free and had since gone to Congress while concurrently running a pro-Douglas paper in Washington.

Lincoln went on to turn his Cincinnati speech into an all-about-Douglas address, even to the point of mocking the Little Giant's purposeful mischaracterization of Lincoln's principles in the *Harper's* article. He also pointedly stated that Douglas had yet to take a position on slavery. "There is not a public man in the United States, I believe, with the exception of Senator Douglas, who has not at some time of his life, declared his opinion whether the thing is right or wrong," declared Lincoln to highlight the absurdity of Douglas's noncommittal stance on such a black-or-white moral issue.[26]

Lincoln employed another new tactic for delivering the middle portion of his speech. He told his audience that he would model his remarks as if he were addressing only pro-Douglas, slavery-supporting Kentuckians. This naturally provided him with a foil that replaced the mundane reading of Democratic newspaper excerpts, as he'd done in Columbus. With only the Ohio River separating North from South, Cincinnati was a perfect place to employ the device. He said he assumed that Kentuckians had mingled in the crowd below him. But even if this was not the case, Lincoln reasoned that "we are on elevated ground, and, by speaking distinctly, I should not wonder if some of the Kentuckians would hear me on the other side of the river." Lincoln well understood that more than 90 percent of the throng below him were Buckeyes. Still, by pretending to speak to an all-Kentucky crowd, Lincoln could highlight Douglas's hypocrisy while presenting a congenial case as if he were addressing all the residents of slaveholding states.

Lincoln appeared comfortable with this method, but some in his audience were not. At one point Lincoln made an inflammatory comment that produced a groan from one of his listeners, leading Lincoln to quip, "That is my Kentuckian I am talking to now." Minutes later an exasperated listener yelled up, "Speak to Ohio men, and not to Kentuckians!" Rather than accede, Lincoln retorted, "I beg permission to speak as I please." The laughter that immediately followed told Lincoln that most of his audience was in synch with his style and he shouldn't adjust it to placate a confused few. It eventually became clear to all, due to Lincoln's frequent reminders, that he was deliberately speaking to "them" and not "us."[27]

Mocking Douglas by imitating the Little Giant's stump-speech style, Lincoln drawled out the "gu-reat per-inciple" of popular sovereignty. He used logic to show that Douglas was debauching public opinion, preparing people to accept a second *Dred Scott* decision that would allow the extension of slavery into Northern states much as the original one had affirmed the extension of slavery into the territories. Lincoln reasoned that Douglas was playing mind games with the country in an effort to permit a national slave code that would allow slavery to extend wherever the people wanted it—including Northern states like Ohio where it had never existed before. Lincoln reiterated how Douglas argued that Northerners would not have slaves because the climate was not supportive of crops requiring slave labor, but at the same time it violated the principle of popular sovereignty to prevent the people from deciding upon it. Lincoln stressed that "whenever your minds are brought to adopt his argument, as surely you will have reached the conclusion that although slavery is not profitable in Ohio, if any man wants it, it is wrong to him not to let him have it."[28]

Taking the argument to its logical conclusion, Lincoln went on to state that since Douglas was effecting the acceptance of slavery into the territories (and perhaps throughout the land), it was natural to conclude that the only way to nourish popular sovereignty was to reopen the slave trade, notwithstanding the existence of a published letter from Douglas opposing this African "market." Lincoln reasoned, "If it is popular sovereignty for the people to have slaves because they want them, it is popular sovereignty for them to buy them in Africa because they desire to do so."[29]

Throughout his speech Lincoln was interrupted, not only by applause and shouts of affirmation, but at least twice by a cannon discharge, immediately followed by breaking glass from the loud report of the weapon. None of this deterred the speaker as he worked his way through his address. But he quickly quelled any attempt to turn this into give-and-take banter. At one point an audience member shouted out a question to him: "Don't foreign nations interfere with the slave trade?" Lincoln apparently thought this came from a Democrat who was attempting to weaken his argument. When Lincoln learned after a brief exchange that the questioner was a Republican, Lincoln admonished, "You and I will be on the best terms in the world, but I do not wish to be diverted from the point I was trying to press."[30]

Lincoln pointed out to his "Kentucky" audience how effective Douglas had been in eroding public opinion to this point. He emphasized how no one five years before ever expressed publicly "that the negro had no share in the Declaration of Independence." Now, in 1859, the entire Democratic Party, including all Northern Democrats, had latched on to this belief. According to Lincoln, this was evidence of how Douglas could trivialize slavery, as also were Douglas's overt attempts to dehumanize slaves. To illustrate, Lincoln repeated Douglas's analogy that in all contests between the Negro and the white man, Douglas was for the white man, and for all the ones between the Negro and the crocodile, he was for the Negro. Lincoln deduced for his audience that Douglas was creating "a sort of proposition in proportion which may be stated thus: as the Negro is to the white man, so the crocodile is to the Negro, and as the Negro may rightfully treat the crocodile as a beast or reptile, so the white man may rightfully treat the Negro as a beast or reptile. This is really the 'knip' of all the argument of his."[31]

He heeded the earlier advice to incorporate all the parties of Ohio in his anti-Douglas thesis. Continuing his tactic of addressing Kentuckians, Lincoln said that they were stuck with Douglas as their candidate, for they would be beaten if they did not take him, and the same result would occur if they did nominate him. "We, the Republicans and others forming the Opposition of the country, intend to 'stand by our guns,' to be patient and firm, and in the long run to beat you whether you take him or not," warned Lincoln as he reverted to partisan stump speaking. "We know that before we fairly beat you, we have to beat you both [Kentucky and Douglas] together . . . and we expect to do it. We don't intend to be very impatient about it. We mean to be as deliberate and calm about it as it is possible to be, but as firm and resolved as it is possible for men to be. When we do as we say, beat you, you perhaps want to know what we will do with you."

The last one of these inflammatory sentences induced the roused-up portion of the crowd to laughter. Lincoln had stirred up the more extreme faction of his audience, who applauded each of the previous four charged statements. Now they wanted Lincoln to throw them the red meat; they wanted him to tell the Kentuckians that they would be forced to submit to the hard-line Republicans' will. Meanwhile the Democrats and moderates who had listened so intently were reduced to silence, likely stunned at how Lincoln's logical address had suddenly turned so partisan, so brazen and bellicose. He had declared his intent to "beat you" five times in less than a minute, perhaps a message directed at none other than Stephen A. Douglas, who was likely to read this speech as soon as one of the Cincinnati papers published it. No doubt everyone in front of him attentively waited for Lincoln to tell what the Opposition would do to the pro-Douglas voters after beating them.

Lincoln's answer, "so far as I am authorized to speak for the Opposition," surprised them all. "We mean to treat you, as near as we possibly can, like Washington, Jefferson, and Madison treated you. We mean to leave you alone." The crowd—this time including the moderates—erupted in cheers as Lincoln completely reverted to the middle-ground message he had consistently been advocating, not only throughout the evening but since the mid-1850s—preserving slavery where it was constitutionally allowed. He told the "Kentuckians" that aligning with Douglas had turned them into "degenerated men," but the principles of the Founders and the authors of compromise legislation allowed them their constitutional rights—including the right to keep slaves.

"We mean to remember that you are as good as we," Lincoln preached in his most conciliatory tone; "that there is no difference between us other than the difference of circumstances. We mean to recognize and bear in mind always that you have as good hearts in your bosoms as other people, or as we claim to have, and treat you accordingly." Likely with Mary—Kentucky born and bred—at his side, Lincoln then humorously and effectively countered another Douglas criticism: that Lincoln favored race mixing. "We mean to marry your girls when we have a chance—the white ones I mean—and I have the honor to inform you that I once did have a chance in that way," he announced to the "Kentuckians." As the crowd responded with a hearty laugh, someone yelled, "Good for you!" which triggered another round of applause.

A citizen studied Lincoln throughout the speech. "Browning's description of the German professor, 'Three parts sublime to one grotesque,' was applicable to this man," asserted the observer in his unflattering portrait of Lincoln's appearance. "The face had a battered and bronzed look. . . . His nose was prominent, and buttressed a strong and high forehead. His eyes were high-vaulted and had an expression of sadness; his mouth and chin were too close together, the cheeks hollow."

Notwithstanding his harsh critique of Lincoln's look, the citizen deemed him an attractive speaker, swayed to that opinion by his expressive voice, his charming manner, his humor, and his simple and direct diction. Rutherford B. Hayes stood in the crowd that night and came to the same conclusion regarding Lincoln's look versus his sound. "Mr. Lincoln has an ungainly figure, but one loses sight of that, or rather the first impression disappears in the absorbed attention which the matter of his speech commands." Hayes raved about Lincoln's calm, easy, and logical style. The reporter for the *Daily Enquirer*, Cincinnati's chief Democratic organ, grudgingly admitted that Lincoln's homely features somehow came across as attractive, crediting him as an "awkward, positive-looking individual, with character written in his face and energy expressed in his every movement."[32]

Lincoln had succeeded in capturing his audience with that expressed energy. The air was electric and Lincoln knew he had won this crowd. No greater stimulant could be administered to an orator than those magic moments when he could sense that his listeners were hanging on to every word he uttered. That is how it was in Cincinnati on the night of September 17, 1859, a speaker flushed with confidence after capturing an audience, not intending to let them go.

"I have told you what we mean to do," declared Lincoln to his fictitious Kentuckians; he now asked what they mean to do. He stated, "I often hear it intimated that you mean to divide the Union whenever a Republican, or anything like it, is elected President of the United States." When he heard someone yell, "That is so," Lincoln wondered aloud if that was one of his Kentuckians. Told that the anonymous responder was indeed a Douglas man, Lincoln queried him on his desire to divide the country. "Well, then, I want to know what you are going to do with your half of it?" He wondered aloud if they were going to widen the current river-sized gap between the South and "us outrageous fellows." He asked if they would build a wall. All of this set up a logical argument Lincoln was sure secession-minded Southerners had not considered. The Fugitive-Slave Law assured that their "moveable property" (Lincoln's facetious euphemism for escaped slaves) would be returned to the Southern slave owners by constitutional decree. But if the South tried to form a separate nation, then Northerners would no longer be bound by law to return their slaves if they fled across the Ohio River into the North.

Lincoln then challenged the saber-rattling sect of Southerners who threatened bloodshed in the wake of any perceived threat to their institutions. "Will you make war upon us and kill us all?" Lincoln asked, obviously in response to hearing these threats metastasize throughout the closing months of the 1850s. Acknowledging the gallantry of Southerners, Lincoln reminded them that it all came down to a numbers game because "man for man, you are not better than we are and there are not so many of you as there are of us." He appeared to use these remarks to illustrate the futility of civil war rather than as a clarion call to Northerners. It is unknown how the crowd interpreted it, but they did reward Lincoln with his loudest cheers of the evening after completing this part of his speech.[33]

Raucous cheering gave way to the longest applause of the evening when Lincoln announced he would direct his remarks hereafter to Ohioans. Lincoln delivered this portion of the speech as he had done in Columbus and Dayton. At this point Lincoln attempted to stomp out any fire Douglas had ignited the previous week with the provocative section of his *Harper's* article. Douglas insisted that Ohio and the other five states (including eastern Minnesota) carved out of the Northwest Territory were created as slave-free entities not because of the Ordinance of 1787, which restricted slavery in the original territory from where the states were formed, but because of popular sovereignty, which empowered the citizens of Ohio, Indiana, Illinois, Wisconsin, Michigan, and Minnesota to vote out slavery when their respective states were formed from the territory.

The Ordinance of 1787 had been Lincoln's trump card against Douglas for five years; it had been his foil for Douglas's acceptance of extending slavery into territories where it had not previously existed. Douglas had offered only a meager response to this until he wrote out his *Harper's* piece. The article turned the table on Lincoln by stressing that slavery had been permitted in Illinois prior to its statehood, and excluding slavery in the territory encompassed by the other five states—including Ohio—did not require excluding it in any of those states when they were formed from the territory. Lincoln had read Douglas's remarks in Columbus and believed that in Cincinnati Douglas had repeated the view that Ohio citizens were responsible for Ohio being a free state "and that the Ordinance of 1787 was not entitled in any degree to divide the honor with them." To counter this Lincoln offered this preamble: "I have no doubt the people of the State of Ohio did make her free according to their own will and judgment, but let the facts be remembered."

Lincoln then structured his arguments as a mixture of facts and logic. Addressing his crowd as the true Ohioans they were and not his fictitious Kentuckians, Lincoln swiftly transitioned from a political speaker to a history teacher. He taught them that their first state constitution in 1802 included a clause prohibiting slavery, a clause made easy to enforce because no slaves existed within Ohio's borders at the commencement of statehood. "Pray what was it that made you free?" asked Professor Lincoln. To answer the question he contrasted Ohio with Kentucky, the neighbor state not part of the 1787 Northwest Ordinance and separated from Ohio by a river less than a mile wide. Lincoln highlighted the fact that because of the course of the Ohio River, the eastern portion of Kentucky included lands north of where they presently stood, yet all of Ohio was free, while all of Kentucky—including the portion *north* of Cincinnati—was "entirely covered with slavery." This excluded climate and soil as reasons for the contrast, thus vanquishing Douglas's assertions that slavery would never extend into Northern territories because the geography was not conducive to it. Lincoln challenged anyone to offer any reason for the difference "other than that there was no law of any sort keeping it out of Kentucky, while the Ordinance of 1787 kept it out of Ohio." Teeming with self-assurance, Lincoln concluded, "This, then, I offer to combat the idea that that Ordinance has never made any State free."[34]

He offered a similar argument for Indiana but added that unlike in Ohio, there had been a movement to include slavery upon statehood, one that had failed because of the tenets of the original ordinance. Then came a harder lesson to teach: Illinois. Lincoln acknowledged Douglas's claim that Illinois's first state constitution allowed slaves to remain in the French settlements where they had already existed for more than a hundred years, and allowed blacks to enter the state as indentured servants, a form of slavery that Lincoln conceded violated the ordinance. Although these facts justified Douglas's assertion that Illinois came into the Union as a slave state, Lincoln scoffed at Douglas's contention that it was currently a free state because popular sovereignty had extinguished the institution.

Lincoln painstakingly contrasted Illinois with Missouri, using the same geographical argument that he did for Kentucky and Ohio. Why, then, was Illinois a free state in 1859 while Missouri was inundated with slaves? Because, Lincoln argued, the limited number of slaves allowed in Illinois in the early years of its statehood was constitutionally legalized with the spirit of the Ordinance of 1787 in mind. The institution was meant to die, since there were few, old slaves in the French settlements; and indentured servitude was a form of slavery that ended with the servants' death and at-tainment of adulthood by their children. By running through the history of the states formed from the Northwest Territory, Lincoln haughtily concluded that it was "a fallacy" for Douglas to insist that the slavery re-striction in the Ordinance of 1787 was trumped by popular sovereignty in those states.[35]

"I have been detaining you longer perhaps than I ought to do," con-fessed Lincoln in mock concern; "I am in some doubt whether to intro-duce another topic upon which I could talk awhile." The time passed 10:00 P.M. More than two hours had elapsed since he had piped out his first shrill words, but Lincoln sensed he still had control of his crowd. His voice and cadence remained strong and smooth. Cries of "Go on! Go on!" rent the air in the marketplace. Lincoln was pleased though not sur-prised at the affirmation. He had set them up for another hard-hitting line, one that had worked to perfection in each of his previous speeches in Ohio, and Lincoln knew it would score again in Cincinnati. "It is this, then," Lincoln declared as the cries died down; "Douglas' Popular Sover-eignty, as a principle, is simply this: If one man chooses to make a slave of another man, neither that other man [nor] anybody else has a right to object."

The audience roared with cheers and laughter at Lincoln's punch line, one that turned Douglas's "gu-reat per-inciple" on its head. Lincoln had completely dissected Douglas with two hours of rhetorical logic. He pro-ceeded to define what "real" popular sovereignty was: "that each man shall do precisely as he pleases with himself and with all those things which exclusively concern him." He transferred the same definition to federal and local governments, replacing "man" and its pronouns with those institutions in each definition. Lincoln placed the discussion of slav-ery within the context of capital and labor. Lincoln argued that the most successful American system of labor existed when a hired laborer worked knowing that he could garner his wages. He accomplished this by a "sober" and "industrious" approach to his labor, and accumulated enough capital either to spend it as he pleased or to hire his own laborers and thus become the type of employer he had originally worked under. Slavery, of course, abolished this successful approach to labor, preached Lincoln, Doug-las and his form of popular sovereignty notwithstanding.[36]

Lincoln felt the natural downward cycle of his speech and he adeptly transitioned to a conclusion. He reminded his audience that for the purpose of his discourse he had assumed himself to be their spokesman—that is, for the Ohioans and not the Kentuckians. He continued with that assumption to insist upon the recognition that slavery was wrong and that no one could prevent its spread without setting up a policy that treated it as a wrong, for its perpetual spread into the territories—those lands intended to be free by the Founders of the American democracy—threatened the destruction of the Union and the government they had created. "Our friends in Kentucky differ from us," Lincoln acknowledged to the Buckeyes. But he recommended that they not make the argument for their slaveholding neighbors, but determine for themselves what actions needed to be taken to preserve the government.

What actions needed to be taken? Lincoln declared that those who recognize that slavery was wrong still must not interfere with it in the states where the interference was constitutionally forbidden, and likewise must not interfere with enforcing the Fugitive-Slave Law, "because the Constitution requires us, as I understand it, not to withhold such a law." Lincoln added this line to his speech with Ohio specifically in mind, for the Opposition was still applying its pressure to add a plank to the Republican National Convention to repeal the Fugitive-Slave Law, a movement Lincoln, in his June correspondences with Governor Chase, had insisted would break up the convention and throw the election to Douglas and the Democrats.

Using the Constitution and the concept of "general welfare" as his guides, Lincoln maintained that neither supported the spread of slavery; therefore, this should be the focus of those who regarded slavery as immoral and wrong. Lincoln claimed that they must snuff out the movements to reopen the African slave trade and to promulgate a territorial slave code. There was only one way to stop those movements. "The people of these United States are the rightful masters of both congresses and courts," Lincoln fired out to his cheering crowd. He told them not to overthrow the Constitution (hence continue to preserve slavery in the South and the Fugitive-Slave Law), "but to overthrow the men who pervert that Constitution."

He entered his closing as an advocate of democracy and not "mobocracy," a term he implied in Cincinnati but had used more than twenty

years earlier to denounce a lawless approach to popular rule. He deftly discussed nominating a presidential candidate that the Opposition could rally
around, one who adhered to the principles he had preached for two and a
half hours. Lincoln did this without mentioning himself as that potential
candidate, which effectively enhanced the reliability and force of his message. As a pure statesman, Lincoln offered up the possibility that a slaveholding state could provide an acceptable candidate for president or for
vice president, provided that this nominee entered the race of his own intent and not by the will of Opposition bosses or handlers. "If such a one
will place himself on the right ground, I am for his occupying one place
upon the next Republican or Opposition ticket. I will heartily favor
him . . . ," insisted Lincoln. "It would do my soul good to do that thing.
It would enable us to teach [the South] that, inasmuch as we select one of
their own number to carry out our principles, we are free from the charge
that we mean more than we say." Lincoln thanked his listeners for their attention and patience, admitting that he "detained you much longer than I
expected to do." And with that he concluded his Cincinnati speech, one
instantly acclaimed by hearty and robust cheers and applause.[37]

All indications are that Lincoln was pleased with his performance, a
strong close to two full days of speeches in Ohio. He felt justified that the
precious days consumed by the trip had been well spent. And the instanta-
neous gratification he received would magnify even before he returned to
Springfield. It would not take Lincoln long to realize that the past thirty
hours in Ohio would bring him more national attention than any thirty
days of speeches he had delivered in Illinois, including any month of the
Lincoln-Douglas debates of 1858. Based on the reaction he would receive,
the geographic extent of that reaction, and the doors that would open for
him based on that reaction, Lincoln's decision to speak in the Buckeye State
and his subsequent performance in Columbus, Dayton, and especially
Cincinnati would rank as one of the most important events of his life.

Four

THE GIANT KILLER

IMMEDIATELY AFTER THE completion of Lincoln's speech in Cincinnati, the organizers of the event called out for one of their newly elected Republican congressman to address the crowd. This was Thomas Corwin, the most respected and revered Ohio politician in Cincinnati that night. The sixty-five-year-old former Whig was one of the most experienced politicians in the country. Not only had Tom Corwin previously served in the U. S. House of Representatives throughout the 1830s, but he had been a governor, a U.S. Senator, and the secretary of the treasury in President Millard Fillmore's cabinet.

Tom Corwin shared Abraham Lincoln's mind-set on the night of September 17, 1859, and he told his audience as much. After forcibly expressing his unqualified approval of Lincoln's sentiments, Corwin encouraged the crowd to take Lincoln's views with them to the polls in three weeks. Corwin and Judge A. G. W. Carter then made their way to the Burnet House, where they met Lincoln after he returned from the speech.[1]

Lincoln and his guests adjourned to a conference room adjoining his private one. Notwithstanding the late hour (it was eleven P.M.) Lincoln was as lively as ever, adrenaline still coursing through his veins. He ordered whiskey punches for his guests, and for the next few hours the three men exchanged anecdotes. Lincoln propped his gangly legs and gigantic feet upon the table as he sat in his chair. "I had heard of Mr. Lincoln as a story-teller," recalled Judge Carter, "but I never heard that he was such a serious, sincere, earnest, funny one as he showed himself that night." When solely in the company of men, Lincoln enjoyed relaying ribald stories and jokes. Earlier that year, when asked by a frequent recipient of his dirty yarns why he did not assemble those stories into a book, Lincoln responded while contorting his face as if he had taken a deep whiff of a decaying animal carcass, "Such a book would stink like a thousand privies." His stories were often so raunchy that friends in Springfield dared not repeat them. As one of them explained to a reporter, "I won't tell you the stories he used to tell me, for I wouldn't want you to put them in the paper."[2]

The hours-long gathering was not restricted to storytelling. Tom Corwin informed Lincoln of something that he had been hearing with increased frequency: "Well, Mr. Lincoln, the people begin to talk about you as a candidate for the presidency." Lincoln attempted to defuse the subject by claiming the talk was not serious and was limited to Illinois; there was really nothing to it. Corwin refused to let the matter drop, correcting Lincoln by asserting that the talk was indeed serious and more widespread. Lincoln fell back on his standard not-fit-for-the-office dismissal, which is the way the talk broke up at two A.M. on Sunday morning.[3]

As the papers and the witnesses debated, described, and discussed Lincoln's performance, the inconspicuous presidential candidate and his wife enjoyed a free day in Cincinnati on Sunday, September 18. They spent the day with William Dickson's family, the same family who had hosted Lincoln during his previous visit in 1855—the only fond memory of that unpleasant experience. The time spent with her kinfolk pleased Mary Lincoln (she and Mrs. Dickson were cousins), who deemed her stay in Cincinnati "a charming visit." She may have changed her mind when her husband received the lodging bill from the Burnet House several months later, an itemized tab including alcohol, extra suppers, and cigars that Lincoln insisted they never ordered or took. The frills ran up Lincoln's hotel bill to $53.50, a cost eventually picked up by the Republican State Central Committee of Ohio.[4]

The first reports of Lincoln's Dayton and Cincinnati performances were published on Monday morning, September 19, and the response continued for several days afterward. As was the case in the larger cities of Illinois, rival newspapers in Cincinnati evaluated his words according to their philosophies, but all acknowledged the strength of Lincoln as a public speaker. The *Cincinnati Daily Commercial*, although partial to Lincoln, appeared the most objective in two editorials. The paper characterized Lincoln's address as "strong and peculiar" and credited him with the unique twist in the speech where he directed his remarks to Kentuckians. But it also considered it folly to place Lincoln on an equal footing with Douglas—"the most noted politician in the country." The *Commercial's* conclusion confirmed the effectiveness of Lincoln's strategy of clandestine influence and impeccable timing: "Mr. Lincoln is not conspicuous as a presidential candidate."[5]

The Lincolns' train ran northwestward late that Monday morning and deposited them several hours later in Indianapolis, where Lincoln agreed to speak that night. He did so with great relish, beginning his performance at Masonic Hall, "Fellow citizens of the State of Indiana . . ." He went on to recount his own Indiana childhood in Spencer County, from 1816 to 1830. He embellished a bit, stating that, armed with an ax, he'd fought the trees of the Indiana wilderness until he was twenty.[6] He then reiterated most of the points he'd made in Cincinnati.

The audience generated a mixed reaction to Lincoln that night. Calvin Fletcher witnessed the speech and left Masonic Hall unimpressed, penning the following observation in his journal: "He is a plain commonsense man without much polish. Evidently a backwoods man."[7] Hugh McCulloch offered a more detailed recollection:

Careless of his attire, ungraceful in his movements, I thought as he came forward to address the audience that his was the most ungainly figure I had ever seen upon a platform. Could this be Abraham Lincoln, whose speeches I had read with so much interest and admiration—this plain, dull-looking man the one of the most gifted speakers of his time? The question was speedily answered by the speech. The subject was slavery—its character, its incompatibility with Republican institutions, its demoralizing influences upon society, its aggressiveness, its rights as limited by the Constitution; all of which were discussed with such clearness, simplicity, earnestness, and force as to carry me with him to the conclusion that the country could not long continue part slave and part free—that freedom must prevail throughout the length and breadth of the land, or that the great Republic, instead of being the home of the free and the hope of the oppressed, would become a by-word and a reproach among the nations.[8]

Lincoln delivered one more speech in Indiana before heading westward to Illinois. During the evening of September 20, merely five days after they had departed for Ohio, the Lincolns stepped back into their Springfield home. With the Ohio elections still three weeks away, the impact of Lincoln's efforts could not be gauged. He could not have been impressed by the size of his crowds. Cincinnati delivered the largest turnout, about 3,500, but this was only a thousand more people than showed up at Jonesboro, Illinois, in 1858—the site of the smallest Lincoln-Douglas debate. Lincoln had been used to audiences exceeding 5,000; sometimes he expressed his thoughts aloud to five-figure crowds. Unfortunately for Lincoln, the *total* number of witnesses to his seven speeches delivered during the third week of September fell below 10,000.

Upon his return to Illinois, and for weeks afterward, it became abundantly clear to Lincoln that the number of people digesting his words perhaps exceeded his total Ohio and Indiana audiences by more than twentyfold. Robert R. Hitt, the *Chicago Press and Tribune*'s stenographer, converted his shorthand notations of Lincoln's Columbus speech into text and sent it to the paper, which published it in its entirety before Lincoln even returned home. Hitt apparently was not in Cincinnati for Lincoln's big speech, but this did not prevent the *Press and Tribune* from reproducing it, this time by republishing the text from the *Cincinnati Gazette*. The *Illinois State Journal* and dozens of other organs in the state reproduced large portions of the *Press and Tribune* reports. In addition, the *Chicago Journal* happened to have a Cincinnati correspondent who took in Lincoln's speech. His glowing report of Lincoln's performance spread to other papers as well.[9]

To Lincoln's delight, his words in Ohio and Indiana spread from coast to coast as issues of the Dayton, Cincinnati, Indianapolis, and Chicago newspapers were perused and reproduced by editors across the country. New York papers churned out large excerpts of the speeches; *The New York Times* reprinted some of the Dayton speech under the subheadline "Senator Lincoln." In Washington, the *National Intelligencer* obtained a copy of the *Cincinnati Gazette*'s version of Lincoln's speech and reproduced it in its entirety on September 22. It took several weeks for Lincoln's words to strike the West Coast, but this did not prevent the *Oregon Argus* from reproducing the entire Cincinnati speech—exactly three months after he delivered it. California newspapers also belatedly monitored Lincoln's Ohio trip. Ohio's State Central Republican Committee ordered ten thousand copies of Lincoln's Ohio speeches printed and distributed.[10]

The three days of speeches in Ohio and Indiana garnered more positive press for Lincoln than he had received the previous year in his debates against Stephen A. Douglas. Since his return to politics in 1854, Lincoln had developed a strong reputation as a tireless speaker. The sheer quantity of his public presentations buttressed that reputation. Lincoln had delivered 160 speeches in the five years from the summer of 1854 through September 1859. No single speech to this point in Lincoln's career received more national attention than his Cincinnati speech. It altered Lincoln's reputation by softening the harsh view of him as the "House Divided" radical and wiping away the stain of a Senate loss. It also established him as a stentorian voice for the conservative center of the Republican Party, the moderate stance between the abolition radicals and those Republicans indifferent to the potential of slavery's spread.

The reduced number of important state election in 1859 compared to 1858 placed more national attention on the goings-on in Ohio. Although Lincoln and the Little Giant never spoke in the same town on the same day, those who read about the Ohio speeches treated the speaking tours as the sequel to the Lincoln-Douglas debates of 1858. Newspaper editorials adhered to their political proclivities in assessing the performances. Lincoln was the beneficiary of papers that were routinely more anti-Douglas than they were pro-Lincoln. For example, the *Aurora Beacon* in northern Illinois raved about Lincoln's performance in Ohio and scorned Douglas's magazine article by comparison. The *Beacon*'s conclusion: "Lincoln is the Giant, he the dwarf."[11]

Lincoln considered Douglas small in stature only, but still a giant in appeal and influence. Overly concerned about the upcoming Ohio elections, Lincoln sent Salmon Chase a letter urging the governor to do whatever possible to prevent "Douglasism" from sweeping his state. "That ism is all which now stands in the way of an early and complete success of Republicanism," Lincoln explained; "and nothing would help it or hurt us so much as for Ohio to go over or falter just now." Lincoln's plea was a complete change of pace from the series of correspondences he had sent to Chase over the constitutionality of the Fugitive-Slave Law. Diplomatically brushing off Chase's snub in Columbus by acknowledging that the governor was "at work in the cause," Lincoln prodded him and his fellow Buckeyes to continue the hard work all the way to Election Day. "You must," urged Lincoln, "one and all, put [your] souls into the effort."[12]

Although the approaching election was his primary marker for his influence in Ohio, Lincoln also had the opportunity to gauge any change in his presidential prospects by the reaction to his speeches. This reaction could be found in letters sent to him and his associates. Ozias M. Hatch routinely received mail from Republican friends, relatives, and acquaintances throughout Illinois and across the country, and many of these letters teemed with political opinions. On the eve of Lincoln's Ohio trip, Hatch received harsh assessments of Lincoln. A cousin in Boston apparently had not forgiven Lincoln for failing to defeat Douglas in 1858. He dismissed Lincoln as a presidential prospect in 1860, believing him a mere lightweight destined to disappoint in a big election "as he is in the habit of doing." Two weeks after Lincoln's return from Ohio, more praise than criticism for Lincoln filled the letters to Hatch. "I have read old Abe's speeches with the greatest pleasure," crowed a Republican in the nation's capital. "Many of the Douglas papers in the South are publishing portions of it. Some of the papers are calling Lincoln 'Abe the Giant Killer.' "[13]

Those Douglas papers that used the term "Giant Killer" apparently did to scoff at the assertions of the Northern press. The *Chicago Times*, the chief Douglas-supporting newspaper in the country, claimed that forty-four Southern newspapers were or would soon be running Lincoln's speech in their issues. With the help of a pro-Douglas Illinois congressman, fifty thousand copies of Lincoln's Cincinnati speech were produced and sent south under the title "Douglas an Enemy to the North"—an ingenious method to court Southerners who felt alienated by Douglas's break with President Buchanan over the Lecompton Constitution in Kansas. The *Chicago Times* boasted that Lincoln's Cincinnati speech "will do Douglas more good than any speech made by a Democrat." The paper asserted, "If Lincoln would go South and 'kill Douglas' a little more, he would doubtless obtain Douglas' eternal gratitude." The point lost on the *Times* was that the portion of

Lincoln's Cincinnati speech directed to the Kentuckians alienated Douglas from Northern Democrats. The Republican press predicted this result. "Mr. Douglas's friends in the South might find it worth while to give Mr. Lincoln's speech the widest possible circulation," acknowledged the *Cincinnati Commercial*; "it would not, however, be palatable to the Douglas Democracy of the North."[14]

The "Giant Killer" sobriquet was indeed premature, for Douglas's popularity had not diminished one iota, as his supporting press made the same claims for him as the anti-Douglas press made for Lincoln. Still, Lincoln made no effort to quell any utterances of his new title. Lincoln was proud of his performance in Ohio and Indiana, particularly his Cincinnati speech. Notwithstanding all of the attention the speech had received in the press and in pamphlets, Lincoln edited the *Cincinnati Gazette*'s version of the speech and submitted it to the *Illinois State Journal* for publication in early October.[15]

Eight months had passed since he revealed his desire for the presidency; five months had elapsed since the strategy was devised to keep his presidential bid "under wraps" to prevent a premature boom and early criticism of his positions. Lincoln likely had not expected to have such rapid, widespread attention heaped upon him in the first weeks of autumn of 1859. But Douglas forced Lincoln out with his *Harper's New Monthly Magazine* article. The tremendous coast-to-coast response to the Ohio speeches was not planned, but from this point on Lincoln would not discourage the press's attempt to hype him as he had the previous April. He had remained the statesman and continued as the undeclared candidate, but there was no mistaking the reality of the moment. The Lincoln boom had begun.

More events allowed Lincoln to magnify his boom. Lincoln struck out for the speaking circuit again at the end of September. After wrapping up light court duties in Springfield for a week, he trained northward, staying overnight in Chicago's Tremont House on September 28 before moving on the following morning for a foray into Wisconsin. Whereas the state fair in Columbus had shrunk Lincoln's audience, the state fair in Milwaukee *was* Lincoln's audience, for he was the featured speaker in this well-advertised event. Back in August, Lincoln had agreed to an invitation from the chairman of the executive committee for the Wisconsin Agricultural Fair to speak in front of the state's agricultural society. Lincoln admitted his trepidation about giving this speech, citing lack of preparation time as his chief concern on August 18. By September 1, however, he had agreed to do it.[16]

This was a puzzling decision to be sure, for his speech would be about agriculture, not politics. The "Discoveries and Inventions" speech had also digressed from the political issues of the day, but Lincoln had had plenty of time to craft that speech. The time-consuming Harrison trial and his swing into Ohio and Indiana had certainly kept Lincoln from preparing enough to feel comfortable delivering this sort of speech. Regardless, Lincoln entered Milwaukee on September 30 determined to edify his audience on an issue about which he had a heightened interest. At eleven o'clock on Friday morning, Lincoln fought a stiff dust-kicking wind all the way to the speaker's stand, looked out over an audience that rivaled the size of the Cincinnati crowd, and began to speak.[17]

"I presume I am not expected to employ the time assigned to me, in the mere flattery of the farmers, as a class," Lincoln stated early in his speech to an audience composed mainly of farmers, whom he acknowledged as the dominant class of workers in the country. He seemingly provoked them when he said, "My opinion of [farmers] is that, in proportion to numbers, they are neither better nor worse than any other people. . . . I believe there really are more attempts at flattering them than any other; the reason of which I cannot perceive, unless it is that they can cast more votes than any other." Despite this assertion and his confessed dearth of bona fides, Lincoln was able to present himself as one to be trusted on a topic outside his expertise. "He inspires confidence," observed a Milwaukee correspondent of a small-town Wisconsin newspaper. "He looks like an open-hearted honest man who has grown sharp in fighting knaves."[18]

Lincoln subtly introduced his antislavery ideas into this discussion. He did so by contrasting theories of labor. Stating that wheat and corn crop yields were only a fraction of what they should be, Lincoln acknowledged that more labor was required to increase those yields, but he claimed that yield per bushel was not the same as yield per acre in regards to labor requirements. "The world is agreed that labor is the source from which human wants are mainly supplied," professed Lincoln, tying his argument in to South Carolina senator James H. Hammond's proslavery "mudsill" theory, which postulated that labor was dependent on capital to induce that labor. Lincoln claimed that mudsill proponents assumed that a hired laborer had no room for advancement, "and thence again that his condition is as bad as, or worse than that of a slave."

He contrasted the mudsill theory with the "free-labor" theory. Defining the latter, Lincoln explained to his audience that labor was independent of capital, preceded capital, produced capital, and therefore was "the superior— greatly the superior—of capital." From this point he returned to the argument he had presented toward the end of his Cincinnati speech. He reiterated the notion of "free labor," where even a "prudent, penniless beginner in the world, labors for wages for awhile, saves a surplus with which to buy tools or land, for himself; then labors on his own account" until he can hire another beginning laborer to help him. This fit into Lincoln's ideal economic system, which afforded the laborer the "right to rise."[19]

Lincoln expanded on these theories and definitions of labor to tie them in with education. "The old general rule was that educated people did not perform manual labor," he stated, but pointed out that uneducated laborers did not treat the system as evil, because the proportion of educated to uneducated supported this notion. "But *now*," continued Lincoln, "especially in these free States, nearly all are educated—quite too nearly all, to leave the labor of the uneducated, in any wise adequate to the support of the whole." This meant that educated people must perform labor, thus destroying the old general rule. All of this tied in to a question Lincoln posed to segue to the next section of his speech: "How can labor and education be the most satisfactorily combined?"

Once again he was able to denigrate slavery by criticizing the mudsill theory. Comparing an uneducated laborer to a blinded horse on a treadmill, Lincoln illustrated how mudsill theorists assumed the incompatibility of education and labor. Just like the horse without a blindfold, which would kick or buck the treadmill, Lincoln said, the educated laborer "is not only useless, but pernicious, and dangerous." Hyperbolically, Lincoln mocked: "In fact, it is, in some sort, deemed a misfortune that laborers should have heads at all. Those same heads are regarded as explosive materials, only to be safely kept in damp places, as far as possible from that peculiar sort of fire which ignites them. A Yankee who could invent a strong handed man without a head would secure the everlasting gratitude of the 'mud-sill' advocates." A witness in the audience spoke for many with his assessment of Lincoln's attack: "He thrust a stilletto [*sic*] into Hammond's 'mudsill' theory."[20]

This easily set Lincoln up to compare the mudsill theory to the free-labor theory in one phrase: "Free Labor insists on universal education." Lincoln claimed that he discussed the labor theories without any bias, although it would have been clear to all paying attention to his speech that he sided with them, for Lincoln spoke for them by declaring, "I shall not be mistaken, in assuming as a fact, that the people of Wisconsin prefer free labor, with its natural companion, education."

Most of Lincoln's address departed from the topic of agriculture—the reason his audience was in front of him. He chose the close of his address as the place to tie in labor theory and education with agricultural pursuits. He insisted that agriculture was the field that offered the most "profitable and agreeable combination" of education and labor. He went on to describe how the field divided into several areas of study: botany, diseases, soil science, animal science, and machinery to name a few. He stressed that this wonderful combination succeeded only with a thorough effort, for a halfhearted approach was a signal for failure. He shunned the notion of large plantations as necessary to accomplish this, bringing the discussion back to heightened crop yields on smaller plots of land. He claimed that this thorough effort in agricultural pursuits protected against oppression, "independent of crowned-kings, money-kings, and land-kings."[21]

When Lincoln finished he was rewarded with loud and lengthy applause. One who must have heard him before proclaimed, "The address was a short, sweet Lincolnism. . . . It did not please everybody, I suppose, and therefore it was something positive and good." Another audience member agreed, calling Lincoln's speech "short, pointed, pithy and interesting," and believed it would gain a wide readership once newspapers published it. "It contained many excellent ideas, which will bear pondering upon by the farmers and laboring classes of our State."[22]

Newspaper editors were incredibly kind to him. The *Milwaukee Wisconsin* characterized him as "a clear reasoner and a popular orator" who "has few superiors in the nation." The *Milwaukee Free Democrat* (a Republican paper) not only called the speech an "admirable" one, but also became the rare paper that praised the look of the speaker. "Mr. Lincoln's appearance is decidedly prepossessing," ran the editorial. "His countenance is pleasing and attractive, and significant both of a high degree of intelligence and goodness, while as a speaker he is dignified and impressive. He is plainly one of the leading men of the country."[23]

As he had in Columbus, Lincoln spoke a second time, that Friday at Milwaukee's magnificent hotel, the Newhall House on Main Street. This was an unscheduled event, for Lincoln was shaking hands with well-wishers in the rotunda when someone called out for him to speak on the political issues of the day. Someone brought him a sturdy dry-goods crate to serve as a makeshift platform. Lincoln stepped upon the wooden box and spoke for over an hour about the defining issue separating Republicans from Democrats: Republicans believed slavery was wrong, and Democrats believed it was right. According to a witness in the Newhall House, Lincoln's succeeded in "keeping them spell-bound by his clear, logical remarks."[24]

Lincoln's words in Newhall House likely were a rehearsal of an address he was set to deliver the following day. On Saturday morning he trained westward to Beloit, Wisconsin, fulfilling an agreement he had made with a member of the city's Republican Club to open its campaign with an address to the citizens of Rock County. Lincoln arrived on schedule at noon that Saturday, but the itinerary changed due to persistent winds. He was originally scheduled to speak from the balcony of the Bushnell House, but blowing dust forced the congregation to move one block over on State Street to Hanchett's Hall, a newly erected building.

The hall was packed with a mostly partisan Republican crowd. Although most were hearing him for the first time, it is likely that several in the hall had made the thirty-mile train ride to Freeport, Illinois, a year earlier to hear Lincoln debate Douglas. The editor of the *Prescott [Wisconsin] Transcript* studied Lincoln's style during the October 1 Beloit speech. "He is neither a fluent nor a graceful speaker," noted the newsman, "but analyses closely, and drives sharper points into the political dogmas of the slavocracy than any other speaker we have heard, and through the whole runs a vein of humor, which pleases while it holds the mind of the bearer to dry argument."[25]

Lincoln's antislavery speech sated his audience. He did not need to pull his punches in Wisconsin, the state that had birthed the Republican Party five years earlier and where Republicans generally adhered to the ideals of the abolition wing. But Lincoln also hammered home themes that he had pursued in Ohio and Indiana, a response to Douglas's *Harper's* article. Whereas Douglas had maintained that the Founding Fathers were the progenitors of popular sovereignty and thus would have endorsed his position to allow slavery to be voted up or down in the territories, even if it risked expanding the institution across the country, Lincoln claimed the contrary. He maintained that the originators of the U.S. Constitution in the 1780s identified with the principles and ideals of the Republican Party of the 1850s and not with the Democrats. Lincoln's political acumen let him tune his speech to his audience. Wisconsin was a product of the Northwest Ordinance of 1787, so Lincoln presented the document as evidence that slavery was intended to be excluded from this extension of U.S. territory. Therefore, the Founding Fathers had intended to contain slavery in the regions where it already existed, prevent its spread, and ultimately allow it to dwindle to extinction.[26]

Lincoln wrapped up his speech using the words of his political idol, Henry Clay. Lincoln had delivered a memorable address eulogizing the famous Whig upon his death in 1852, and in Beloit he employed Clay's prophetic denunciation of the pro-Douglas segment of the Democratic Party as the authors of ruin for the country. An observant listener to one of Lincoln's Milwaukee speeches compared Lincoln to the late Kentucky senator. "I think he is very much like Clay without the light complexion and fiery enthusiasm," noted the observer.[27]

Lincoln closed his midafternoon address to prolonged applause and cheering, a response he had begun to grow accustomed to from his out-of-state crowds. To no one's surprise the Democrats in Beloit were not impressed with Lincoln, characterizing his performance as "lame." A gushing editor of a pro-Republican paper in southern Wisconsin countered swiftly by lauding Lincoln's skewering of Douglas's principles. "The lance he drove into Douglas was barbed and after it had entered into his victim it was turned and twisted in the body of the impaled sufferer," crowed the newsman. "The 'little giant' finds a hard customer in the long backwoodsman bard because he deals out justice to him and in doing so never descends to the blackguard or falsifier."[28]

With Beloit sitting on the Wisconsin-Illinois border, Lincoln expected to wrap up his tour of the Badger State that afternoon and then return home to Springfield. But a persuasive cortege of Republicans from Janesville,

Wisconsin, convinced Lincoln to come north with them to speak there that evening. Lincoln acceded and boarded the carriage of William H. Tallman, a real estate profiteer and an ardent abolitionist who owned a majestic Italian-villa-style home in Janesville. The twelve-mile jaunt sparked Lincoln's memory, as he was able to identify landscapes last seen twenty-seven years before when, as a captain of militia, Lincoln had led a company into this region during the Black Hawk War.[29]

Lincoln largely repeated his Beloit speech at Myer's Hall in Janesville that night. The reaction from the press was so consistent with that in Ohio and Indiana as to be noteworthy. "His style of oratory is plain and unpretending and his gesticulations sometimes awkward," reported the *Janesville Gazette* of what they called the "homespun, backwoods Abe Lincoln." But as disappointed as the Wisconsinites were by the appearance and mannerisms of the heralded messenger, they were gratified by his message. The *Gazette* summed up his effect: "You are compelled to revolve his ideas over and over in your mind (whether you will or not)." The paper summarized in one sentence the mind-set of all of his audiences in the three states where he spoke: "No one can forget Mr. Lincoln, his manner or his logic."[30]

He returned to Illinois on Monday morning, October 3, and slowly worked his way back to Springfield via the courts. One month earlier he had fretted over invitations, agreeing to a quick two-city swing in Ohio. He had not forecasted the enormity of his speaking responsibilities outside Illinois: seven speeches in Ohio and Indiana, followed by four more in Wisconsin. Those eleven speeches delivered between September 16 and October 1, 1859, were intended to bolster the Republicans in the former Northwest Territory and covertly bring Lincoln out from the confines of Illinois, where he had been hidden for most of his political life. He hoped the two weeks of work away from his lucrative practice were worth the effort.

He could not have anticipated how important those two weeks were to his political ascent. The election results were clarified by the middle of October with astounding results in Ohio. Republicans swept the state, capturing the governorship, both bodies of the state legislature, and all statewide offices. Lincoln received some of the credit for those victories. (Douglas's lengthy appearances in Ohio also helped, for his constant visibility appears to have been detrimental in a state leaning heavily toward Republican ideals.)

More important for Lincoln was how he was received. His overt purpose had been to aid the Republican Party; but Lincoln's covert goals—to increase his exposure, broaden his popularity, and nationalize his political positions—were all achieved, as indicated by the nationwide newspaper coverage he received. His argument to counter Douglas had not been fully developed, but he was able to deliver his phrases without a debater present to immediately counter him, and he made sure that no "House Divided" remarks marred his speeches to provide endless fodder for the Democratic press. He had been dubbed "the Giant Killer" without ever debating on the same platform with the Little Giant in 1859. Furthermore, Lincoln's presentations, under the guise of a Republican spokesman rather than a canvassing candidate, attracted less criticism from Republicans supporting other potential nominees in 1860. Lincoln's strategy for getting the nomination had bounded forward in Ohio, Indiana, and Wisconsin, a leap that advanced his name into the minds of future voters.[31]

With the election results confirming the power of his message, Lincoln discovered he was the hottest commodity in the state of Illinois.

Five

BIRTH OF A BOOM

"LINCOLN'S GOING TO speak."

Those four words were relayed and repeated by citizens rushing to the town square of Clinton, Illinois, the seat of De Witt County. The news caught most by surprise. Lectures and speeches normally received a few days of advertisement, both in the local papers and by drawn-up handbills posted throughout the town. But Clinton's October 14 Republican Party courthouse celebration received only a few hours of advanced billing. The event was decided upon that very day; the occasion was the recent off-year election victories in Ohio, Pennsylvania, Iowa, and Minnesota. The decision to hold the evening event appeared to be based on one factor—Abraham Lincoln was in town.[1]

This was Lincoln's second trip to Clinton in nine days. He first arrived on October 5 for four days of circuit-court duties on his return from Wisconsin. Normally, his frequent visits to Clinton went unnoticed by newspapers, but this time Lincoln's bubbly demeanor could not be overlooked. "The old familiar face of Abraham Lincoln is again amongst us," noted the court reporter for Clinton's weekly paper, "and we cannot help noticing the peculiarly friendly expression with which he greets everybody, and everybody greets him. He comes back to us after electrifying Ohio, 'with all his blushing honors thick upon him,' yet the poorest and plainest amongst our people, fears not to approach, and never fails to receive a hearty welcome from him."[2]

One week later, the concrete news of the election victories in states where Lincoln had dazzled his audiences had made him an instant celebrity. Thus, his return to Clinton for four more days of court duties—he even presided as judge on nine cases—sparked the decision for a political celebration. At seven P.M. on Friday, the Clinton Sax Horn Band set up in the courthouse and delivered soul-stirring strains of patriotic music as residents flocked to the center of the town square to hear the words of Lincoln, the man now dubbed "our gallant standard-bearer." The organizers had been concerned that afternoon that the short notice would result in an embarrassingly small crowd. By nightfall, those fears disintegrated. A witness insisted the court room "was rammed, jammed and crammed from stem to stern."[3]

Lincoln was the first of three speakers scheduled for the evening, but rather than being a warm-up speaker, he was the main attraction. In fact, he was supposed to arrive escorted by the serenading band, but he showed up too early for the pomp. Still, great fanfare accompanied him to the stage. As soon as his telltale lanky form negotiated through the crowd to the front of the room, the band struck up "Hail the Conquering Hero Comes," and according to a reporter, "cheer upon cheer ascended to the dome, uttered by stentorian lungs," as Lincoln mounted the stand.

The crowd hushed momentarily as he began to speak. He informed them that demonstrations like this were transpiring throughout the North due to the Republican victories and predicted that St. Louis would celebrate as well, notwithstanding its being in a slave state. He then went on to repeat many of the remarks he had delivered in Ohio, Indiana, and Wisconsin over the past month, showing his audience his newly developed thoughts about the issues of the day, primarily the view that his position—and that of the Republican Party—was consistent with the intent of the Founding Fathers, while Douglas and the Democrats had radically departed from the traditional landmarks.

Lincoln hailed the Republican victories as a benchmark for the return of the doctrines of the Founding Fathers. "Our position is right," he declared, "our principles are good and just, but I would desire to impress on every Republican present to have patience and steadiness under all circumstances—whether defeated or successful. But I do hope that as there is a just and righteous God in Heaven, our principles will and shall prevail sooner or later." When he closed the speech the crowd erupted. A participant claimed that the loud and prolonged cheering "made the rafters of the court house ring again." Clinton's Republican paper, the *Central Transcript*, reported on all the speeches that night, rating Lincoln's speech an "eloquent and masterly exposition." The *Transcript* also contributed to what was becoming a growing movement throughout Illinois—it endorsed Abraham Lincoln for president of the United States.[4]

The celebrations continued into the weekend. Lincoln arrived in Springfield on the Saturday-evening train and returned to his home expecting a quiet evening. But word traveled swiftly, and before Lincoln turned in for the night, an impressive procession of several hundred city Republicans, headed by a music-blaring band, serenaded Lincoln's success on the stump. Lincoln greeted the multitudes, who flattered him with cheer after cheer on the street corner. Lincoln followed them to the capitol, where he repeated the Clinton speech to the assembly in the rotunda.[5]

The late-night event represented more than a disruption of Lincoln's neighbors. Since Lincoln's return to politics in 1854, he had continually been hailed for the quality of his speeches. Always respected in Springfield, even by and large by his political opponents, Lincoln had been viewed by Springfielders and those on his law circuit as an honorable man with a logical message. But that cool Saturday night on the corner of Eighth and Jackson, Lincoln had transcended beyond "Honest Abe." For perhaps the first time, the messenger was more important than his message. Lincoln had become the pride of the Illinois Republican Party, the "favorite son" of the state.

The *Illinois State Journal* hyped Lincoln as a "giant killer" for besting the Little Giant in Ohio. Lincoln's role in the Republican victory was not lost on prominent Republicans in Ohio. William T. Bascom updated Lincoln on the numbers in a letter from Columbus that Lincoln received a few days after his serenade. Looking ahead one year, Bascom crowed, "We think [the results] dispose of all the hopes for Douglas in Ohio." He thanked Lincoln. "We feel that some of the credit is due to you," he acknowledged, promising Lincoln, "In the future of the Republican Party in Ohio your visit to the Buckeye State will be held in grateful remembrance."[6]

Sam Galloway agreed in a letter also sent the same day from Columbus. "We all think that your visit aided us," he claimed, "and we are grateful for your services." But Galloway went much further than that. He opened up his thoughts to Lincoln in regards to Governor Chase's White House prospects. "His nomination as our Candidate for the Presidency would sink us," he maintained. Galloway believed Chase generated hard feelings, and he turned to Lincoln as the candidate of Ohio Republicans. "Your visit to Ohio has excited an extensive interest in your favor," insisted Galloway. "Whilst I would desire to have you remain as you are unobtrusive, at the same time, tis my . . . advice that you treat kindly and respectfully all requests for the use of your name."[7]

Galloway's words could only buoy Lincoln's already-uplifted spirits. He was fast becoming a hot prospect. As pleased as he was to be regarded as a national figure, he must have been irritated to see himself more frequently given only vice-presidential consideration. Operatives looked ahead to the election and realized what states needed to be won for them to achieve total victory in November 1860. With the belief that Douglas would become the Democratic nominee, they sought Lincoln to steal Illinois away from him (based on the vote total that tilted in Lincoln's favor in the 1858 Senate contest). Rather than look toward Lincoln as the Republican presidential candidate, they continued to put him second on the ticket.

One linkage that started to grow in popularity was a prospective Simon Cameron–Abraham Lincoln ticket. Although Senator Cameron had not accumulated much support outside his home state of Pennsylvania, his commanding support in his state—the third-largest delegation in the country—made him one of the front-running candidates for the Republican nomination. The belief prevailed that the Cameron-Lincoln pairing would win for the Republicans Pennsylvania and Illinois, two of a handful of states considered essential to claim the White House. Pennsylvania newspapers began to circulate this ticket, and Illinois papers reported it. Still holding back an official endorsement—it was only October 1859—the *Illinois State Journal* may have tipped its hand by proclaiming, "We think this ticket would suit the Republicans of Illinois better if the names were transposed."[8]

Lincoln sought to quell the entreaties of the Cameron supporters. "As to the ticket you name," responded Lincoln to one of the persistent

Pennsylvanians, "I shall be heartily for it, *after* it shall have been fairly nominated by a Republican national convention, and I can not be committed to it *before*." Lincoln repeated his mantra of working for the party and not for the self, but he allowed a glimpse into his ambition when he told the Cameron operative, "I shall labor faithfully in the ranks, unless, as I think not probable, the judgment of the party shall assign me a different position." Although Lincoln felt assured he had snuffed out the predetermined ticket talk, the Cameron-Lincoln movement would continue to dog him for the remainder of the year.[9]

Cameron's people were not the only ones seeking Lincoln as a vice-presidential link to their Republican candidate. On October 20, Thurlow Weed, the omnipotent campaign manager of William H. Seward, sent Norman B. Judd a curt telegram: "Send Abram Lincoln to Albany immediately." Forwarding Weed's message instantly to Lincoln, Judd confessed, "[W]hat it means I don't know nor do I know what to advise. I take it that Thurlow Weed is not so green to think he can get you into a combination with his pet Seward and it must be something else and probably of importance—I am in a fog about it." That fog did not envelop Lincoln, who must have believed that Weed indeed was seeking to snatch Lincoln up as Seward's vice president. The best evidence for Lincoln's interpretation of Weed's message is what he chose not to do—he never responded to the presumptuous wire.[10]

As irritated as Lincoln must have been to be continually talked of as vice-presidential timber, the second-place prospect aided his strategy of cloaking his ambition. By the end of October, at least several months away from the Republican National Convention (site and date still unknown), Lincoln's status had already changed dramatically since the beginning of 1859. He no longer was the Senate loser. He could now claim broader appeal than he did during the 1858 Senate campaign and, at least indirectly, he had helped to influence elections. The fact that he was not universally considered a top presidential prospect worked in his favor. He could continue to build a strong reputation with his mainstream address and work to solidify his base in Illinois while he remained somewhat hidden from national scrutiny.

At the same time, Lincoln sought to broaden his national exposure. While he never accepted Weed's order to proceed to Albany, he did entertain another opportunity to visit New York State. This one came from a

Chase supporter in Seward's state, who was apparently so impressed by Lincoln's performance in Ohio that he telegraphed an invitation to deliver an address "on any subject you please" in Brooklyn in late November. Lincoln savored this offer. The appeal of the invitation was its flattering tone as well as the opportunity to strike the Northeast—Seward's backyard—much as he had done to Salmon P. Chase in Ohio. The other appealing feature in the offer was money—Lincoln was to be paid two hundred dollars for the effort. Lincoln's only qualm was the proposed date—late November was still too early for him, so he proposed to move it back to the winter of 1860.[11]

While the final arrangements of the Northeastern trip were being worked out through the mails, Lincoln remained active. In addition to carrying out his circuit-court duties, he tried to be as politically influential at home as he had been in Ohio, writing and speaking on behalf of John Palmer, who was contesting Democrat John A. McClernand for the U.S. House of Representatives. (Ironically, Lincoln wrote his former client Peachy Quinn Harrison asking him to support Palmer, the prosecuting attorney who had opposed Lincoln in the murder trial.) Lincoln's influence was unable to carry Palmer; McClernand won the November 8 election.[12]

Interest in local politics suddenly collapsed due to the force of the national reaction to events in Harpers Ferry, Virginia. An abolitionist fanatic named John Brown had helped to accentuate the notorious reputation of "Bleeding Kansas" in 1856 when he formed a band of eight renegades (including four of his twenty children) to abduct and murder five innocent proslavery men in retaliation for the murders of free-soil men. Brown escaped prosecution to stir the pot again three years later. In October 1859 he enacted a months-long plot to start a slave insurrection in Virginia. With a band of twenty-two recruits (including three sons and five black men), Brown descended from the mountains upon the U.S. arsenal and armory at Harpers Ferry in an attempt to seize it and distribute arms to slaves, who he expected would rally to him when they heard the news.

John Brown and his "army" launched their attack against the federal installation at dark on October 16. It was an utter failure. Innocents were killed, no slaves rose up, and after the escape of some of his band, Brown and the remainder were surrounded as they hid behind the protective walls of the engine house. Thirty-six hours later, a company of U.S.

Marines—led by Colonel Robert E. Lee and accompanied by Lieu-
tenant J. E. B. Stuart—successfully stormed the engine house, captured
the wounded Brown and several members of his gang who had failed to
escape, and escorted them to jail in nearby Charles Town. Brown and the
six men captured with him were swiftly tried, convicted, and sentenced to
death for murder, treason, and insurrection. John Brown's hanging was set
for Charles Town on December 2, 1859.[13]

John Brown's insurrection reverberated across the country. Its political
ramifications could not be ignored. While some believed the trial worked
in favor of the Republicans, most saw the whole event as a fiasco for the
party. Under these circumstances, one of Lincoln's more frequent correspondents pleaded for his friend's intervention. "The Harpers Ferry affair
doubtless to some Extent hurt us in New York," assessed Republican
newspaperman Mark W. Delahay of Kansas Territory. He had been disappointed that Lincoln was forced to cancel a planned spring trip to Kansas
to speak at the territory's Republican convention in May. Half a year later
he considered Lincoln's presence in the territory imperative to prevent a
Democratic landslide in the December elections for seats in the territorial
legislature. Delahay sent Lincoln an invitation signed by dozens of mer-
chants, bankers, and businessmen to implore him to conduct a speaking
tour in the territory. Territory Republicans were hoping against hope to
prevent Kansas from entering the Union as a Democratic state. "You can
probably save us two U.S. Senators and our State Ticket," claimed
Delahay—overconfidently—adding, "I *trust* you may regard the *Exigency*
as demanding some sacrifice on your Part by accepting this appeal from
our Friends."[14]

Lincoln agreed to do it. He appeared to be affected by Delahay's appeal, having already disappointed him the previous spring. Delahay was
more than a friend to Lincoln, for he had married a Hanks, a distant
cousin of Lincoln's birth mother. Lincoln also saw this as an opportunity
to test the rough edges of the new speech he had been crafting to present
in Brooklyn in February. The trip to Kansas would also be Lincoln's first
and only trip to the territory whose very origin by the Kansas-Nebraska
Act had brought Lincoln back to politics in 1854.

Lincoln also looked ahead. Based on the response of appreciative Republicans in Ohio, who thanked him profusely for the speaking tour he

conducted there in September, Lincoln likely saw the Kansas trip as an opportunity to curry favor with party activists in the territory. Lincoln understood many of them to be adherents of Seward, but he hoped his intervention might plant a seed to effect a change of opinion about him, as his trip to Ohio had won over some Chase backers. At least he hoped that the delegation sent to the Republican National Convention would not be committed as a unit to Seward, or to their geographically nearest candidate, Edward Bates of Missouri.

He headed out on November 30, traversing Missouri on the newly completed Hannibal & St. Joseph, Railroad. At the depot in St. Joseph, Lincoln greeted his two Kansas escorts, Delahay and D. W. Wilder, the latter the publisher of the Republican paper in Elwood, the town across the river where Lincoln was scheduled to stay. In St. Joseph Lincoln took the time to get shaved and acquire New York and Chicago newspapers before heading out toward Kansas. Lincoln's brief visit in St. Joseph did not go unnoticed by the *Gazette*, the town's Democratic paper. It wryly reported, "The Republicans of Kansas must be getting badly frightened when they send for big guns from other States to assist them. Abe will be lucky if he succeeds in doing for the Republicans of Kansas what he was unable to do for himself in Illinois—beat the Democracy."[15]

Lincoln and his companions packed themselves in a stage and rode out to the ferry. Wilder recalled Lincoln's distinctive attire, including buttons missing from his shirt, and a felt stovepipe hat. Most unusual, thought Wilder, were Lincoln's gangly legs. "They were legs you could fold up," he noted. "The knees stood up like the hind joints of a grasshopper's legs." The threesome ferried over to Elwood, where Lincoln registered in the Great Western Hotel, the largest one in the territory, with seventy-five rooms in the three-story building.

Although he was feeling under the weather after his jarring ride, Lincoln agreed to speak in the dining room of the hotel that evening. There wasn't time to advertise the speech, nor was advertising needed in the three-year-old town of two thousand inhabitants. The speech was announced all afternoon by a man pounding a gong on the town streets.[16]

Enough of Elwood's citizens heard the gong and spread the word to produce a large gathering in the hotel that evening. Their eyes were glued to the celebrated speaker. "Your territory has a marked history—no other territory has had such a history," noted Lincoln after warming up the crowd with his introductory remarks. He went on to fault both parties equally for producing "Bleeding Kansas." He strove to maintain the middle ground throughout the short address. Most noteworthy about Lincoln's speech were his first public remarks about John Brown and his failed insurrection at Harpers Ferry. He told the crowd it was wrong on two fronts. Not only was it a clear violation of the law, stressed Lincoln (Brown was scheduled to be hanged in two days), but it also was a futile act that would have no effect on the extinction of slavery. "John Brown has shown great courage, [and] rare unselfishness, as even Governor Wise testifies," continued Lincoln, "but no man, North or South, can approve of violence and crime." Always adhering to the Constitution, Lincoln preached using the ballot box to express opinions on slavery rather than illegal means.[17]

Lincoln played it safe and did not attempt any new additions to the address at Elwood, for it was an unplanned speech for him. Still, his remarks were reproduced—particularly the moderate assessment of John Brown—in the Elwood Free Press two days later. But Lincoln did not stay in town to see the issue. On Thursday morning, December 1, he, Wilder, and Delahay climbed into an open carriage and rode onto a wind-swept prairie. Winter weather had frozen eastern Kansas, and now it tormented Lincoln on the road to Troy. Although accustomed to nearly thirty years of frigid prairie temperatures since his first winter in Illinois—the infamous winter of the deep snow in 1830–31—Lincoln found that his heavy overcoat failed to break the knifelike winds stabbing through the open carriage.

The ride was uncomfortable, but it turned ironic for the guest and his party. They came upon a two-horse wagon bearing two passengers and heading eastward. One of them stopped the wagon in front of Lincoln's vehicle, called Lincoln by name, and jumped out to shake hands with him. Lincoln had no idea who this bearded man, decked out in winter pioneer garb, was until the man finally gave him his name. It was Henry Villard, the Cincinnati Commercial reporter who had called upon him eleven months earlier in his law office, just two days after his Senate defeat. Villard had been returning from a stint in the Rockies, reporting for the Commercial about gold in Colorado. "Why, good gracious!" a stunned Lincoln exclaimed. "You look like a real Pike's-Peaker."[18]

Villard lent Lincoln one of his buffalo robes, and after a brief chat Lincoln and his companions rode on to Troy, a town of shanties, a single tavern, and a small frame courthouse. Perhaps forty people gathered in the courthouse to hear Lincoln speak. His address, less than two hours in length, likely repeated most of what he had said at Elwood. But his words would eventually be transmitted in the most influential city in the country. Albert D. Richardson was there as a western correspondent for the *New York Tribune*. Richardson penned a mixed critique of Lincoln's performance: "Neither rhetorical, graceful, nor eloquent, it was still very fascinating." What fascinated the reporter most was a surprising response to the speech provided by the largest slaveholder in the audience, if not the entire territory. Stressing that he disagreed with Lincoln's doctrines and his politics, this audience member still rated Lincoln's speech as the most able and logical one he had ever heard.[19]

Lincoln did not stay in Troy but instead proceeded twenty miles south to Doniphan, a settlement of about 1,000 inhabitants on the west bank of the Missouri River. Lincoln registered at the hotel there and stayed overnight. Like in Elwood, Lincoln spoke in the hotel that night, but no one left a record of his speech, the size of his audience, or its reaction to his arguments. The next morning he was off to his fourth speech in three days, this one in Atchison, five miles down the river from Doniphan. This was the largest and fastest-growing town he had seen thus far in Kansas Territory, with 2,500 inhabitants. Until 1859, Atchison was a proslavery town, considered the headquarters of the Border Ruffians. Although the free-state men had won control of the region by the time Lincoln traversed Kansas, he found that the Republicans there were not pro-Lincoln men. They included the mayor, Samuel C. Pomeroy, a passionate Seward supporter, and John A. Martin, the editor of Atchison's Republican newspaper. Although even late in 1859 neither of the two would have considered Lincoln a threat to Seward's bid for the presidency, Martin in particular made sure that no one would make inroads against Seward. He refused to play up Lincoln's speech in his newspaper. According to Edgar Watson Howe, an Atchison resident destined to become a leading editor himself in Kansas, Martin "hoped to kill off" Lincoln by not giving him a notice in his paper.[20]

Regardless of the lack of print he would receive, Lincoln attracted a great deal of attention in Atchison. Shortly after his arrival in the mid-morning, a handbill was printed and posted to advertise the evening talk in the Methodist church. Lincoln could shed his borrowed buffalo robe this day, for the temperatures had warmed enough to make the afternoon comfortable. The day was made more momentous when telegraph messages reached eastern Kansas to inform the townspeople that John Brown had been executed that day. During the evening Lincoln was escorted from the hotel to the church, preceded by a brass band. By eight P.M., there was hardly any standing room left in the church; the band members were forced outside, where they joined the latecomers who circled the church and strained to hear Lincoln's words.[21]

Lincoln spoke for two hours and twenty minutes, longer than he had in the previous three addresses in Kansas. He apparently introduced some of the material he was preparing for his New York speech, but by and large he reproduced the Elwood, Troy, and Doniphan speeches in an effort to rally disheartened Republicans to the polls in three days. "His talk was as eloquent as it was sound and logical," proclaimed an impressed Republican in the crowd.

Escorted back to the hotel, Lincoln shot billiards with the proprietor, a little Irishman who bested him. He also laughed and joked with proslavery and freedom advocates alike, displaying his humor and quick wit to the visitors in the hotel parlor. While discussing Nebraska Territory, someone mentioned a prominent stream there called "Weeping Water." Immediately conjuring up the image of the Minnesota waterfalls with the mesmerizing Indian name in Henry Wadsworth Longfellow's epic poem, *The Song of Hiawatha*, Lincoln quipped that if Longfellow's Minnehaha translated to "Laughing Water," then "Weeping Water" must have been translated from "Minne Boo-hoo."[22]

On Saturday, December 3, Lincoln followed what was now a routine of boarding the open carriage and riding twenty miles southward down the west bank of the Missouri. The road passed through a settlement called Kickapoo and the expansive Fort Leavenworth before arriving at the town of Leavenworth, the featured stop of Lincoln's territorial venture. Even before he entered the boundaries of Leavenworth, Lincoln well understood his appearance there was a meticulously prepared and advertised event. One mile from the town he was greeted by a large procession including citizens, dignitaries, and a band. Lincoln was the feature of this parade, entering the town amid the multitude of carriages and horses.

Leavenworth in 1859 was the largest city in the American West between St. Louis and San Francisco, with a population approaching 7,500—roughly the size of Lincoln's Springfield. The Republicans of Leavenworth were out in full force at noon, packed so densely on the city streets that they slowed the passage of the carriages. The parade deposited Lincoln at the Mansion House, the hotel where Lincoln would remain for that Saturday afternoon. Hearing his name chanted by the crowd outside, Lincoln walked out onto the hotel balcony to greet them. Breaking through the raucous cheers, Lincoln thanked them for the warm reception, flattered them by extolling the virtues of the beautiful country in which they resided, and teased them with a prelude to his evening's planned address with brief references to politics. He promised to expand on those ideas in several hours and disappeared from the view of the adoring crowd. The editor of the Democratic paper dismissed Lincoln's brief balcony appearance: "He was probably afraid he would explore his 'one idea' and leave no capital for the evening."[23]

Representatives from both rival newspapers positioned themselves that night within a crammed Stockton's Hall on the corner of Fourth and Delaware streets. Lincoln knew that like in Atchison, this was a Seward crowd, speckled with some proslavery Democrats. After an effusive introduction by Mark Delahay, Lincoln stepped up to the dais, took out his notes, and began to speak. A Democrat in the crowd observed him carefully to paint a word picture of "Old Abe" as a speaker. "The personal appearance of the individual is altogether different from any idea which a stranger would form," he noted. "So far from appearing 'old' he bears the appearance of a man well in his prime, but without dignity or grace. . . . His style of delivery, though concise, and striking plainly on the bearer, bears the impress of labored efforts to collect a smooth and easy flow; while his ideas are put forth in language totally at variance with all rules of grammar."[24]

Lincoln spoke for about ninety minutes, half the time he'd required at Atchison, but since he had already dispensed with his usual introductory comments on the balcony of the Mansion House, his remarks at Stockton's Hall were more focused upon the political issues of the day. As he had done the previous night, Lincoln introduced some themes he planned to expand upon in New York in February. He pointed out that the Democratic Party had changed dramatically to a radical party with views divergent from those of the Founding Fathers. By contrast, he declared that the Republican Party adhered to the doctrines and ideals of Washington, Madison, and Jefferson. He then made his remarks topical, with a statesmanlike approach to maintaining harmony between Kansas Territory and its neighbor, the slave state of Missouri. He warned the Kansans not to agitate the slaveholders in Missouri, advice consistent with his position of noninterference with the institution where it existed through the hard-fought Compromise of 1820. He closed his speech with a plea to head to the polls, proclaiming that it was more than a privilege—it was a duty.[25]

Lincoln's actual speaking time might have been closer to an hour than an hour and a half, but his speech was interrupted every several minutes by spontaneous applause. At the close of his address the audience in the hall responded with prolonged clapping and cheering, followed by grateful handshaking. The reviews of his performance were predictable, based on the political proclivities of the newspapers. The *Weekly Herald*, the Democratic organ of Leavenworth, told its readers:

> *[W]e have seldom heard one where more spurious argument, cunning sophistry, and flimsy evasions, were mingled together, and made to work out all right—no doubt to the satisfaction of the audience. He seized the slavery hobby in the beginning and rode it out to the end; starting out with the presumed facts, which the man could not know were points in dispute in the war of the parties, and by the surreptitious adoption of which he cunningly evaded any charge of the inconsistency in his erratic and blundering harangue. His remarks throughout were but the reproduction of the same old Illinois stump speeches with which he bored his audiences in that campaign which made him famous, and gave him the notoriety which he is not entitled to, owing to the position of his opponent.*[26]

The Republicans ate up Lincoln's performance, praising his style as well as his words. The Republican paper, the *Leavenworth Daily Times*, hailed his truthfulness, his common sense, his statesmanship, and the hope and faith he exuded about the future of the party and the nation. "Oratory is an art . . . ," ran the editorial, raving over Lincoln's mastery of it.

"No man can speak as he speaks or work as he works, without sowing seed which will bear rich fruits."[27]

As in the other Kansas towns where he spoke, Lincoln's formal performance was not his final discussion of the evening. He ventured to a room across the street from the hotel and sat around a woodstove with Marcus L. Parrott, the territorial delegate to Congress; Daniel R. Anthony, the editor of a Republican newspaper in eastern Kansas; and two other Republicans. There the five talked well into the night, with Lincoln swapping tales while tilting his chair back on its two rear legs. For Lincoln this evening would have been reminiscent of the winter nights in Springfield's town square twenty years before, where he would hold court with his friends in the back room of a dry-goods store, engaging in serious and not-so-serious discussions while sharing the warmth of a wood-stoked stove.

The wood supply in the Leavenworth room was exhausted long before the conversation. Rather than bear the cold outdoors on a wood hunt, Lincoln's companions began tossing the sacks of patent-office reports originally sent by Parrott for distribution. As these books were torn up and tossed into the fire, one of the men asked Lincoln if, as president, he would sanction the burning of government documents by cold Kansans. Lincoln smiled and responded, "Not only will I not sanction it, but I will cause legal action to be brought against the offenders." Most noteworthy about this friendly banter was the assumption that Lincoln would render this decision from the White House.[28]

Lincoln remained in Leavenworth for the next two days as a guest in the home of Mark Delahay. On Monday, the day before the election, Lincoln disregarded the bad weather and took to the streets, greeting citizens walking by and visiting them in their offices and shops. He immersed himself in their interests, beliefs, and convictions. Late that afternoon he returned to Stockton's Hall, packed again with a crowd waiting to hear him deliver another speech. Lincoln took the opportunity to expand on a theme he had introduced two days earlier. This speech also drew no praise from the Democratic paper. "To sum up the whole," critiqued the *Weekly Herald*, "we characterize his efforts as weak in the extreme and himself an imbecile old fogy of one idea; and that is—nigger, nigger, nigger."[29]

Clearly, this speech irked the editor even more than Lincoln's Saturday address. Lincoln was less a statesman in the Monday speech and more a

Republican partisan, trying to distinguish Douglas Democrats from Republicans by way of a history lesson. Lincoln evoked the Founding Fathers again, proclaiming that they had not attempted to interfere with slavery where it already existed, but had striven to prevent its extension. (Although no specifics were reported, Lincoln likely used the Northwest Ordinance as an example of the latter.) He proclaimed this as the key principle of the Republican Party as it prepared to enter the year 1860.

Lincoln then dug into the Democrats in regards to slavery, impugning their morality by repeating Douglas's line that he "didn't care whether it was voted up or voted down." Using that statement as the policy of the entire Democratic Party, Lincoln concluded that the slave power believed it had the right to extend slavery into the territories and future states of America, in spite of the intent of the Founding Fathers. Spinning a new metaphor reminiscent of a "House Divided" Lincoln likened the difference between North and South to a house on fire. Republicans were in favor of putting out the fire, while Democrats—particularly those adhering to Stephen A. Douglas's version of popular sovereignty—would prefer to stand aloof and let the fire spread to the point of burning down the house.

Lincoln then provided new remarks concerning John Brown and the attempts by Kansas Democrats on the eve of the election to identify his illegal act as a policy of the Republican Party. Lincoln pointed out that elections were held in New York, New Jersey, Minnesota, and Iowa after Brown's failed attempt at starting an insurrection in Harpers Ferry, and all of these states enjoyed Republican victories. This, Lincoln declared, was solid evidence that Democrats underrated the good sense of the people in those states, who realized Brown was insane. Lincoln challenged the crowd to find the first Republican who endorsed Brown's murderous act. If one was found, Lincoln suggested, he should step out of the ranks and correct his errant policies.

Lincoln continued to labor to counter damaging preelection claims by Democrats in regards to slavery. One was that Republicans favored the mid-nineteenth-century taboo of "amalgamation"—race mixing. Lincoln said that he wanted the races kept distinct; that he did not want a Negro woman to be kept as a slave did not mean that he wanted to marry her. He used state populaces as an example of the folly of the claim. The Republican state of New Hampshire had a mere 179 mulattoes, Lincoln pointed out, while the Democratic state of Virginia teemed with 79,000 mixed-race men, women, and children. He also countered the Democratic argument that Republican states allowed free blacks to vote, citing Massachusetts and New Hampshire as examples of this controversial policy. Lincoln shot down this argument by informing his audience that the voting laws had been enacted by Old Whigs in Massachusetts and by Democrats in New Hampshire. He went on to note that under current Kansas voting law, heavily influenced by Republicans, only white males were allowed to vote in the territory.

Lincoln's speech was crafted to uplift the spirits of the Republicans by indicating that their position was morally sound, and he gave them the ammunition to counter the fire of their most rabid Democratic neighbors. He closed the speech with a reinforcement of Republican principles to rally his audience to the polls. The *Leavenworth Daily Times* concluded, "He sought to make no display, but gave home-bred truths in a home-bred style that touched the hearts of his hearers and went home to all. . . . At the close of his speech he was greeted with a cordial round of cheers which made the old hall ring."[30]

Lincoln had saved his best for last. The second Leavenworth speech, on December 5, was Lincoln's most provocative, forceful, and convincing effort. It offered a glimpse of the more tailored argument that he was preparing to present in Brooklyn in 1860, and it demonstrated Lincoln's ability to provide historically educated, logical counterarguments to Democratic positions. Ironically, the Leavenworth speeches were linked with the poorest results, while the Elwood, Troy, Doniphan, and Atchison addresses were linked with happier outcomes for Republicans. On election day Republicans enjoyed gains in Atchison and Doniphan counties, while Leavenworth Democrats smothered the Republicans at the polls.[31]

The day after the election, on the morning of December 7, Lincoln bade farewell to his gracious hosts, the Delahay family. Before saying goodbye to Mary Delahay, the little girl of the house whose irresistible charm captivated Lincoln, he could not resist her request to leave her his autograph. "With pleasure I write my name in your album," penned the presidential hopeful, offering his best advice to her: "Ere long some younger man will be more [than] happy to confer his name upon you. Don't allow it, Mary, until fully assured that he is worthy of your happiness."[32]

Lincoln exited the warm Delahay house and boarded another open carriage, this one already seating three others, including W. H. Gill, the Democratic editor of the *Leavenworth Weekly Herald*. The trip to St. Joseph (including the carriage ride across the frozen river) softened Gill's impression of Lincoln. "Judge Lincoln was the soul of the company," confessed Gill in a letter to his paper. "Whilst we abhor the political heresies to which he adheres, none can deny that he is a high-toned, honorable and dignified gentleman." Lincoln regaled his carriage companions with anecdotes and insights, which Gill claimed "did much to relieve the monotony of our otherwise rough and tedious trip." Gill observed an abrupt souring of Lincoln's demeanor when the topic switched to politics, a product of the Republican losses in Leavenworth. According to Gill, he and his celebrating companion "sought to relieve [Lincoln] on this point, however, by assuring him that he had instilled all the spirit and enthusiasm in his party that had been manifested, and that the Democratic majority would have been five hundred instead of three, had he not aroused his sluggish, slumbering Abolition brethren."[33]

Lincoln arrived in St. Joseph at four P.M. that Wednesday. He may have learned how much he had disappointed Republican leaders there by not showing up a day earlier. O. A. Benjamin had met Lincoln at Elwood back on November 30, and was so impressed with him that he planned a large celebration for Lincoln in St. Joseph to launch his return trip. He wrote Lincoln on December 3 to inform him of the election night plans, insisting "there will be much disappointment if you fail to be here." There is no indication that Lincoln received the pretentious invitation in time to respond that he would not be able to step onto Missouri soil until the day after the planned event. Judging by the last line of the demanding invitation, Lincoln may have met with cold stares instead of a parade: "we feel otherwise than certain that you *will* be here *and you must not disappoint us*."[34]

The railroad from St. Joseph beelined Lincoln back to Springfield. The daylong trip gave him enough time to himself to contemplate what had worked and what had not in Kansas. The Kansas excursion had served as a dress rehearsal of sorts to develop his new speech, but he knew that he needed to do much more with it before it was presented in front of a New York audience and before it was evaluated by the New York and Northeastern press. Although he felt he had made gains with the argument that the Founding Fathers supported the Republican ideal of containing slavery, Lincoln realized he needed to prove this as best he could. This would require research into the earliest Congresses and the votes on legislation appropriate to this point of view.

As Lincoln's train pulled into the Springfield depot on Thursday night, December 8, Lincoln should have been satisfied that he had completed a great forward step toward his nomination. But waiting for Lincoln in his pile of mail was a growing obstacle to his candidacy, one that threatened the fragile composition of the Republican Party in Illinois.[35]

Six

WINTER HEAT

A BRAHAM LINCOLN HAD been hoping for a respite from the ardors of traveling and speaking in four states and one territory in less than three months, but the mail awaiting him upon his return to Springfield snuffed out those expectations. A week-old letter directed him to a festering problem, one that formed fissures in the foundation of the Republican Party in Illinois. The feud between "Long John" Wentworth and Norman B. Judd had boiled over.[1]

The rivalry between these two strong-willed Republicans had been growing for over a year. Wentworth used the influence of his newspaper to diminish Judd's power. Throughout 1859 the *Chicago Democrat* denounced Judd for mismanaging state funds and accused him of fraud. By the fall of the year, Wentworth spewed more venom in his editorials, highlighting Judd's 1855 vote against Lincoln for U.S. Senator while accusing him of secretly undermining Lincoln again during the 1858 campaign to purposely ruin his political career, a strategy by which Judd could support Lyman Trumbull for president in return for the senator's support of Judd's bid for governor. The routine and rhythmic sparking of anti-Judd pieces in the *Democrat* started to catch fire among state Republicans, who began to turn against Judd after reading them or hearing about them.[2]

Judd determined his only recourse was through legal channels. He sued Wentworth for libel on December 1, seeking $100,000 in damages, and wrote Lincoln that same day to vent his spleen. "I am berated in the newspapers, slandered in private conversations, and the uninitiated made to believe that I cheated you," wailed Judd, blaming Lincoln for letting the accusations go this far without intervening. He went on to claim that Lincoln's passive role in this affair had widened this division within the Republican Party of Illinois.[3]

Lincoln answered Judd on December 9, the day after his return from Kansas Territory. Lincoln broke down each part of Judd's accusation, "which I think is not quite just." He reminded Judd that he [Judd] had indeed voted for Trumbull in 1855, so how could Lincoln intervene on that issue? As to the charge of bungling Lincoln's 1858 campaign, Lincoln advised Judd, "The vague charge that you played me false last year, I believe to be false and outrageous; but, it seems, I can make no impressions by expressing that belief." Here, Lincoln was wrong, for he clearly carried enough clout to confront Wentworth and the accusing parties, and if he could not convince them that Judd was not to blame for the defeat, he could at least cease their public accusations. Lincoln's peacemaking strategy was to stand back and let things take care of themselves, which in this case exacerbated the issue until it seemed out of control.

Most interesting in Lincoln's response was how he dealt with Wentworth's third charge—that Judd was conspiring with Trumbull against Lincoln for president in 1860. Here he placated Judd by stating that he knew Judd well enough "to believe you would not pretend to be for me while really for [Trumbull]." Lincoln revealed to Judd that he did not consider Trumbull to be his rival, reminding Judd of the pledge he had made never to challenge Trumbull for his Senate seat. To underscore his own loyalty, Lincoln insisted that he had made this pledge even though he would rather be a U.S. Senator than the president, a claim made to point out that if Trumbull chose to run for the presidency, it would hardly matter to Lincoln.[4]

Lincoln's confession to Judd that he preferred a Senate seat to the presidency was not an admission that he had lost his ambition for the latter. On the contrary, he was prepared for the first time to advertise his candidacy and more publicly—yet indirectly—declare his presidential ambitions. He did this by completing a favor for a friend, fulfilling a request one year after it was made. In Bloomington the previous December Lincoln had steadfastly refused the entreaties of Jesse Fell to write his autobiography for circulation as a campaign document. Smarting over the disappointing end of the Senate campaign, Lincoln had hardly been proud of himself, his pedigree, and a life story blemished by failures. However, the shattered dreams that closed 1858 had dissipated, superseded by the recovery of 1859 and anticipation of brighter days ahead for the presidential campaign year of 1860. Gone were the self-pity, the gloom, and the "Why me?" approach to his life. Replacing them were self-confidence, sanguinity, and a "Why not me?" outlook.

It was a rejuvenated Abraham Lincoln who carved out a short version of his life story on the eve of the winter season. He wrote it in the first person, and structured it in the traditional style: "I was born . . . My mother . . . My father . . . I was raised . . ." He took pains to avoid embellishments concerning his ancestry, noting for instance that his grandfather—for whom he was named—was killed by Indians, "not in battle, but by stealth." Although he chose not to spruce up his past, Lincoln used his uninspiring childhood to his advantage. Falling back upon his opening remarks made in Indianapolis in mid-September, he described his wilderness upbringing in Indiana and how that had limited his formal education. "Of course when I came of age I did not know much," he wrote self-effacingly. "Still somehow, I could read, write, and cipher to the Rule of Three; but that was all." Knowing that a growing readership was learning about Lincoln through his speeches, he cleverly illustrated to them that the intelligence radiating from his phrases, analogies, and historical backgrounds was not the product of a privileged education, but from the dedicated determination of a self-made man.

To continue with the Western tradition of presenting himself as a man of the people, Lincoln went on to chronicle the many hats he wore as a young man after he moved to Illinois: store clerk, a captain of volunteers during the Black Hawk War ("a success which gave me more pleasure than any I have had since"), his several stints in the Illinois legislature, his law practice, and his 1846 election to the U.S. House of Representatives. He chose against a labored description of his two Senate defeats, but made a veiled allusion to the 1858 popular vote by mentioning that his first attempt at the Illinois legislature in 1832 was his sole unsuccessful race, "the

only time I have been beaten by the people." The final of his four paragraphs included a folksy description of his physique: "If any personal description of me is thought desirable, it may be said, I am, in height, six feet,
four inches, nearly; lean in flesh, weighing, on an average, one hundred and
eighty pounds; dark complexion, with course black hair, and grey eyes—
no other marks or brands recollected."[5]

Satisfied with his effort, Lincoln wrote a brief cover letter to Jesse Fell
on December 20, admitting in his characteristic downplayed style, "Here-
with is a little sketch, as you requested. There is not much of it, for the
reason, I suppose, that there is not much of me." He pointedly instructed
Fell to take it out of the first-person style to make it appear as a biography
and not an autobiography. He did not want the story enhanced, save for
the addition of speech excerpts. His modest view of his life story was
practical, for Lincoln felt that his past was not going to make him president. He also recognized that the talents of his associates were necessary
for his success. For this reason, he delegated the responsibility of his biography to Jesse Fell, allowing him some leeway in how to circulate the personal sketch to the greatest possible advantage.[6]

It would be another friend charged with an even greater responsibility
for taking the Lincoln boom to a new level. As the ink dried on Lincoln's
life sketch, Norman Judd was on a train to New York City. As the Illinois
member of the Republican National Central Committee, Judd attended
the meeting to choose the site and date for the 1860 Republican convention. Judd's mission was to bring that convention to Illinois. He would do
this by recommending Chicago as the site. Judd and Lincoln were on the
same page again after Lincoln finally addressed the accusations against
Judd in an effusive letter acknowledging his supreme confidence and faith
in Judd's judgment and abilities. But Lincoln's intervention was hardly
self-inspired. He chose to act only after being pressed by three Chicago
businessmen who questioned Lincoln about Judd's conduct. The letter
was eventually published in the *Illinois State Journal* and appeared to placate
Judd on the eve of his all-important trip.[7]

Judd's political skills in New York would be Lincoln's only reasonable
chance to win the nomination, a realization Lincoln had expressed to his
confidants in Springfield. One week earlier Lincoln wrote Judd, "I find
some of our friends here, attach more consequence to getting the National

convention into our State than I did, or do. Some of them made me promise to say so to you." Although on its face Lincoln's statement indicates that
he didn't appreciate the importance of the convention site, it may just reflect his typical indirect style, a style that Judd was accustomed to; Judd understood fully that Lincoln was prodding him to make extraordinary efforts
to land the convention in Chicago. But Lincoln placed an even higher pre-
mium on the convention's date than on its location, preferring it to be held
after the Democrats met in April in their convention in Charleston—"the
later the better," he instructed to Judd.[8]

Judd took his seat with the other committee members at New York's
Astor House at noon on December 21. The nine hundred miles that separated him from "Long John" Wentworth also distanced him from the feud
and sharpened Judd's focus on the task at hand. He was one of twenty-one
delegates representing all the Northern states and the District of Columbia, Maryland, and Virginia. The committee agreed to set the date of the
convention for June 13, 1860, but the locale proved more problematic. No
fewer than eight cities were bandied about as potential host sites, including three in Pennsylvania, a testament to the dogged determination of Simon Cameron's crony Thomas Williams. Presidential hopefuls Chase and
Bates were also well represented with bids by Cleveland and St. Louis.
(Surprisingly, no New York venue was placed in contention, despite the
advantage of having the state's delegate, Governor Edwin D. Morgan, presiding over the committee.)[9]

The session dragged throughout the afternoon and into the early evening. Indianapolis had been talked up in the press as a preferable site, but it
was eventually eliminated due to lack of hotel space. By 7:30 P.M., the list of
sites was whittled down to two: St. Louis and Chicago. St. Louis also was
aided by members of the Francis P. Blair family, influential supporters sitting
in the meeting as invited observers. Chicago made the short list primarily
because Lincoln's name had not resonated as a serious presidential candidate
within the ranks of the committee, a huge benefit for Norman Judd, who
could promote Chicago as a neutral site, while St. Louis—the home base of
Edward Bates, a more respected candidate in 1859—could not claim the
same status. Although St. Louis was the next best thing to Chicago as a close
site for Illinois delegates, Lincoln adherents would likely be overwhelmed in
St. Louis by Bates supporters. Furthermore, in Missouri, Judd could not pull

strings—for example, reduce train fares—as he could in Illinois to assure a huge Lincoln-supporting crowd, one that would by increments overpower the supporters of any other candidate. If St. Louis was chosen as host city— and it was the odds-on favorite—it would be inconceivable for Lincoln to win the nomination.[10]

No one recorded exactly what Judd said to appeal for Chicago that night, but he proved to be the right man for the job. He established a strong case for the delegates to vote for Chicago based on three strengths: it had tremendous and new railroad transportation, it was teeming with hotels to comfortably house a flood of delegates, and it was neutral territory to placate the top-tier candidates. Judd also convincingly argued that the convention would be wasted in St. Louis, in a slave state, one that the Republicans had no chance to carry in the national election.

Judd's political hallmarks, zeal and persuasive arguments, won over members who must have been predisposed toward St. Louis. The final vote commenced near eight P.M. Judd's own vote proved to be the decisive one—Chicago received eleven votes and St. Louis garnered ten. In the midst of personal turmoil back home, Judd achieved an incredible coup by placing Chicago at center stage for national party politics in 1860.[11]

Judd returned home a few days later fresh from his victory, one that was trumpeted by Chicago papers before he set foot on Illinois soil. But Judd's conflict with other Republicans in Chicago was displayed between the lines in these otherwise joyous reports. Charles L. Wilson, the editor of the *Chicago Evening Journal*, crowed over the final vote in his editorial but refused to acknowledge Judd as the man responsible for it. Predictably, "Long John" Wentworth took an audacious turn in his editorial in the *Chicago Democrat*. Not only did he refuse to credit Judd for his coup, but he accused Judd of supporting Indianapolis over Chicago, requiring a late-hour petition campaign by Chicagoans to convince the national committee that it offered much more than Indianapolis. (Wentworth conveniently failed to explain how this list of names favoring Chicago over Indianapolis was able to wrest the convention from front-running St. Louis.)[12]

Republicans outside of Illinois were also pleased. "I rather like Chicago as the place for the Republican Nat. Convention, and the time is perhaps about right," assessed a Republican in Kansas Territory upon learning of Judd's accomplishment. This was the reserved reaction of someone ignorant of the importance of Illinois as the site and of the powerful combination of skill and serendipity that had allowed Judd to land it. Lincoln and his supporters were not lost in that fog. They knew that no Republican presidential candidate would win a slave state in the 1860 election, that hopes for victory rode on winning four out of the five free states that John C. Frémont had lost as the first Republican presidential candidate in 1856: Illinois, Indiana, Pennsylvania, New Jersey, and California. Election returns from the fall of 1859 offered hope for the Republican Party to win the precious Electoral College votes of those states, but Illinois would be doubtful if, as most people expected, Stephen A. Douglas sealed the Democratic nomination. Judd's convention coup for Chicago improved the odds for Republicans to steal Illinois from Douglas Democrats.[13]

Most Democrats were indifferent to the meeting of the Republican National Central Committee, but some became outright conspiratorial over it. If Lincoln read the rumors published in Democratic organs, he must have been amused to learn that he too was at the Astor House prior to the meeting of the committee, in secret caucus with fifty Republican bigwigs. The newspapers spun this tall tale by claiming that the caucus decided to cast Seward aside for his "irrepressible conflict" stance and to replace him with Edward Bates, whose moderate views were less offensive to Southerners. According to the fanciful story, reported first by the *New York Herald* and picked up by newspapers in other states, for helping to dump Seward, Lincoln would be rewarded by being named secretary of the interior in Bates's cabinet. Seward would be sent overseas as minister to England, "and take his chances in 1864." This wild rumor did reveal the perceived acceptance of Bates's candidacy by some Democrats, the belief that Republicans favored that candidacy as an appealing moderate ticket, the regard held for Lincoln as a ranking national leader, the overall hostility to Seward, and the fear of Democrats that Republicans would—in a moment of clarity—prevent their flawed front-runner from winning the nomination by replacing him with a more moderate candidate.[14]

Notwithstanding these reports, Lincoln was never in New York and would never have agreed to a cabinet position in someone else's administration, particularly now that he was racking up impressive presidential endorsements from Republican newspapers both in and outside of Illinois. By the end of the first week of the new year of 1860 more than a score of dailies and weeklies from Illinois, Indiana, Ohio, Pennsylvania, and Wisconsin had either run his name for president near their mastheads, or prominently endorsed him in their political editorials. Lincoln had been reading and reviewing them in the *Illinois State Journal* and the *Chicago Press and Tribune*, which reported upon the endorsements whenever they received them. Although pleased at the faithful and dedicated approach by his hometown's paper, Lincoln must have been vexed that the *Journal* had yet to express its opinion on the presidential candidates of 1860.

That all changed on Saturday, January 14. Lincoln was most likely at home when he opened his copy of the *Journal* to page 2. There, in the first column and immediately under a report about the pending Republican National Convention, Lincoln was transfixed by the headline "Mr. Lincoln and the Presidency." Having reported earlier that week that Ohio Republicans had picked up the once-defunct project of publishing Lincoln's debates with Douglas, and that the Young Men's Republican Club in Springfield had met on Thursday and changed its name to the "Lincoln Club" as its formal endorsement, the *Journal* followed suit. Lincoln read with pleasure the *Journal*'s acknowledgment that he was "the favorite son of Illinois" and that "in all directions, the public press are making him their first choice of the nomination."

The article developed the thesis that the next president should come from a state closer to the Mississippi River than to the Atlantic Ocean; what came next had to rank as one of the most pleasing paragraphs Lincoln had ever read. "ABRAHAM LINCOLN has arrived at that period of life when a man's mental and physical powers and faculties are in their prime," chimed the Saturday editorial, which went on to laud Lincoln's strength of mind, patriotism, ability, integrity, and conservative approach to Republican politics. Calling him "one of the great men of the land," the *Journal* ended its piece with the endorsement: "The Republicans of Illinois will sustain and support, with their full strength, the Presidential nominee of the Chicago Convention whoever he may be; but they respectfully, yet earnestly, call upon the Republicans of the Union to weigh the claims, estimate the qualifications and availability, and consider the fitness and propriety of giving the nomination to ABRAHAM LINCOLN of Illinois."[15]

This was the endorsement Lincoln had sought and expected, and now, at the start of the great campaign year, it had finally arrived. The Lincoln boom was growing; all his hard labor to restrain blanket endorsements early in 1859 had paid off, for he had not peaked too early; he had not peaked at all. He was a growing snowball rolling down a hill, the center of which was the rock—Lincoln's ambition—while the packed coat of snow, formed by the legions of supporters, strengthened the force of the ball with momentum.

That January more and more packing snow coated the ball, doubling its size toward the end of the month. During that last full week of January, a secret caucus met in the state capitol. Unlike the fictitious private Republican meeting at New York's Astor House that was recounted in Democratic newspapers one month earlier, this actual one received no newsprint—not even from Republican papers. The opportunity to meet arose when prominent Illinois Republicans migrated to Springfield to conduct their day jobs as attorneys with cases to present before the Illinois Supreme Court or to have their arguments heard before the U.S. circuit court. At least ten of them, including Lincoln, gathered at the secretary of state's office on the second floor of the building.

One year earlier, Lincoln had planted the seed of his presidential run at a similar caucus in the basement of the capitol. Back then, however, no one present except for Jesse Fell had entertained the notion that Lincoln was a serious prospect. No doubt that opinion had changed throughout 1859, and the endorsement by the *Journal* less than two weeks before this meeting had been read and appreciated by the caucus members. Many of the participants gathered with the notion to endorse Lincoln for president and to develop a strategy to give him the best chance at the upcoming convention.

But Jackson Grimshaw, who likely initiated the caucus, had other ideas, and Lincoln knew it. Grimshaw was a thirty-nine-year-old Quincy attorney in Springfield to attend the courts. After bumping into Lincoln in the basement library of the capitol, Grimshaw called the meeting in Secretary Hatch's office, which doubled as a committee room. Grimshaw's stated purpose at this caucus was to discuss Lincoln's prospects for the presidency, but his clandestine one was to get Lincoln to run as Simon Cameron's vice presidential candidate. This was made apparent by Grimshaw's overt labors to form Cameron-Lincoln clubs statewide. Lincoln declined to be anyone's vice president, as he had for a full year. Unable to ignore the burgeoning Lincoln boom, Grimshaw asked Lincoln if the caucus members, all influential in their regions of the state, could advertise Lincoln as their preferred nominee. Lincoln officially consented and the caucus broke up, its members completing their court duties in Springfield before fanning out on their return trips to their hometowns.[16]

This caucus was Lincoln's catapult. He needed the backing of these influential colleagues, who had unofficially formed into a team of managers. They, in turn, would sway other influential politicos in their towns and counties. The goal was twofold: to spread the word of "Lincoln for president" across the state, and to assure that the delegates who would meet in Decatur for the Republican State Convention in May were resolved to endorse Lincoln's candidacy on the eve of the national convention upstate in Chicago.

Although Chicago could be the site of Lincoln's salvation in the spring of 1860, it was the source of the greatest obstacle for Lincoln's success during the preceding winter. The Wentworth-Judd rivalry had yet to be resolved, and the libel suit remained active. State Republicans were choosing sides, creating a greater rift in the fragile young party and worrying Republicans across the state. With no resolution nearly three months after Judd sued for libel, some fretted that the festering feud would ruin their chances later in the year. "What has come over Chicago, and what effect upon the state nominations is this unexpected move going to have?" wondered an Alton party member about Judd's lawsuit.[17]

Wentworth either had a tin ear about the issue or was completely shameless when he dared ask Lincoln to defend him in the suit. "You must not decline until you have taken proper time to think of it," pleaded Long John in his attempt to retain Lincoln as his lawyer. Lincoln refused to bite on this proposal. Realizing the detrimental effects of this very public feud, he did offer to mediate an agreement by which Judd would drop the suit in return for Wentworth's publishing a retraction of the charged rhetoric that had initiated the suit in the first place. To assure Judd that Wentworth's retraction would be simple and unambiguous, Lincoln crafted it himself and sent it to Wentworth. He also suggested that the *Democrat* and the *Press and Tribune* abandon their attacks on the suit's subjects: "Let the papers, as such contend with one another on measures of policy as much as they like; but John Wentworth and N. B. Judd to be absolutely let alone in both of them."[18]

Wentworth balked at Lincoln's proposal, claiming that it failed to guarantee that Judd would drop the suit, but more concerned with how eating his words would affect his standing with both his allies and his adversaries. Although he was unable to pull Lincoln over to his side, Wentworth succeeded in persuading David Davis to side with him. Davis's support of Wentworth was born out of frustration with Judd as well as his confidence in Long John's political skills. Judge Davis was savvy enough to realize that this fight was as much between rival Republican newspapers as between rival Republicans. He confessed to Lincoln in February, "I need not say to you that I should be *rejoiced*, if the Libel Suit could be settled honorably, & that at least between this time & next November, that a stop could be put to the personal animosities of the Democrat & Press & Tribune."[19]

As much as Lincoln lamented how the battling Chicago newspapers affected the cohesiveness of the Republican Party in Illinois, he clearly favored Charles Ray and Medill's *Press and Tribune* over Wentworth's *Democrat* and Wilson's *Chicago Evening Journal*. Throughout 1859, the *Press and Tribune* had closely followed Lincoln's activities. Curiously, the paper chose not to report on his Chicago speech in March, but it rarely missed from that point on. His 1859 speeches had routinely been reproduced or excerpted in the *Press and Tribune*, even his nonpolitical agricultural address in Milwaukee. When not reporting on his travels and speeches, the paper still found reasons to drop Lincoln's name in analyses and editorials, even while remaining neutral regarding Republican presidential candidates (a testament to Judd's loyalty, influence, and support). Although Lincoln had not officially been endorsed for president by the paper, the *Press and Tribune* saw fit to republish endorsements from other papers, much as the *State Journal* had done. In the twelve months between February 1, 1859, and February 1, 1860, Lincoln's name appeared 120 times in the *Press and Tribune*, 34 times in the headline of a column, and nearly every mention of him was favorable. The paper was clearly a pro-Lincoln organ in the winter of 1860.

On the other hand, both the daily and weekly issues of Wentworth's *Chicago Democrat* strove to avoid promoting Lincoln as a presidential candidate. Not only did the paper neglect to reproduce or excerpt Lincoln's autumn speeches in Ohio, Indiana, and Wisconsin; the paper failed even to mention that Lincoln had ventured out of state on a speaking tour. Although Wentworth published Lincoln's Jefferson birthday letter in April, he did it without prefacing the letter with a Lincoln accolade as had most Illinois papers that had also reproduced the letter. Lincoln's letter was dwarfed in the *Democrat* by a full supporting editorial in the same issue on Edward Bates that prefaced a letter Bates had written to redeem himself from criticism of his policies. True to his inconsistent form, Wentworth predicted late in December (shortly after asking Lincoln to defend him against Judd's lawsuit) that the upcoming Republican National Convention would draw a huge crowd to Chicago "the day Lincoln is nominated." Lincoln and anyone else paying attention to Wentworth's political fluttering could easily discern that the purposely omitted end of the sentence was the words "for vice president" and not "for president."[20]

By publicly supporting Judd in a December letter to three Chicago businessmen, published in papers across the state, Lincoln had taken a political risk. Since Judd was running for governor, Lincoln's words of praise for him did not go unnoticed by the two other gubernatorial candidates, Leonard Swett of Bloomington and Richard Yates of Jacksonville, and by their supporters. Lincoln made sure Judd understood this sacrifice, informing him, "Some folks are pretty bitter towards me about the . . . letter." Although Judd expected more from Lincoln, he must have understood that Lincoln was walking a tightrope to keep the peace among the rival Republican factions in Illinois.[21]

In order to maintain the precarious balance, Lincoln was forced to clamp down upon his junior law partner. Billy Herndon had suddenly entered the political fray as an outspoken critic of Norman Judd, parroting accusations that Judd was misappropriating treasury funds to support his statehouse candidacy. Lincoln confronted Herndon over this and received only a denial from him. But Herndon could see how displeased Lincoln was over the matter, and he seemingly retreated into hibernation that winter, rarely showing his face on the political scene in what was destined to

become a crucial and exciting election year. Given that his law partner—
a man he had admired and marveled over for twenty years—was clearly
starting to boom as a presidential candidate, it was incredibly strange that
Herndon disappeared from politics early in 1860, and indicates either an
extreme case of bad luck on his part or a calculated decision not to par-
ticipate in an event he believed would result in utter failure for "Mr. Lincoln."[22]

Not only did the infighting within the ranks weaken the solidarity of
the political powers of Illinois, but some members stood rock solid for
candidates other than Lincoln. Orville Hickman Browning, a prominent
Quincy lawyer and state senator for the past twelve years, remained
unswayed in his support for Edward Bates. Browning met with Norman
Judd and others in an attempt to gain a consensus to take to the state convention. Others toiled in other parts of the state, vigorously representing
Bates or Chase, Seward or Cameron, and a smattering of others.

But despite Browning's entreaties, Norman Judd and the other members of the Republican State Central Committee remained in Lincoln's
corner. Judd had just returned to Springfield from a trip to Washington,
where he had gauged Republican prospects from the nation's capital. The
site and date of the state convention were the top agenda items for the
committee when Judd convened it in Springfield on the morning of February 8. The date agreed upon was May 23, subject to change if the date
of the national convention was moved up from June. The state convention
had two purposes: to nominate candidates for state offices and presidential
electors, and to select delegates to the national convention in Chicago.
Decatur, the seat of Macon County, was chosen for the locale, likely because the town was centrally located in Illinois.[23]

That evening Lincoln decided to visit Orville Hickman Browning in
his hotel room, ostensibly to gauge the strength of Browning's support for
Bates. Browning was in the midst of crafting a letter to a Bates associate in
St. Louis when Lincoln arrived. "I am more and more convinced that Mr.
Bates is stronger with the people of this state than any other man we can
nominate," penned Browning, "and firmly believe that if nominated we
will carry this state for him against Douglass [sic], or any other man."
Browning's allegiance to Bates was so well known that he apparently was

not invited to join the caucus that threw its support to Lincoln, but Browning saw the results of the late-January caucus differently. Browning fretted that Bates would not have the full support of Illinois delegates on the first ballot, even though he was "the first choice of our people" for the presidency.[24]

Likely catching wind of the sway Lincoln now had with the caucus and with the Republican State Central Committee, Browning claimed that "prominent men who are for Mr. Bates as their 'First Choice' are still inclined to give Lincoln what they call a complimentary vote of the first ballot, and this may occur. I hope not. It is childish and may do a great deal of harm." Browning named gubernatorial candidate Richard Yates as one of the prominent men who favored Bates over Lincoln, jotting down his name just before Lincoln knocked on his hotel room door. Ironically, Dick Yates was one of two people who joined Lincoln in Browning's room that evening for an informal political discussion (the other was David L. Phillips). The topic was the presidency, and Lincoln was dismayed to discover that the caucus decision had had no influence on Browning. According to Browning, who entered the gist of the discussion into his diary that night, Yates and Phillips agreed with him. Browning was also convinced that even Lincoln was for Bates, a mistake he had made four months earlier when he felt Norman Judd shared his desire to nominate the Missourian.[25]

After Lincoln and the other guests left, Browning finished his letter. "I have just had a very free conversation with Mr. Lincoln," he wrote. "He says he is satisfied there is a large class of voters in this state who would go for Mr. Bates . . . and that by the time the National Convention meets it is not improbable he may think with me that Mr. Bates ought to be nominated." Lincoln clearly had decided to placate Browning rather than risk alienating him, but Browning's support of Bates warned of the threat the Missourian posed for Lincoln in Illinois. Bates's strength was further revealed to Lincoln by his contacts that winter. Ozias M. Hatch had begun receiving letters indicating the preference for Bates in the southern part of the state. Long John Wentworth found out that the Missourian's team was already running its political machine out of the Tremont House in Chicago. "The man you have to fear is Bates," warned Wentworth. Horace Greeley had also become a Bates supporter that winter.[26]

Lincoln would have been more discouraged to learn that even Judge

Davis thought Bates had a better chance than Lincoln to win the Republican nomination. "Of course I [should] like it, if Lincoln could be nominated, but I am afraid that is a foregone conclusion," a pragmatic Davis revealed in a letter to a Beardstown lawyer. "It seems to me from this standpoint now, as if it would either be Mr. Bates or Gov. Seward." Davis probably kept this prediction from Lincoln's ears and revealed it only in confidence.[27]

Lincoln realized that Browning and perhaps other Bates supporters would attend the Decatur convention in three months, and his own chances for the presidency depended on a unanimous vote of the Illinois delegates—known as a unit vote. Browning had made his pro-Bates views known to Norman Judd a few months before the February 8 meeting with Lincoln; it is likely Judd and Lincoln privately discussed Browning and the potential troubles he caused.[28]

The day after seeing Browning in his room, Lincoln wrote to Judd about the tenuous situation. In his characteristic understated style Lincoln claimed, "I am not in a position where it would hurt much for me not to be nominated on the national ticket; but I am where it would hurt some for me to not get the Illinois delegates." He revealed his concern that his open support for Judd had embittered some of Judd's enemies—and Judd had many throughout the state, "and they will, for revenge upon me, lay to the Bates egg in the South, and the Seward egg in the North, and go far towards squeezing me out in the middle with nothing." Satisfied that he had inflicted pangs of guilt upon his manager, Lincoln looked to him for a favor: "Can you not help me a little in this matter, in your end of the vineyard?"[29]

Judd's end of the vineyard was Chicago, more specifically the *Chicago Press and Tribune*. Not only was this newspaper the most influential of the three Republican organs in the city, it was highly regarded outside of Illinois as "undoubtedly the ablest commercial and political journal of the great West." A Fort Wayne, Indiana, paper declared, "As a political paper it is not too much to say that it has not its equal for ability West of New York," while another Hoosier paper raved, "We prefer it in every respect to its great prototype, the *New York Tribune*."[30]

The *Press and Tribune* had run chiefly positive pieces on Lincoln over the past two years, but he now sought a greater commitment from it, a public stance that would carry eastward and westward. Judd knew exactly what Lincoln was looking for, and Lincoln soon learned something positive was coming his way. "Don't be surprised if the *Press & Tribune* break ground for you," tantalized a Chicago insider to Lincoln in a letter he received a few days after his fifty-first birthday. Immediately afterward, on February 16, the newspaper officially endorsed him for president of the United States. The endorsement, on the heels of the *Illinois State Journal*'s, sealed the support of the two most influential Republican newspapers in the state. Shortly after the endorsement was published, Judd coyly asked Lincoln, "You saw [what] the Tribune said about you—was it satisfactory?"[31]

It certainly was. Perhaps it seemed inevitable to Lincoln that the *Press and Tribune* would endorse him, but it required one of its coeditors to undergo a political metamorphosis for this to happen. Joseph Medill would later insist he was for Lincoln since the spring of 1859, but his correspondence to his years-long friend, Samuel P. Chase, later in the season convincingly disputes his assertion. Over the latter half of 1859 and into the first two months of 1860, Medill took a pragmatic approach to the presidency. He had become convinced that his man Chase could not claim the states that were key to a Republican victory. Although his political beliefs, particularly regarding abolition, aligned more with Chase's than with Lincoln's, Medill became more comfortable with Lincoln's opinions and realized that his middle-ground position was a consistent one and one more likely to prevent moderate voters from jumping over to Douglas's camp. He also appreciated Lincoln's efforts against Douglas in 1858, and knew that the presidential race would be won by a popular vote in Illinois and not a legislative one. The *Press and Tribune* calculated that in 1858 pro-Lincoln legislators received four thousand more votes statewide than pro-Douglas ones. Lincoln, therefore, had the best chance of all Republican candidates to win Illinois in November 1860.

But what about the other key states? All of them were deemed doubtful for Republican pickups, but Medill became convinced that only a candidate adhering to a middle position could claim them by attracting the abolitionists without alienating the antiabolition sects. This eliminated Seward as well as Chase, and for Medill, only Lincoln and Bates could resonate within the party ranks. Lincoln superseded Bates for Medill, based partly upon his impressions of him from 1858–59. Medill considered Lincoln the most "available" candidate for Republicans to rally around.[32]

To Lincoln's supreme benefit, Medill was not bogged down by the fatalistic predictions made about Lincoln's prospects. Instead, he embarked upon a personal campaign to make Lincoln a household name. The winter of 1860 found Medill in the nation's capital as the *Press and Tribune*'s special correspondent, under the pseudonym "Chicago." Medill later claimed that his real mission there was to promote Lincoln's nomination. "I began preaching Lincoln among the Congressmen," Medill proudly recalled; "I urged him chiefly upon the ground of availability in the close and doubtful States."[33]

Medill claimed success in the mission, one he trumpeted in a letter he wrote four days after his paper officially endorsed Lincoln. He extolled Lincoln's virtues and compared his moderate views to those of the better-known but more radical front-runners. "I will say, in conclusion, that I hear the name of Lincoln mentioned for President in Washington circles, ten times as often as it was one month ago," reported Medill, not revealing to his readers that he made great efforts to circulate Lincoln's name to generate that interest. "The more the politicians look over the field in search of an available candidate, the more they are convinced that 'Old Abe' is the man to win the race with. If the States of the Northwest shall unite upon him, and present his name to the Chicago Convention, there is a strong probability that he will receive the nomination, and as certain as he is nominated he will be President."[34]

Medill's report was full of wishful thoughts, for Lincoln's nomination prospects were nowhere near the "strong probability" the newsman claimed in February 1860. Lincoln appeared to be a dark horse even in Illinois, having yet to receive an endorsement from either of the remaining Republican papers in Chicago or to sway all prominent Prairie State Republicans to him. But despite the opposition to Lincoln within Illinois, the newspaper endorsements and the support of Republican caucus placed him in a much stronger position in the winter of 1860. The enlarging Lincoln snowball was nearly halfway down the hill. Obstacles still impeded the path, but now the ball was large enough to bust them up until it reached the strong, thick wall at the bottom—the Republican National Convention in Chicago, a wall reinforced by the bricks of Seward, Chase, Bates, and their operatives.

Medill's report helped to enlarge the snowball and weaken the wall at the same time. It was published in the *Press and Tribune* at the end of February. As heralded as Lincoln had become throughout the states of the Old Northwest Territory, his popularity and name recognition had diminished drastically beyond the eastern border of Ohio. Throughout the winter of 1859–60 Lincoln had with increasing frequency been linked to the presidency in newspapers published not only in Illinois, but in Ohio, Indiana, Michigan, Wisconsin, and the states and territories west of the Mississippi River: twenty-nine newspapers had officially endorsed Lincoln for president by February 1860. But as large as that number seemed at first glance, it represented only a minute fraction of the thousands of newspapers in circulation throughout the United States.[35]

For the 1860 election, Pennsylvania's nickname as the Keystone State was apropos, for it was one of four keys necessary to unlock the White House for Republicans in 1860. Thus far in Pennsylvania, Lincoln was considered merely a possible vice president on a ticket headed by one of the state's most prominent politicos, Simon Cameron or John Hickman. Only the *Reading Journal* tepidly suggested Lincoln's name at the top of the ticket. Jesse Fell activated the Lincoln campaign there during the second week of February when he persuaded an editor and friend to publish Lincoln's autobiography as an article in the *Chester County Times*. The article was picked up by other newspapers, and Lincoln's life story began to spread. Fell's efforts had taken root, but Lincoln could hardly be considered a household name in Pennsylvania that winter.[36]

In New York and the Northeastern states, very little ink was splurged associating Lincoln with the presidency. He was relegated to a subject of conjecture. For example, in a wintertime column appropriately titled "Short Paragraphs," the *Hartford Courant* briefly passed him off as a source of gossip: "It is said the Illinois Republican delegates will be in favor of Abraham Lincoln." The *New York Herald* went further, relaying from its Chicago correspondent the rumor that the city's Lincoln advocates "now declare that his nomination is a foregone conclusion." Given Lincoln's inability to sway the likes of Orville Hickman Browning in his direction, the *Courant* and *Herald* reports were premature. But the fact that these papers were printing Lincoln's name as a nebulous national figure was progress.[37]

Still considered a Western curiosity by most in the Northeast, Lincoln was most familiar to northeasterners who had migrated to Illinois, but he still had not won over even *their* hearts. One of those Prairie State transplants revealed that winter, "As a New Yorker, my preferences are very naturally for our own Seward; but if I was asked who would make the strongest Republican candidate in the United States, I should say unhesitatingly—Abraham Lincoln of Illinois."[38]

This was Lincoln's dilemma in the winter of 1860, one that he confronted head-on by reading the New York native's letter in the *Illinois State Journal* or the *Press and Tribune*. In the midst of ringing endorsements and widespread support, he had to break the bond that linked state delegates to their favorite sons. Even worse for Lincoln was the regional influence of politics. Those delegates of second- and third-tier candidates (Lincoln was in the latter category in the first months of 1860) would eventually shed their loyalties to support a winner, and in the case of the Pennsylvania and northeast nominators, Seward was most likely that candidate. Seward still held the cards in New England as the front-runner and as the candidate receiving the most press coverage. The convention skills of Seward's manager, Thurlow Weed, seemingly rendered inevitable the solid voting block of the Northeast for the prominent New York senator.

New York natives residing in Illinois in the 1850s still felt loyal to Seward in 1860, one of them admitting to Ozias Hatch that he had "for years looked up to Wm. H as the great light of our country." What chance did Lincoln have to sway the opinions of New Yorkers remaining in their native state if he could not break their bond to Seward after they moved to Illinois? Lincoln was about to find out. Just as Seward men resided in Illinois, New Yorkers were hardly "anti-Lincoln"; in fact, he had many admirers in that state. "Mr. Lincoln has hosts of friends here," wrote a supporter from New York City in mid-February. "His discussions with Douglas in Illinois in [1858] won for him *golden opinions*."[39]

The task before Lincoln was to spread those "golden opinions" throughout the East. Back in October he had agreed to speak at Plymouth

Church in Brooklyn on any topic of his choice. Although he had not purged the topic from his mind, he certainly would not reprise "Discoveries and Inventions"—much to the relief of his friends. "I believe, after all, I shall make a political speech of it," decided Lincoln.[40] His New York speech had been rescheduled for the end of February.

Merely days from taking the eastern trip, Lincoln realized how fortuitous the timing of this speech was to him. The Lincoln boom had begun to make waves that rippled in all directions into the states neighboring and close to Illinois. The effect was magnified in those states where Lincoln had spoken in the late summer and autumn of 1859. Although Ohio had three potential candidates for president, Lincoln's speaking tour had persuaded some to consider him the state's favorite "outsider" candidate. His press coverage increased in Ohio in the winter of 1860 as his book of 1858 debate compilations neared publication by an Ohio publishing firm. Lincoln also received favorable press in the most prominent papers of Indiana, Wisconsin, and Kansas Territory. His decision to speak in the largest cities of those states (even Dayton ranked in the top 10 percent of most populous cities in the country) aided his cause, mainly because of the widespread circulation of the cities' newspapers. Could he achieve the same benefit in Brooklyn, the third-largest city in the country in 1860, neighboring the largest one—New York City?[41]

What had become abundantly clear to Lincoln by the eve of his trip to New York was the power of the press. Newspapers were a politician's lifeline, more so in 1860 than during any previous campaign. More than three thousand newspapers circulated throughout the United States in 1860, nearly double the number of papers twenty years before. Not only were there more newspapers, but advances in transportation and communication improved the speed and thoroughness of reporting the news. In 1860 the *Chicago Press and Tribune*, for example, fielded reports throughout Illinois and neighboring states within a day of their creation by a system of rail transportation that was unavailable to it ten years earlier. Indiana and other adjacent states to Illinois reprinted more *Press and Tribune* reports than ever before because of the improved access. Daily circulation of the paper surged past twenty thousand and it was likely read by more than one hundred thousand people.[42]

But the greatest benefit for all newspapers in the mid-nineteenth century was the telegraph. Nearly fifty thousand miles of telegraph lines were strung across the states in 1860, transmitting more than five million messages each year. The creation of the New York Associated Press by several major New York newspapers in 1849 improved the speed of wiring news to New York City through a dedicated line. The news gathered by this wire service was sold to Boston, Philadelphia, and other major cities in the Northeast. Lincoln's debates with Douglas in 1858 were widely read by this avenue of communication, as were the speeches of his Ohio trip one year later.[43]

As an avid reader of newspapers both at home and on the speaking circuit, Lincoln had become increasingly appreciative of how the papers dropped his name and spread his message, while at the same time updating him on the success and failures of his rivals. His speaking tours in Ohio, Indiana, Wisconsin, and Kansas Territory expanded his name recognition in those regions, not just because people saw him for the first time, but especially because newspapers excerpted and reproduced his performances and sent that news across the country.

This exposure was bound to influence the Republican delegates from those states, those future conventioneers who would read Lincoln's message and gauge how their fellow citizens felt about the messenger. No more than twenty-five thousand people attended at least one of Lincoln's seventeen speeches in September, October, and December 1859; but the number of people across the country who read at least a snippet about one of these Lincoln events likely exceeded half a million.

That number was destined to at least double before the ides of March as Lincoln began his trip to New York. By happenstance, the lack of familiarity of Lincoln to the citizens of the Northeast—the prime Republican voting block in the country—would work to his favor as he boarded a train for New York City to deliver the most important speech of his life. His audience would view him as an Illinois Republican statesman, not as a rival candidate to William H. Seward, one who was clandestinely launching his campaign in the region. Many of Lincoln's correspondents were unaware he was heading east but knew how powerful his out-of-state performances had been in 1859 and urged him to return to the speaking circuit early in

1860. "You must get yourself in training for the Presidency," advised one of Lincoln's Chicago boosters during the second week of February. Lincoln politely thanked him "for your anticipations of the future for me."[44]

Lincoln's response was more noteworthy for omitting self-deprecating remarks about the presidency. He no longer claimed a lack of fitness or desire for the job.

Seven

SEWARD'S BACKYARD

LINCOLN'S TRIP EAST averaged less than twenty miles per hour between Springfield and New York City, three days of jarring train rides interrupted by several depot changes and marred by late departures. For most of the journey, he was accompanied by his brother-in-law's sister and her eighteen-month-old child, who parted company with Lincoln in the Philadelphia depot before dawn on Saturday, February 25. Before hopping on board the next train, Lincoln made his way to a nearby hotel in Philadelphia to meet with Senator Simon Cameron and Congressman David Wilmot. Neither politician was there, although they had somehow learned that Lincoln would be passing through the city and had left messages at the station for him to meet them. The fruitless detour consumed little time, and later that morning Lincoln boarded his fifth and final train, which pulled away from the station and headed northward to New York.[1]

Alone in a passenger car for the first time since leaving Springfield, Lincoln could immerse himself in the carefully prepared manuscript of the speech he was to deliver in Brooklyn in two days. He had put more study and effort into this address than into any of the other 175 speeches performed over the previous five years. This address needed the extra attention, for Lincoln well understood that his presidential hopes would improve if he performed well in front of a New York audience.[2]

Unlike most of the previous addresses, particularly the seventeen speeches he delivered late in 1859, Lincoln afforded himself several weeks to carefully craft this speech. He used the time wisely, building on the framework of his performances in Ohio and Kansas Territory with research made necessary by Stephen A. Douglas's assertions in *Harper's New Monthly Magazine*. Had Douglas not published his article, and had Lincoln not sharpened and honed the message he first presented in Chicago nearly one year before this trip, he would likely have developed a rather ordinary speech. Now the pages of blue foolscap in his hands contained rhetoric unlike anything he had ever crafted before. Not only was he confident that he had produced a powerful counter-argument to Douglas's version of popular sovereignty; he also had discovered in the piles of books he pulled from the shelves of his home bookcase, the ones in his law office, and the shelves of the library in the basement of the Illinois state capitol a nearly perfect foil to the 1857 *Dred Scott* decision. From these discoveries he prepared a thesis that vanquished Chief Justice Roger B. Taney's decision in the three-year-old case as well as dismantled the assertions published by Stephen A. Douglas.

Lincoln's train journey ended Saturday afternoon at the Jersey City terminal. He retrieved his luggage and stepped onto a ferry that plied the waters of the Hudson River to Manhattan. As impressed as he must have been at the sight of the sprawling skyline, the awe was supplanted by the realization that no one was there to greet him in Manhattan. After the ferry deposited him on Cortlandt Street, Lincoln made his way to the Astor House, the huge gaslit hotel where two months earlier Norman Judd secured the national convention for Chicago. Lincoln checked himself into one of the three hundred rooms offered by this premier establishment.

It would not have taken Lincoln long to acquire a copy of that Saturday's edition of the *New York Tribune*, Horace Greeley's top-notch paper, considered the gold standard of Republican organs in the country. The February 25 issue included a laudatory biography of Lincoln, but this commendation did not open Lincoln's eyes nearly as much as did the first sentence of the piece, for it notified him that his speech would not be presented in Brooklyn's Plymouth Church. Instead, the article said, "Abraham Lincoln of Illinois will, for the first time, speak in this Emporium, at Cooper Institute, on Monday evening."[3]

"When I reached New York, I, for the first time, learned that the place

was changed to 'Cooper Institute,'" Lincoln revealed six weeks later. Although the new venue—the Great Hall of Cooper Union had officially
opened less than one year before—might seem to mean little to a speaker,
Lincoln felt compelled to alter his speech. Less than two weeks before he
left for the trip, Lincoln had been warned by his sponsors, the Young
Men's Central Republican Union of New York City, that his speech
would have to be adjusted to conform to their intended audiences.
Charles C. Nott, a member of the sponsoring organization, wrote Lincoln
on February 9 to inform him not only that his speech should be "a political lecture," but also that the recipients of this lecture would be an audience unlike "that of an ordinary political meeting." Nott wrote, "These
lectures have been contrived to call out our better, but busier citizens, who
never attend political meetings. A large part of the audience would also
consist of ladies." In the same letter Nott revealed that Lincoln's would be
the third of an 1860 series of lectures, following addresses by Missourian
Francis P. Blair Jr. and the famous Kentucky orator Cassius M. Clay.[4]

Nott's letter likely arrived in Springfield after Lincoln had already
completed his speech, thus forcing a revision to comply with a less partisan and informed audience than he had originally expected. The fairly
late notice appears unintentional, for Nott also tried to push the political
lecture back two more weeks to the middle of March. But Lincoln responded in a letter insisting that he hold to his February 27 date. That request was accepted and acknowledged in a letter Lincoln received before
he departed, but the letter failed to inform Lincoln of the change of location to Manhattan. But Lincoln's discomfort with the text of his speech
appears to have been caused more by the lack of time afforded him in
Springfield to adjust it from a speech for partisans to a lecture for a general-
interest audience of New York's elite men and women, than by the change
of location from Brooklyn to New York City.[5]

Not to be overlooked in the factors affecting Lincoln's need to craft his
speech was his desire to have his words published verbatim. Changing the
venue from Brooklyn to New York assured that America's most influential
newspaper editors would be covering the address. To make sure of nationwide attention, Lincoln planned to submit a version of his speech to
one of the pro-Republican organs in Manhattan.

Any thoughts Lincoln had of reworking his speech that Saturday were wiped out by the constant stream of callers to his room, one of whom later claimed to entertain well-wishers while Lincoln edited his speech. Chances are he made little headway on his revisions. He left his room sometime that day to visit the office of newspaperman Henry C. Bowen, the editor of the antislavery *New York Independent*. Although Lincoln was weary, he understood the importance of greeting influential editors—particularly those who shared his ideals. But Bowen was less than impressed with the unkempt appearance of the unusual man he had advertised so heavily for New Yorkers to hear on Monday night. "For an instant I felt sick at heart over the prospect, and could not greet my visitor with any warmth of manner," admitted the editor. Lincoln was able to soften the harsh first impression by entertaining Bowen with his repertoire of anecdotes and jokes, delivered while Lincoln rested on a lounge.[6]

Lincoln took Bowen up on his offer to attend Plymouth Church the following morning to hear the Reverend Henry Ward Beecher's sermon. Lincoln ferried across the East River to Brooklyn early on Sunday and entered the church that had been the originally intended site for his Monday-night lecture. Perhaps as many as two thousand parishioners joined Lincoln to hear the most famous antislavery minister in the country deliver his weekly sermon from the church he had led for a dozen years. Beecher, whose sister wrote *Uncle Tom's Cabin*, did not fail his congregation, enlightening them with a strong speech. Afterward, Lincoln shook his hand as scores of churchgoers remained to meet Lincoln and greet the clergyman. Lincoln excused himself from a lunch invitation at Henry Bowen's house, as he was antsy to return to the Astor House to focus on his address.[7]

By early afternoon Lincoln was back in his room, perfecting his speech. The original version has not survived for posterity, so the degree of rewriting will never be known. But it is apparent that Lincoln was eager to reveal what the views of the Founding Fathers were in relation to extending slavery into the territories. Lincoln's edited version of the speech addressed that question immediately. He also felt the vehicle he had employed in the Cincinnati speech—addressing his remarks directly to the South by talking to the Kentuckians—was something he wished to attempt again in front of his New York audience. He crafted his speech to tackle complex political issues without condescending to his audience. He also reworked his remarks to distinguish his views not only from those of Douglas and the Democrats, but also from those of New York's own William H. Seward.

Lincoln needed to deliver this speech as a statesman for the Republican Party and not to come across as an ambitious presidential candidate with an agenda to win over future delegates and win the nomination. The Democratic *New York Herald* exposed his true intent when it announced in its Monday-morning edition that Lincoln "makes his bid for the nomination this evening." Visitors at the Astor House that day treated him as a candidate. Admirers crowded into his room, and out-of-state delegations deluged him with invitations to address their citizens. "I have talked with Republicans here, and am convinced that he is the strongest man in the Republican list," opined one of his visitors that day.[8]

Lincoln occupied Monday afternoon by strolling the streets of Manhattan with some of his hosts. He bought a new stovetop hat to replace the well-worn hat he had brought from Illinois. He also stopped to have a new photograph taken by the nationally renowned master of his craft, Mathew Brady, who had a temporary gallery on the corner of Bleecker Street and Broadway while his permanent studio farther down Broadway was under construction. Lincoln had had several images taken in 1857 and 1858, but considerably fewer in the past year. So, for the first time in 1860, Lincoln met Brady on Monday afternoon to have his image—Lincoln called it his "shadow"—captured on plate.

The full-length photograph Brady took of Lincoln that day was the finest one to date of him. Brady's trained eye and modern equipment teamed up to place Lincoln in the best possible light. He made sure Lincoln's hair was combed (his second image in Chicago in 1854 set the standard for his notoriously unruly hair), and fissures and furrows in his weather-beaten face would be softened. Brady also instructed Lincoln to pull up his collar so his unusually long neck would not mar the image. After the photograph was taken, Lincoln left the studio, not realizing that the picture would not materialize for several months; but when it did it would have an impact on his career unlike any other image of him.[9]

Lincoln entered Cooper Union that night accompanied by one of his sponsors and descended the stairs to the basement, where the Great Underground Hall was located. This immense auditorium—equipped for seating 1,800—was not filled to capacity this night, as a few hundred empty seats could be counted. At least one Democrat mingled with the overwhelmingly Republican audience: Mason Brayman, a friend of Lincoln's, was charged with the task of sitting in the back and cuing Lincoln to speak louder if necessary by raising his hat on his cane. Shortly after eight P.M. William Cullen Bryant, the editor of the *New York Evening Post*, introduced the speaker at this meeting by hailing Lincoln as "a gallant soldier." Pointing out that the Westerners (referring to the states surrounding the upper Mississippi River) stood in the front lines of the antislavery armies, Bryant enunciated the well-known name "Abraham Lincoln of Illinois," which triggered explosive applause for the featured speaker sitting on a chair on the elevated stage.

The New York audience was about to link the face with the oft-heard name for the first time. Lincoln unfolded himself from his chair and slowly walked to the wrought-iron podium near the southern edge of the stage, a lectern decorated in velvet and trimmed with gold-colored tassels. He was facing one of his largest indoor audiences ever, but Lincoln would have been more taken by the spectacular Great Hall than by the size of his crowd. Mirrors lined the walls to reflect the light emitted by the twenty-seven chandeliers over the heads of the seated crowd. Each chandelier was fueled by six gas burners, which triggered Lincoln to realize that his voice needed to compete with the audible hiss of the modern lighting system.[10]

He also had to compete with the recent history of Cooper Union as a venue for some of the most renowned Republican orators in the country. The Young Men's Central Republican Union had landed Francis P. Blair Jr. and Cassius Clay the previous weeks to dazzle the crowds in the Great Hall. Tom Corwin had spoken at Cooper Union in November. Corwin based part of his presentation on the intent of the Founding Fathers to restrict slavery in the territories by using the Northwest Ordinance as the proof. This was the same thesis Lincoln had presented in Ohio, and it appears that Corwin borrowed heavily from the theme of the speech he had witnessed Lincoln deliver in Cincinnati in September. Whether Lincoln was aware of Corwin's November 3 Cooper Union speech or not, he was fortunate to come prepared with a brand-new lecture and thus avoid being branded a copycat by the prominent New York newspaper editors in attendance.[11]

The audience was aghast at the unkempt appearance of Abraham Lincoln. His hair, combed for the Brady photograph earlier that afternoon, had returned to its usual disheveled state. His black suit, albeit new, was wrinkled and ill-fit his spindly frame. The coat ballooned from his back while both of his forearms protruded from his sleeves. His trousers looked just as bad as the suit; one wrinkled pants leg was hiked two inches above his foot. The only benefit of such an ugly suit would be to distract the viewer from Lincoln's physical anomalies, but these clothes magnified Lincoln's ungainly features, from his long head to his enormous hands and feet. One witness noted drily that Lincoln's overall appearance "made a picture which did not fit in with New York's conception of a finished statesman."[12]

Thus, Lincoln had dug a hole for himself even before he opened his mouth. Silent until the applause had completely abated, Lincoln opened his speech the way he began most of the speeches before it—with a shrill, high-pitched voice that must have been as troubling to the crowd as his appearance. This was no Cassius Clay or Tom Corwin facing them. The harsh tone of his voice and the grating frontier accent deepened Lincoln's hole. The only way he could climb out of it was to present a soothing and stirring message.

He had prepared to do this in the opening minutes of the presentation. No winding lead-in to his theme was in the offing here. Lincoln was set to stun the crowd with the results of his research. The third sentence out of his mouth quoted Stephen A. Douglas—the ubiquitous foil of most of Lincoln's speeches since 1854—from the text of the Little Giant's September address in Columbus, Ohio: "Our fathers, when they framed the Government under which we live, understood this question just as well, and even better than we do now." This time he chose not to criticize Douglas's claim. "I fully indorse this," agreed Lincoln, "and I adopt it as a text for this discourse." The line triggered the audience to the first of many rounds of applause that night, but no one in the crowd had any inkling of how often Lincoln would make Douglas pay for that phrase. Lincoln would quote the Douglas sentence, in excerpt or in total, thirty more times in the course of his speech as proof of his endorsement.[13]

Rather than reveal the question, Lincoln chose the sentence to first define what "the frame of government under which we live" and who "our fathers" were, the omniscient originators whom Douglas clearly held in reverence. In his Columbus address, Douglas did not pinpoint his definition of "our fathers," but the text of his address indicated that they were an expansive group that included not only the revolutionaries of the late 1700s but also the original American colonists of the 1600s.[14]

Lincoln tightened the definition of "our fathers" to fit the powerful message he planned to lay out early in his lecture. He explained first what the frame of government meant. The Declaration of Independence had fit this definition in most of Lincoln's previous speeches regarding the immorality of slavery. But at Cooper Union, Lincoln did not use the Declaration as the definition of "the frame of government." Instead, he chose the Constitution of the United States, including the twelve amendments added to the document during the seventy-three years that had passed since it was created. Lincoln defined "our fathers" as the original framers of the 1787 document, revealing that there were thirty-nine who signed the Constitution. He expanded the definition to include the seventy-six legislators who subsequently passed the Bill of Rights, the first ten amendments to the Constitution.

Having applied his own definition to the points of the Douglas sentence that surrounded the question alluded to by the Little Giant, Lincoln revealed the question to the New York audience: "Does the proper division of local from federal authority, or anything in the Constitution, forbid our Federal Government to control as to slavery in our Federal Territories?" Lincoln posed the question using legal wording, and the question sounded clumsy and tedious. But Lincoln chose his words carefully, setting up both a swipe at Douglas's version of popular sovereignty and an attack on the *Dred Scott* decision. Lincoln's version of the question—where the word "control" meant to prevent the spread of slavery into the territories—did not take Douglas's line out of context. Douglas had addressed the issue more plainly in his Columbus speech: "We Democrats maintain that the federal government has no right to interfere with the question, either to establish, to protect, to abolish, or to prohibit slavery; but that the people in each State and each Territory, shall be left entirely free to decide it for themselves."[15]

What Lincoln did next was a rarity in politics. He pulled the ace from his sleeve and convincingly presented evidence that the majority of the "fathers" who signed the Constitution and the Bill of Rights supported the ideals of the Republican Party: that the federal government should control slavery by preventing its spread into the federal territories. He first demonstrated this with a review of the voting record of the thirty-nine "fathers" who signed the Constitution. He painstakingly reviewed the three votes involving the formation of the slavery-free Northwest Territory in 1784, 1787, and 1789. He added to this the 1804 congressional vote for the territorial organization of a small portion of the Louisiana Purchase (a vote to prevent the import of slaves) and finally tagged on the Missouri Compromise of 1819–20; which prohibited slavery north of thirty-six degrees, thirty minutes. For of these votes, Lincoln had successfully researched the names of the members of Congress who were among the original signers of the Constitution.

Summarizing all of these instances in which territories were acquired and organized with the explicit exclusion of slavery, twenty-eight aye votes were cast by senators and representatives, and by slave-owning President George Washington (he signed the 1789 bill to enforce the Ordinance of 1787, "thus completing its validity as a law"); all were by original Founding Fathers of the U.S. Constitution. After excluding double and triple votes, Lincoln still named twenty-one of the framers of the Constitution who had subsequently voted to forbid slavery from entering into territories owned by the government they had established—a majority. Only two out of the thirty-nine had voted nay, but Lincoln stressed that their reasons for voting this way were unknown and should not be taken as support for popular sovereignty, as Douglas would have liked to claim.[16]

Barely half an hour into the Cooper Union address, Lincoln had proven that a majority of the Founding Fathers, by his definition, not only intended for the federal government to prohibit the spread of slavery into the territories, but actually documented their intention by voting for the exclusion in legislation before and after the formation of the Constitution. This revelation not only crushed the thesis of Douglas's *Harper's* article, but also weakened Chief Justice Roger Taney's opinion in the *Dred Scott* decision when Taney proclaimed that when a U.S. citizen entered a federal territory, "the Federal Government can exercise no power over his person or property, beyond what that instrument confers, nor lawfully deny any right which it has reserved."

No one in the Cooper Union audience had ever received this novel presentation of the issue over the constitutionality of the right of the federal government to prohibit slavery in the territories. This was the most revealing and convincing claim they had yet heard that most of the originators of the United States government would have been on the side of the Republican Party in regards to the question of excluding slavery from the territories of America. Lincoln never took credit for this discovery, and perhaps he was not the first to investigate the voting records of the Founding Fathers. He had prefaced the revelation by admitting that the facts that he was portraying may have been revealed before. "If there shall be any novelty," he explained about his research findings, "it will be in the mode of presenting the facts, and the inferences and observations following that presentation."[17]

Lincoln had not finished presenting his historical case. He strengthened his argument and the stringency of his message by invoking the names of Benjamin Franklin, Alexander Hamilton, and Gouverneur Morris, three signers of the Constitution whom Lincoln was forced to categorize as Founding Fathers with unrecorded positions on territorial slavery despite their fame as antislavery patriots. For the sake of objectivity and statesmanship, he also tossed out the name of South Carolinian John Rutledge, one of the unrecorded sixteen founders who likely would not have supported any bill creating territories that excluded slavery. The inference, however, was that the majority of the framers with unrecorded positions would have supported the ability of the government to prohibit the extension of slavery into the federal territories.

By now Lincoln's vocal cords warmed up enough to minimize the piping and squeaking that characteristically marred the first minutes of his speeches. His audience also grew accustomed to the awkwardness of his appearance, and noticed that unlike other speakers, Lincoln chose to remain at the podium and did not roam around the raised stage as he laid out his facts. His dialect became less distracting as the message superseded the messenger. His voice also conquered the hissing gas burners, so his friend in the back was never induced to signal Lincoln to speak louder.

Lincoln piled on more weight to his evidence. He reiterated that the seventy-six-member Congress that passed the antislavery Ordinance of 1787—including sixteen of the original framers of the Constitution—were exactly the same men who passed the Bill of Rights. Thus, by Lincoln's original definition, this entire Congress fit into his definition of "our fathers who framed the part of 'the Government under which we live.'" By linking these Bill of Rights "fathers" with the originators of the 1787 Northwest Ordinance, Lincoln embarrassed Chief Justice Taney and Stephen A. Douglas at the same time, for both men cited a specific reading of the Bill of Rights to support their respective positions of why it was the intent of the Founding Fathers to allow slavery to enter into the territories. Entirely confident in his thesis, Lincoln haughtily asked, "Is it not presumptuous in any one at this day to affirm that the two things which that Congress deliberately framed, and carried to maturity at the same time, are absolutely inconsistent with each other?" He immediately followed this by rhetorically asking if it was not "impudently absurd" to suggest that the same seventy-six congressmen would—to a man—pass these two landmark pieces of legislation, believing that they were inconsistent with each other. Lincoln finished the thought by reminding his audience that the Little Giant declared that the Founding Fathers understood this issue "better than we," then struck down Douglas with another rhetorical blow: "better than he who affirms that they are inconsistent."[18]

The Cooper Union crowd soaked in every word and thought, responding with appreciative applause and laughter. Supremely confident, Lincoln summarized that the members of the early Congresses who framed the Constitution and the Bill of Rights together were the Founding Fathers. He defied anyone to show that any of these legislators, revered by Douglas as "our fathers who framed the government under which we live," ever declared that the federal prohibition of slavery in the territories was unconstitutional. "I go a step further," declared Lincoln:

> I defy any one to show that any living man in the whole world ever did, prior to the beginning of the present century, . . . declare that, in his understanding, any proper division of local from federal authority, or any part of the Constitution, forbade the Federal Government to control as to slavery in the federal territories. To those who now so declare, I give, not only "our fathers who framed the Government under which we live," but with them all other living men within the century in which it was framed, among whom to search, and they shall not be able to find the evidence of a single man agreeing with them.

Lincoln destroyed Douglas's entire thesis and rubbed salt in the gaping wounds he had opened by constantly repeating Douglas's exact words to highlight the hypocrisy and shallowness of thought informing his position. He uttered the Douglas phrase "better than we" ten times in the first hour, the last time to remind his audience that he agreed that the Fathers did indeed understand the issue better than anyone else, and so everyone else should "speak as they spoke, and act as they acted upon it." As the statesman of his party that night, Lincoln announced, "This is all Republicans ask—all Republicans desire—in relation to slavery." He seized on the opportunity to remind the crowd that although slavery was "an evil not to be extended," it was constitutionally protected in the Southern states where it existed. "Let all the guarantees those fathers gave it, be, not grudgingly, but fully and fairly, maintained."[19]

This punctuated stroke positioned Lincoln firmly away from the radical positions of Douglas and Taney, and the equally radical abolitionists who sought to defy the Founding Fathers by wiping out slavery where it was constitutionally permitted. But by doing this as the undeclared spokesman of the Republican Party, Lincoln not only strengthened the case that moderate Republicans aligned more with the positions of the revered founders of American democracy than did Democrats; he also presented the attractive and safe middle-ground position of the party that appealed to anyone concerned with the more extreme views of the two front-runners for the Republican presidential nomination, William H. Seward and Salmon P. Chase.

Now at the halfway point of his prepared text, Lincoln reverted from the brand new to the tried and true. He had been praised for the rhetorical device he used at Cincinnati when he spoke as if he were exclusively addressing the residents in the South through the Kentuckians across the Ohio River. But the South was hundreds of miles from him at Cooper Union, not hundreds of yards from the Fifth Street Market in Cincinnati where he had spoken in September. No longer blessed with the geographic convenience, Lincoln still stubbornly repeated the acclaimed device that had succeeded in Cincinnati. He chose a somewhat clumsy segue. "And now," proclaimed Lincoln, "if they would listen—as I suppose they will not—I would address a few words to the Southern people."

The audience did not immediately understand that Lincoln was not really directing his remarks to Southern people. As was the case in Cincinnati, Lincoln's real intent was to accentuate the differences between him and Douglas to a Northern audience. Knowing that Douglas campaigned for Southern Democratic support by circulating Lincoln's Cincinnati speech, Lincoln altered the speech in New York to reiterate Douglas's Southern-friendly positions without mentioning his name. Here he succeeded by referring specifically to Douglas only once in his remarks to "the Southern people," while at Cincinnati he had brought up Douglas forty-seven times in the portion of the speech addressed to "you Kentuckians." In New York as in Cincinnati, Lincoln's words directed to the South embodied his attempt to distinguish moderate Republicans from radical elements of the Democratic Party in an attempt to woo moderate Democrats to his middle-ground message.

Although the text of the message to the South was altered between Cincinnati and New York, Lincoln still presented a similar theme, perhaps more effectively at Cooper Union on the backbone of his heavily researched thesis regarding slavery and the Founding Fathers. In Cincinnati, Lincoln essentially opened his speech with his dialogue to Southerners and ended it with his logical approach to the intent of the Founding Fathers. It appears he flipped the topics in New York, realizing that the differentiation between North and South was made clearer by first revealing what the Founding Fathers (hailing from both sections of the country) had done about issues considered sectional in 1860.

Lincoln poked fun at Southerners for using the phrase "Black Republicans" to condemn the party. "Indeed," he deduced, "such condemnation of us seems to be a prerequisite—license, so to speak—among you to be permitted to speak at all." Lincoln implored Southerners to specify what positions earned that condemnation. He haughtily challenged them: "Bring forward your charges and specifications, and then be patient long enough to hear us deny or justify."

Lincoln then brought up the charges and refuted them in turn, as if he were conducting a two-way conversation. "You say we are sectional. We deny it," he declared. Southern claims that the Republicans were a sectional party (a charge actually supported by the Electoral College votes for president in 1856) were hypocritical; the lack of Republican votes in Southern states was a sectional decision by them and therefore was not the fault of Republicans. Lincoln added a sound counterargument by invoking George Washington. Acknowledging that some Southerners delighted in repeating Washington's warning against sectional parties in his Farewell Address in 1797, Lincoln reminded his New York audience that Washington endorsed the slavery prohibition of the Ordinance of 1787, which established the Northwest Territory, the same lands that spawned the formation of six slave-free states. He added a little-known fact about Washington and the ordinance to slam the door shut on any opportunity Southerners had to use George Washington against Republicans: "he wrote La Fayette that he considered that prohibition a wise measure, expressing in the same connection his hope that we should at some time have a confederacy of free states."[20]

Lincoln reversed the Southern charge that Republicans were revolutionary while Southern Democrats were conservative. "What is conservative?" queried Lincoln; "is it not adherence to the old and tried, against the new and untried?" He had already rendered his question rhetorical by the effectiveness of the first half of his presentation. He belittled the attempt by Southerners to hold up John Brown as the icon of Republican revolutionaries. Brown's failed insurrection at Harpers Ferry had occurred the month after Lincoln's Cincinnati speech, but Lincoln had spoken about it in Kansas Territory in December, and now he offered a more severe denunciation of John Brown. He reiterated that Brown was no Republican, nor did any Republican aid his Harpers Ferry raid. To counter the Southern claim that Republican positions induced insurrection, Lincoln reminded the Southerners that there were more deadly slave insurrections—referring to Nat Turner's bloody uprising in Virginia in 1831—a quarter of a century before the Republican Party was born.

As Southerners cited George Washington's warning of sectionalism to castigate Republicans, Lincoln quoted Thomas Jefferson to turn the tables on Southerners. He cited Jefferson's desire for Virginians "to direct the power of emancipation, and deportation," in a peaceful and slow manner, "as that evil will wear off insensibly," and be replaced "by free white laborers." Lincoln showed through this passage that Jefferson wished slavery to disappear, and so did Republicans and moderate Democrats in 1860—by a process of containment within the states where it was constitutionally protected, to allow those states slowly to emancipate their slaves and replace them with white workers. He repeated that this emancipation was to be directed by states—as Jefferson had urged—and not enforced by the federal government.[21]

Lincoln's approach and presentation were intended to be more statesmanlike than partisan, but the speech was definitely political and purposely shunned complete and contextual objectivity. He had altered Douglas's intended definitions at the beginning of the speech and conveniently neglected to tell his audience that his version of "our fathers" was not the same as what Douglas intended. Lincoln also cherry-picked Jefferson's words and positions to invoke him to his Cooper Union audience. He wisely stayed well away from Jefferson's positions in his later writings, where Jefferson seemed to support the spread of slavery into the territories and criticized federal attempts to interfere with it. Lincoln chose not to muddy the waters at the expense of damaging his own argument. A Democratic critic was not fooled by Lincoln's tactics at Cooper Union, noting, "It is a customary thing with Mr. Lincoln to lay down false premises and draw false conclusions, to mistake the position of his adversary, and by special pleading and sophistical reasoning to lead the mind of his hearer or reader from the true facts in controversy."[22]

Lincoln reminded the Southerners (through his Cooper Union audience) that a million and a half voters agreed with Jefferson that slavery was "that evil" that should be ended throughout the country. Lincoln declared, "Human action can be modified to some extent, but human nature cannot be changed." Lincoln went on to declare that moderate Republicans were not abolitionists, but sought specific "human action" to put slavery back on the course of ultimate extinction. That action focused on seating a Supreme Court that would reverse the *Dred Scott* decision, a decision based on an interpretation of an amendment that Lincoln proved errant in his well-researched presentation. He asked, "When this obvious mistake of the Judges shall be brought to their notice, is it not reasonable to expect that they will withdraw the mistaken statement, and reconsider the conclusion based upon it?" As in Cincinnati, Lincoln chided the South for threatening to break up the government. But he employed a new metaphor to highlight the absurdity of the claim that it would be the fault of Republicans if the South dissolved the Union in the wake of their election. "That is cool," remarked Lincoln to great laughter. "A highwayman holds a pistol to my ear, and mutters through his teeth, 'Stand and deliver, or I shall kill you, and then you will be a murderer!' "[23]

Lincoln followed the template of his Cincinnati speech to transition from his message to the Southerners into his rallying cry. Addressing his remarks specifically to Republicans, Lincoln advised a pacifist approach to this threat: "*Even though much provoked, let us do nothing through passion and ill temper. Even though the southern people will not so much as listen to us, let us calmly consider their demands, and yield to them if, in our deliberate view of our duty, we possibly can.*" Lincoln's solution was antithetical to what he had said in Ohio, where he used bellicose language to rousing partisan cheers. But he did repeat the desire to "let them alone" in regards to slavery within their states. He added the importance of convincing Southerners that they would indeed be left alone if a Republican won the White House.

Lincoln entered his conclusion shortly before 10:00 p.m.. He reiterated what had been his mantra since his debates with Douglas in 1858: the immorality of slavery. "Wrong as we think slavery is," declared Lincoln to the New York Republicans, "we can yet afford to let it alone where it is." He expressed the importance for Republicans to do all they could to contain slavery, to stand by their constitutional duties (including adherence to the Fugitive-Slave Law), but to do so without yielding on the issue of declaring slavery a moral wrong. "Neither let us be slandered from our duty by false accusations against us, nor frightened from it by menaces of destruction to the Government nor of dungeons to ourselves," demanded Lincoln in conclusion. "LET US HAVE FAITH THAT RIGHT MAKES MIGHT, AND IN THAT FAITH, LET US TO THE END, DARE TO DO OUR DUTY AS WE UNDERSTAND IT."[24]

Fifteen hundred awed spectators rose to honor Lincoln with a standing ovation, many waving hats and handkerchiefs, all repeating rousing cheers to thank Lincoln for the unprecedented remarks. Lincoln, of course, absorbed the accolade, a satisfying reward for the presentation he prepared longer and more thoroughly than any other in his life. But it is what he didn't hear that would have floored him. As the audience ascended the stairs to exit the basement hall of Cooper Union, one of them admitted how Lincoln's presentation had left "my face glowing with excitement and my frame all aquiver." When a friend asked this bedazzled eyewitness

Abraham Lincoln, the confident Republican nominee, photographed in Springfield on August 13, 1860, by Preston Butler. *Courtesy of The Lincoln Museum*

THE PRESENT LAW OFFICE OF ABRAHAM LINCOLN, THE PRESIDENT ELECT, IN FIFTH STREET, WEST SIDE OF THE PUBLIC SQUARE, SPRINGFIELD, ILL.—FROM A SKETCH BY OUR SPECIAL ARTIST.—SEE PAGE 74

Interior view of the Lincoln and Herndon Law Office near the corner of Fifth Street and Washington Avenue. This sketch, published in *Frank Leslie's Illustrated Newspaper,* shows the office in a much more organized state than normal. *Courtesy of The Lincoln Museum*

Mary Lincoln with son Willie on the left and Tad on the right. Lincoln doted on his two youngest boys (Robert was away at school) throughout 1859 and 1860. *Courtesy of The Lincoln Museum*

"Long John" Wentworth. The first Republican Chicago mayor lived as large as he looked. His erratic temperament and political passions were the source of tremendous friction within the Republican Party of Illinois. *Courtesy of the Abraham Lincoln Presidential Library*

Lincoln's Cincinnati speech. This oil painting by J. C. Moerschel captures the excitement at the Fifth Street Market on the evening of September 17, 1859. Lincoln can be seen speaking from the balcony on the right side of the image. *Courtesy of Cincinnati Museum Center-Cincinnati Historical Society Library*

The Lincoln home on Eighth and Jackson streets. This 1860 photograph shows Lincoln standing on the porch with his son Willie. Tad Lincoln is obscured behind a post. *Courtesy of The Lincoln Museum*

LEFT: Lincoln in New York. This Mathew Brady image, the first of many by this famous photographer, was taken hours before the Cooper Union speech on February 27, 1860. It is believed that this image of Lincoln was taken to the national convention in Chicago three months later.

RIGHT: Lincoln in Decatur. This image was taken at the Illinois State Republican Convention on May 9, 1860, the day that Lincoln became the "Rail Candidate." *Courtesy of The Lincoln Museum*

PROMINENT CANDIDATES FOR THE REPUBLICAN PRESIDENTIAL NOMINATION AT CHICAGO.—[FROM PHOTOGRAPHS BY BRADY.]

Republican candidates for the presidential nomination. This *Harper's Weekly Illustrated* composition, published four days before the start of the national convention, captures the long road that Lincoln had to travel in a very short time to reach the top of his party's ticket. Pictured at the bottom, second from left, Lincoln appears as an also-ran. *Courtesy of The Lincoln Museum*

LEFT: Richard Oglesby. This young Decatur Republican was responsible for creating the image of Lincoln as "the Rail Splitter." Oglesby enjoyed a distinguished career as a Civil War general, governor of Illinois, and U.S. senator.
RIGHT: Judge David Davis. The Bloomington native enjoyed a twenty-year friendship with Lincoln and came to the Chicago convention as the unofficial head of the Lincoln team. He would enjoy a distinguished career as a U.S. Supreme Court justice and U.S. senator. *Courtesy of the Abraham Lincoln Presidential Library*

Chicago's Great Wigwam. This two-story building housed the Republican National Convention in 1860. It stood near the corner of Lake and Market streets. It was the scene of one of the most momentous events in American history. *Courtesy of The Lincoln Museum*

Lincoln the nominee. This Springfield image, photographed by William Church on May 20, 1860, is believed to be the first image of Lincoln as the standard-bearer of the Republican Party. *Courtesy of The Lincoln Museum*

what he thought about Abraham Lincoln, he responded with the highest single-sentence tribute Lincoln ever received: "He's the greatest man since St. Paul."[25]

Nearly two hours after he departed the Great Hall at Cooper Union, Abraham Lincoln stepped into the Tribune Building and entered the printing office. It was nearly midnight, and galley proofs for the Tuesday-morning edition of the *New York Tribune* were ready for proofreading by Amos Jay Cummings. Lincoln had earlier gained permission to review his speech to ensure that his words were published without alteration. He took a chair and pulled up besides Cummings at the proofreading table. According to Cummings, Lincoln "adjusted his glasses, and in the glare of the gas light read each galley with scrupulous care." Lincoln had earlier submitted the foolscap manuscript of his Cooper Union speech, a text held by Cummings as he proofread the galleys. Using his memory as his guide, Lincoln helped Cummings correct the errors in typesetting. He remained in the office to oversee the final proof production, which he scrutinized again before allowing it to go into print.[26]

The *Tribune* was one of four New York newspapers that reproduced the Cooper Union speech for publication on February 28. The other three papers either used the *Tribune*'s original proof or relied on a shorthand reporter to record Lincoln's words. Regardless, Lincoln chose to scrutinize Greeley's paper, assuming it would reach the largest number of readers directly, or indirectly in excerpts reproduced in other papers across the North. At least 150,000 copies of Lincoln's speech were available less than ten hours after he delivered it, circulating within the pages of the *Tribune*, the *New York Times*, and even the Democratic *New York Herald*. That night thousands of additional copies of the speech were published in the *New York Evening Post*. Lincoln hoped that these issues would multiply in other newspapers across the Northeast.[27]

The text of Lincoln's speech and the initial reaction to it were read throughout the Northern states within a week of the Cooper Union address. Predictably, Lincoln was lauded by Republican papers, both for his logical message and for the tremendous historical research that went into it. Most surprising, however, was the grudging praise offered by the Democratic press. The *Illinois State Register*, for example, found much to criticize in Lincoln's argument but in the end was forced to praise his performance.

"This speech of Mr. Lincoln is a more maturely conceived effort than any of his speeches during the Douglas campaign," admitted the paper's editorial. "It is more Jesuitical, abounds with more sophistry and special pleading, and withal is more ingeniously constructed, than any of his speeches that we have ever heard or read."[28]

Lincoln departed New York City before he had time to cull and digest all the available city papers to gauge the reaction to his speech. Before 8:00 a.m. he was aboard a train bound for Rhode Island. The journey into New England had two purposes. One was to visit his oldest son, Robert, attending Phillips Exeter Academy in New Hampshire, a preparatory school for Harvard University. The other reason was to deliver several speeches in the upper Atlantic Coast states. He had delivered numerous speeches over a few days in Ohio and Indiana, in Wisconsin, and in Kansas, but he had never attempted this over a period of two weeks. The venture would be an exhausting one to be sure, but Lincoln's keen sense of political timing demanded the exertion. As the New York speech coverage expanded into New England, Lincoln intended to magnify his growing boom by keeping his name in the papers.

In the middle of the afternoon of February 28, the train deposited Lincoln in Providence, Rhode Island. Providence was first on the list of speaking venues, although the exact location for the featured event in the city was not established until that Tuesday of Lincoln's arrival. He spoke at Railroad Hall that night. By and large, Lincoln's address was the Cooper Union speech, but he worked his way into his historical argument by personalizing his remarks to Rhode Islanders. He did so by quoting from two local papers that had critiqued his "House Divided" speech, then using that speech to explain the intent of the Founding Fathers. "He showed that he occupied only the ground which was taken by the founders of our government," reported the Republican paper of the city, "and triumphantly vindicated himself and the Republican party against the false charges which are so unscrupulously brought against them."[29]

Perhaps as many people heard the speech in Providence as did in New York City. His address opened the Republican campaign in the state, and was so well received that some of its prominent citizens sought a repeat performance—and they would not take no for an answer. Lincoln agreed to return to the tiny state the following week to rouse Republicans in the town of Woonsocket. The following morning (February 29, the extra day of leap year) Lincoln took a train to Exeter, New Hampshire, the town where his oldest son, Robert, had been attending school.[30]

It was likely on this leg of his Northeastern tour that Lincoln shared a seat with Cassius Clay, the famous Kentucky orator who not only had spoken at Cooper Union, but was also embarking on his own New England speaking tour. Lincoln had seen Clay before, at a speech he made in Springfield in July 1854, but according to Lincoln, the train ride "was my first opportunity to take him by the hand." During the trip the two men engaged in the inevitable discussion about slavery. Lincoln found the perfect—albeit unsightly—metaphor for the institution. An older gentleman sat in the row of the passenger car directly in front of Lincoln and Clay with a downturned shirt collar that exposed a large cyst protruding from the back of his neck. Lincoln pointed out the abnormality to Clay and said that the cyst "bears the same relation to that man that slavery does to the country." Lincoln explained that the cyst "is a great evil. The man that bears it will say so. But he does not dare cut it out. He bleeds to death if he does, directly. If he does not cut it out; it will shorten his life materially." Lincoln went on to rationalize that this analogy applied only to those who considered slavery a moral wrong; those that supported it would look at the cyst not as a severe malady, but as an ornament.[31]

Robert Lincoln insisted well into his twilight years that his father's trip from Illinois to New England was primarily intended to visit him, and the speeches that he delivered along the way and afterward were afterthoughts, ones that suddenly generated a boom for his father's presidential prospects. The reverse appears more accurate, for it is unlikely that Lincoln would have traveled two thousand round-trip miles to visit his son if there were no speeches to deliver on the route. Still, the trip to Exeter induced more speaking engagements in New Hampshire. Word spread that Lincoln was heading there from Rhode Island. A telegram asking him to speak in Exeter reached him before he left Providence, and as soon as Lincoln stepped off the train in Exeter, he was surrounded by Republicans from three other towns asking him to speak at their meetings. Thus, the visit to his son added four events to his New England speaking tour that may not have been available if Lincoln had not visited his firstborn.[32]

Lincoln had agreed to give all four of these speeches during the first three days of March. This left the remainder of Wednesday as a free day to relax with sixteen-year-old Robert Lincoln. Not only was February 29 an odd date for the calendar year; it turned out to be an unusual day for Lincoln, the first of only two days in two weeks when Lincoln delivered no speeches. The following morning Robert and a school chum accompanied Lincoln to the first half of his four New Hampshire speeches in Concord, at Phenix Hall. The speech was over before the afternoon ended, and Lincoln and his young companions headed out to Manchester, where he spoke in Smyth's Hall to a large, appreciative crowd that evening. From there he trained to Dover, depositing his school-age tagalongs back to Exeter along the way. He spoke for two hours at City Hall that evening.

Lincoln returned to Exeter on Saturday, March 3, to comply with the telegraphed request to address the townspeople in an evening speech. Several Phillips Exeter Academy students joined Robert in the building that night to hear his father speak and take in the unusual form of the speaker. Although his appearance disappointed them, the crowd was more than gratified by the message, which helped them warm to the unattractive messenger. According to one of the students, Lincoln learned the difference between speaking in New England and in Illinois or Ohio. Exasperated after getting no response to questions he threw out to the crowd, Lincoln declared, "You people here don't jaw back at a fellow as they do out West."[33]

Lincoln queried the crowd and read local newspaper editorials to them throughout the New England tour. The opportunity called for the revamped speeches, and Lincoln was making a conscious effort to avoid repetitiveness. He was not nearly as concerned about this in Ohio, Wisconsin, and Kansas Territory during his 1859 speaking tours. The problem for Lincoln in New England was that his Cooper Union speech had been studied by many whom he faced in New Hampshire in the first days of March. During his second dormant day, March 4, Lincoln explained the contrast in a letter to his wife. "The speech at New York, being within my calculation before I started, went off passably well, and gave me no trouble whatever," wrote Lincoln in his typical understated style. "The difficulty was to make nine others, before reading audiences, who have already seen my ideas in print."[34]

Lincoln's letter reads more like an official report than a personal mis-
sive from a husband to his wife. (He was able to muster the closing word
"Affectionately" above his signature.) He revealed the frustration he felt
over long train rides and longer waits for trains to take him from one
speaking venue to another. "I have been unable to escape this toil," he
wrote with weariness. "If I had foreseen it I think I would not have come
East at all." Restoring some vigor into Lincoln's body that day was the re-
ceipt of the $200 honorarium for speaking at Cooper Union. He also en-
joyed spending the day with his son, including attending church with him
and listening to his boy's friend play the banjo that night. Little did he realize at the time he wrote Mary that his four upcoming speeches planned
over the next four days would grow to six speeches in six days. He received several other offers to extend the tour with more speeches, but Lincoln demurred, believing "I must hurry home."[35]

The performances on the platform beginning on Monday, March 5,
betrayed Lincoln's weariness. He began the week of speeches at City Hall
in Hartford, Connecticut, and remained in the state for two more days
with performances in New Haven on Tuesday and Meriden on Wednesday. Lincoln took pains to alter the speech, both by incorporating local
news and by using pithy anecdotes and heady metaphors to highlight his
principles. At New Haven, the home of Yale University, Lincoln likened
the issue of slavery and the territories to snakes in the bed with children.
Lincoln told his audience that if he found a venomous snake in a bed with
his neighbor's children, and he had given his neighbor a solemn pledge
not to interfere with the children, he was bound by his promise not to do
so. But if there was a newly made bed where the children were supposed
to be placed, and several snakes were going to be put in the same bed with
them, there was no doubt about what he should do. "That is just the
case!" declared Lincoln in explaining the metaphor. "The new Territories
are the newly made bed to which our children are to go, and it lies with
the nation to say whether they shall have snakes mixed up with them or
not." He closed the analogy with supreme confidence: "It does not seem
as if there could be much hesitation what our policy should be!"[36]

Lincoln was tickled and tantalized to learn about one particular audience member, an unidentified professor of rhetoric at Yale. After hearing
and taking notes on Lincoln's performance at New Haven, the professor

used the speech as the basis of his lecture to his Yale students the following day, likely with an emphasis on Lincoln's snakes-in-the-bed slavery
analogy. Lincoln never met the man but learned from others that the same
professor was back the following night at Meriden to listen to and study
Lincoln's lecture at Town Hall. "Now, if this is so," remarked Lincoln
upon hearing this story, "it is to my mind very extraordinary."[37]

On Thursday, March 8, Lincoln was back in Rhode Island. His crowd
that night at Harris Hall in Woonsocket exceeded one thousand, as it had
in Providence the week before and for most of his speeches on this tour.
With the exception of Cincinnati, Milwaukee, and Cooper Union, these
were the largest audiences Lincoln had seen outside of Illinois. However,
aside from his Cooper Union speech, Lincoln's addresses in the East were
not circulated nationwide in newsprint as the Ohio speeches had been six
months earlier. The speeches still made their way into Illinois newspapers,
particularly the *Illinois State Journal* and the *Chicago Press and Tribune*.

Five days earlier, Lincoln had believed his Woonsocket speech would
close the northeastern tour. But during the week, he consented to two
more speeches in Connecticut on consecutive days. On Friday he took a
train to Norwich, where he spoke at Town Hall, and then he headed to
Bridgeport for his final tour speech. Joining him on this train ride was the
Reverend John Gulliver, a minister who had been captivated by Lincoln's
Woonsocket performance and was dazzled by Lincoln's ability to remember his face from the immense crowd that had heard him the evening
before.

Although Gulliver was not as famous a riding companion as Cassius
Clay had been, he was undoubtedly the most intriguing and pleasant person with whom Lincoln shared a ride during his New England trip. Lincoln was drawn to Gulliver's descriptive analysis of Lincoln's speech—he
obviously had no problem with the minister fawning all over his performance of the previous night. But Gulliver so impressed Lincoln with his
ability to pinpoint what Lincoln had striven to accomplish with his address that Lincoln opened up to him about how he had developed his or-
atorical skills and style. Lincoln revealed to Gulliver something that he had
learned as a young boy overhearing discussions between his neighbors and
his father. He would determine the meaning of their discussion and then
simplify it, repeating it as many times as necessary until he was satisfied

that he had converted it into a language that boys his age could understand. "This was a kind of passion with me," admitted Lincoln, who confessed that he still practiced something similar, consulting a dictionary to
compare the definitions of words. "Perhaps that accounts for the characteristic you observe in my speeches," he reasoned to Gulliver, "though I
never put the two things together before."[38]

Lincoln's Saturday speech at Bridgeport came off without a hitch. He
trained back to Manhattan's Astor House overnight and on Sunday morning he returned to Plymouth Church in Brooklyn to hear Henry Ward
Beecher preach again. After the sermon, Lincoln was escorted to the infamous Five Points slum, notorious for its unsavory combination of crime
and poverty. Accompanied by two hosts, Lincoln toured a mission charged
with housing and protecting abandoned children in the slum. Lincoln observed the children in a Sunday-school class and, asked if he wanted to say
something to the children, he agreed and gave a short and simple speech to
them. Again, he spoke at the level of comprehension of his audience. He
also incorporated anecdotes about his own humble upbringing to share
with an audience that not only could relate to them, but could appreciate
them more than any other group Lincoln could address.[39]

On Monday morning, March 12, Lincoln headed back to Springfield.
This was the culmination, his fifth speaking venture outside of Illinois in
seven months. The Northeast trip was the most arduous, for he delivered
twelve speeches in four bordering states over thirteen days to larger
crowds than he had seen in Iowa, Ohio, Indiana, Wisconsin, or Kansas Territory. But most significant about this trip was the role he assumed upon
his return from it. There was no official declaration, nor did there need to
be. From this point on Abraham Lincoln was no longer identified merely
as a statesman or the middle-ground spokesman for the Republican Party.
Instead, he was recognized as a candidate for president of the United
States.

Eight

THE CANDIDATE

NORMAN JUDD AND Long John Wentworth battled in Chicago throughout the first two weeks of Abraham Lincoln's eastern speaking tour. The very public feud had been ignited by Wentworth's caustic editorials throughout 1859 and was fueled by Judd's libel suit in December and, despite Lincoln's attempt at mediation, it burned red hot early in February. Fanning these flames late in the winter of 1860 was Wentworth's decision to run for mayor of Chicago again.

To win the right to run the city, Wentworth had to win the Republican primary before staving off the Democratic challenger in a general election. Few Republicans had more enemies within their party than Wentworth. Leading the faction against him was Norman Judd, backing fellow lawyer Isaac Arnold. When party leaders suggested that Wentworth step aside to harmonize the party, he raised the stakes of his rivalry with Judd by declaring that he would do so only if Judd dropped his bid for governor. Neither man blinked and nothing happened.[1]

On February 17, Chicago Republicans voted for delegates to attend the next day's convention to officially nominate their candidate. To Judd's dismay, Wentworth-supporting delegates crushed their opposition in eight of ten wards, barely losing the other two and guaranteeing Wentworth's nomination. Wentworth twisted the knife he plunged into Judd by winning the First Ward—Judd's home turf.

Wentworth's primary victory squeezed Judd into a predicament. Prominent Republican politicians in Chicago despised Wentworth enough to betray their party and declare in favor of the Democratic nominee, Walter Gurnee (another former mayor). If Judd followed suit, he would appear a traitor to the party, thus damaging his candidacy for the statehouse. He could stay silent on the matter, but this would be akin to supporting the Democrats. The only other option was to openly support Wentworth, "eat dirt" in Judd's words. To do so, he worried, risked the possibility that Lincoln's stock in the state would drop in favor of a Wentworth candidate, who Judd feared could be Sam Houston or even Stephen A. Douglas. It also would crush him personally, for it would pull the teeth out of his libel suit. Judd also maintained that whether he supported him or not, Wentworth would use all his power to thwart Judd's gubernatorial bid later that spring.[2]

In the end Judd chose to "eat dirt" for the sake of the party. He ceased action on the libel suit, allowing it to languish and eventually disappear. More dramatically, Judd spoke out in favor of Wentworth's election in public meetings, appearing with the nominee and working for his victory. The March 7 election became Wentworth's triumphant moment for 1860. He trounced all of his enemies within the Republican ranks and coasted to an easy win over Gurnee. Once again he was mayor of Chicago, vying to be the most influential politician in Illinois—and, as Judd had forecasted, committed as strongly as ever to crushing Judd's bid to be governor.[3]

Lincoln was touring and speaking in New England in the period between Wentworth's nomination and his election. This did not prevent Wentworth from trying to woo him into Chicago to speak on his behalf. Wentworth even reported in his newspaper that Lincoln would appear to deliver a speech before the election, a claim without any evidence to support it. David Davis got into the act, acting as Long John's surrogate. The judge sent two letters to New York late in February (one of them fourteen pages long), pleading with Lincoln to intervene again in Judd's libel suit by convincing him to withdraw it, and also to support Wentworth's mayoral bid. "If Judd . . . and the rest of them Succeed in beating Wentworth,"

Davis warned Lincoln, "the prospect of [you] carrying Illinois would not be worth a groat—You had better turn your head immediately to Chicago. It may be that your presence alone would be our Salvation." Davis sent the letters to New York while Lincoln prepared for the Cooper Union address, but the letter requesting him to appear in Chicago did not get delivered to the Astor House and was subsequently redirected to Springfield—six months later.[4]

Although Lincoln didn't receive Davis's plea in time, Wentworth's easy victory proved it did not matter. But the letter was evidence of how party men thought Lincoln could help turn the tide in local races, and of the calming presence he was in the midst of heated political disputes. Lincoln did receive the fourteen-page letter from Davis, which placed Davis firmly at Wentworth's side and against Judd. By the time Lincoln returned to Illinois he had learned about Judd's magnanimous efforts for Republican success in the Chicago mayoral race. This showed Lincoln that Davis's suspicions of Judd were dated and moot, and that the esteemed judge was not impervious to bad judgment.

The first day of spring in Springfield was marked by a somber event—the funeral of Governor William Bissell, the first Illinois governor to die in office. Bissell succumbed to pneumonia on March 18, and the funeral of the forty-nine-year-old Republican took place three days later. "In the procession were several of the most prominent men of the State," reported the *Chicago Journal*, "men renowned in politics, education, military history and the law." To the surprise of none of the readers of the paper, it named Abraham Lincoln first in the list of dignitaries at the funeral.[5]

Even if Bissell had survived his bout with pneumonia, the governor's status would have fallen behind that of Lincoln, now the most popular figure in Illinois. Lincoln had delivered thirty speeches in eight states and one territory over the previous seven months. The effort had not been wasted. Seemingly each and every day, another endorsement from a newspaper or a county Republican organization was reprinted in the *Illinois State Journal* or the *Chicago Press and Tribune*. As noteworthy as the frequency of the endorsements was the positioning of the candidate's name. Rarely was Lincoln trumpeted as the vice-presidential candidate as he had been in 1859. Now Lincoln's name frequented the top of the ticket on their wish lists.

Lincoln's popularity in Illinois surged in March, as news of his New York and New England trip rolled off the presses. "I have been highly delighted at Seeing the perfect Success of your tour East," crowed a Jasper County supporter in his letter to Lincoln (the man was so dedicated to the candidate that he named his newborn son after him). Another supporter declared to Ozias M. Hatch that "Lincoln is the surest chance for an election—he can carry all the Free States East of Indiana certain." R. D. Shelton, a Republican from Warren County, was so certain that Lincoln would be elected in a national contest against Douglas that he challenged anyone through the newspapers to bet him a thousand dollars that Lincoln would lose.[6]

Lincoln had successfully expanded his popularity outside his home state. Not only were Lincoln's twelve speeches in New York and New England subjected to extensive press coverage east and west, but his Cooper Union speech was reproduced as a sixteen-page pamphlet under the title "The Demands of the South—The Republican Party Vindicated." Adding to Lincoln's popularity was the long-awaited publication of the 1858 Lincoln-Douglas debates, released at the end of March as a single-volume compilation for fifty cents. Together, these publications boomed Lincoln's name across the country—or at least the Northern half of it.[7]

Lincoln's confidants apprised him of the strength of his candidacy. Sam Galloway insisted that Lincoln was second only to Chase in Ohio, and many preferred him to the state's native candidate. Senator Trumbull in Washington assured Lincoln on March 26, "You made a great many friends by your Eastern trip—Have not heard a single man speak of your speeches but in the highest terms."[8]

Joseph Medill also measured Lincoln's pulse in Washington while he attempted to heighten Lincoln's familiarity with a series of favorable letters about him. Medill's efforts were not without consequence. While in Washington late that winter, Medill attended a reception hosted by William H. Seward. The senator pulled Medill aside and berated him for hyping Lincoln at his expense, particularly in regards to states Medill believed Lincoln could carry and Seward could not. Reminding Medill that he had always considered him "one of my boys"—a reporter he had trusted for years—Seward declared, "Henceforth you and I are parted." Close to the same time Lincoln returned to Springfield, Medill returned to Chicago, replaced by another *Press and Tribune* correspondent with a pseudonym, "Waldo." The fresh reporter followed Medill's template. The *Press and Tribune* exaggerated even the briefest mention of Lincoln by "Waldo" under a subtitle: "Lincoln's Stock Rising."[9]

Lincoln was pleased by the positive effects of his speeches and the endorsements he received. He could picture the electoral map as states like Indiana were reportedly moving in his direction. He did not mind at all that he was not considered the top candidate by the leading Republicans in Ohio and New York, for he was optimistic enough to not consider this an effort to make him vice president. On the contrary, he felt that it left the door open for him if the top candidates in these states should falter. "My name is new in the field," Lincoln explained to an Ohio confidant, "and I suppose I am not the *first* choice of a very great many." He revealed that this fed into the strategy of the Republican State Central Committee of Illinois. "Our policy," he explained, ". . . is to give no offence to others—leave them in a mood to come to us, if they shall be compelled to give up their first love."[10]

But he did offend others, or more accurately stated, he started to worry the "first loves" in the presidential race enough to generate some negative press. Seward supporters seethed when they learned that Lincoln was paid two hundred dollars for the Cooper Union speech. This could be achieved only by a door charge, considered indecent for political speeches in the mid-1800s. Seward's supporters pummeled Lincoln in print for demanding a fee and his Cooper Union hosts for charging the audience "the regular circus rate of twenty-five cents' admittance fee" to hear him. The press had a field day with the issue. The *Washington Constitution* ridiculed Lincoln as "the fellow that charged his own friends two-shillin' apiece to hear him talk about politics," thus tagging Lincoln with an unflattering moniker: the two-shilling candidate. An Erie, Pennsylvania, newspaper had fun with the fact at Lincoln's expense. Quoting the *New York Tribune*'s short report on Lincoln's address to the children at Five Points, the editor wryly added, "The *Tribune* does not say how much Mr. Lincoln charged for his speech—as it was delivered to children. We supposed he asked only 'half price,' say $100."[11]

The negative press rippled westward. From a Republican newspaper editor in Middleport, Lincoln received a clipping of a Democratic newspaper from the same Illinois town that reproduced a *New York Herald* critique of the two-hundred-dollar honorarium. Caught off guard, Lincoln was forced to address the issue, but he did so only by responding to the Middleport editor, Cornelius McNeill. Lincoln explained to McNeill that he had not asked for the fee; it was offered to him in October when he was first approached to give a speech. This point was true, but Lincoln was either clueless or dishonest when he insinuated to McNeill that, since he had decided to give a political speech and not a lyceum lecture, he had not expected to receive the honorarium. "I made the speech and left for New Hampshire," explained Lincoln, ". . . neither asking for pay nor having any offered me." He acknowledged receiving the unexpected check while he was in New Hampshire and accepting it, stressing that he *"did not know it was wrong."*

Lincoln went on to claim—again with a lack of candor—that he had been unaware at the time that the audience had paid an admission fee to hear him. But the fact was—and it was inconceivable for Lincoln not to have seen the advertisement the day of his Cooper Union speech—that the audience was charged twenty-five cents per person. Lincoln suggested that he learned of this afterward, and he told McNeill he was unconcerned about any impropriety because "they took in more than twice $200," thus leaving the impression that he was paid as an afterthought out of gratitude by an organization that raked in several hundred dollars that night from an appreciative crowd. But the actual profit for the sponsors, after paying Lincoln, was a mere seventeen dollars. So although Lincoln could stand by his claim that he personally never "charged anything for a political speech in my life," the evidence was clear that his audience was charged to hear him at an event where Lincoln received most of the evening's profit as an honorarium, a stipend that he accepted and swiftly deposited into his bank account as soon as he returned to Springfield.[12]

Lincoln wisely chose to not publicize this letter through the newspapers. "I have made this explanation to you as a friend; but I wish no explanation made to our enemies," he instructed McNeill. "What they want is a squabble and a fuss; and that they can have if we explain; and they can not have if we don't."[13] Lincoln refused to fuel a fire he hoped was flickering out of existence. As irritated as he must have been by the attention his Cooper Union honorarium had received, he should have taken solace that this controversy was hardly a campaign killer.

The Lincoln boom did not take the candidate's attention away from his legal work. Lincoln entered Chicago for the first time in 1860 on March 23 to partake in a suit before the United States district court. The case was *William S. Johnson v. William Jones and Sylvester Marsh*, but it was better known as the "Sand Bar" case. This was the fourth trial of a ten-year-old dispute over ownership of title to sandy barren lands off the Lake Michigan shoreline. Lincoln was one of four lawyers representing the defense, a client of the Illinois Central Railroad who wanted the land as lots for depots. This case would bring to a close what a newspaper considered "a plump foot-ball of a million dollars in value" that had been "bounced to and fro between the contestants."[14]

A downturn in the weather made it easier to focus on his legal work in Chicago. Two inches of snow fell in northern Illinois, squelching any hints of spring fever in the inhabitants of the region. Lincoln's toils in this case carried him through the end of March and into the first week of April. "I am so busy with our case on trial here," he complained to an attorney asking his opinion about another case, "that I can not examine authorities near as fully as you can there."[15]

Despite his protests to the contrary, Lincoln found plenty of time for diversions in Chicago. "I spent nearly every evening with him," asserted Henry C. Whitney, one of the opposing attorneys in the Sand Bar case. They dined out together one night; on another they attended a minstrel show at Metropolitan Hall. Believing (incorrectly) that the building would house the mid-May Republican National Convention, Whitney said to Lincoln shortly before the performance, "Possibly in a few weeks you will be nominated for President right here." Lincoln demurred, insisting it was an honor merely to be considered for the nomination. The show ended the discussion. Lincoln was captivated by a mesmerizing musical performance—a number called "Dixie." According to Whitney, the song had Lincoln clapping and calling for an encore. "I never saw him so enthusiastic."[16]

Lincoln began a unique morning routine during this Chicago trip. Two years earlier Lincoln had met Leonard W. Volk, a Chicago sculptor who happened to claim Stephen A. Douglas as kin (by marriage). Lincoln promised back then to sit for a life mask, and in 1860 Volk found Lincoln and reminded him of his earlier promise. Each day for a week between breakfast and the beginning of court at 10:00 a.m., Lincoln hiked up five flights of stairs to Volk's studio and sat for a sculpture of his unique features.[17]

Most important, Lincoln made sure during his Chicago trip that his political operatives worked to magnify his boom. Neither Lincoln nor Norman B. Judd discussed the meeting they had during this particular trip, but the gist of what they covered was made clear by Judd's subsequent correspondences. The two likely got together during the weekend of March 31–April 1. This was the eve of the convention season for Illinois, one that would begin with a series of county Republican conventions to choose the delegates to send to the state Republican convention in Decatur, moved up to May 9 to adjust for the earlier national convention, rescheduled one week later.

On April 1, the national convention was merely seven weeks away, a fact well known to Judd and Lincoln when they met to discuss strategy and potential outcomes. Both men must have been aware of the scenarios necessary not only to upend the front-running Seward, but to win the nomination for Lincoln:

1. The convention balloting needed to begin with fewer than half of the state delegates committed to Seward to prevent him from winning on the first ballot.
2. Those state delegates not committed to Seward on the first ballot needed to be prevented from moving to him on subsequent ballots.
3. No other front-running candidate—particularly Chase, Bates, or Cameron—could garner enough support outside his home state to place himself so strongly behind Seward as to become the obvious second-choice candidate for the anti-Seward delegates to converge upon.
4. Lincoln needed to be surprisingly strong—second or third out of at least ten candidates on the first ballot—in an effort to be the rallying candidate in the anti-Seward movement.

Although Judd was an eternal optimist, and Lincoln was beginning to get caught up in his own boom, the fact was that on April 1, none of the four scenarios seemed likely. An ill-boding sign had appeared northwest of

Chicago back in February, when the Minnesota state Republican convention launched the political season. The state's delegates pledged "to use all honorable means" to nominate Senator Seward for president of the United States. This outcome prodded Judd to action, for he realized that a strong alignment of state delegates pledged to Seward at the national convention would ease him to victory in Chicago. Seward could still garner enough support to meet the minimal requirement on the first ballot. Judd perhaps did not expect this to occur, but Lincoln needed to have much more than Illinois's twenty-two delegates committed to him after the first ballot to persuade other states to shift their allegiance to him.

Lincoln expected the Illinois delegates chosen at the state convention to be pledged to him, an expectation made more plausible by Lincoln's growing popularity nationwide. Nearly two months earlier, Lincoln had confessed to Judd that "it would hurt some for me not to get the Illinois delegates." The Illinois Republican State Central Committee determined that 637 delegates would be chosen from the 102 counties in the state to meet at the state convention. By April 1 Lincoln and Judd were more confident than ever that more Illinois counties that passed resolutions for the presidential nominee would be pledged to him than to Bates, Seward, Chase, Cameron, or other recognized candidates. Those who were noncommittal or pledged to a candidate other than Lincoln would need to be persuaded in Decatur to support him as a unit vote, dedicated to unanimously vote for Lincoln at the national convention in Chicago.

Given the strong support voiced for Bates in the southern counties of Illinois, Judd was surprisingly confident, even on April 1, that he and the other party leaders could achieve the unanimous support from the 637 delegates necessary to send 22 delegates to Chicago as a unit vote for Lincoln, rather than spread out between two or three candidates. He assured Lincoln that although support for Bates was still significant in Illinois, it paled in comparison to what the Lincoln boom had achieved throughout the autumn and winter, the influence and power of Orville Browning notwithstanding. Judd's greater concern, as he relayed to Lincoln, was Lincoln's as well: William Henry Seward.

Senator Seward had spent the last eight months of 1859 in Europe and the Middle East. His extended overseas tour removed him from public attention in America. He overcame his long absence from the country by delivering a rousing and highly publicized speech in the U.S. Senate on February 29. The address not only succeeded in giving him headline attention, but helped assuage some fears of his earlier "irrepressible conflict" position. Judd sensed that Seward still had too many negatives dripping off of him to comfort Republican delegates nationwide, and he had a month to do all he could to take advantage of that uneasiness. Judd also was savvy enough to know that these concerns about Seward would be swept under the rug at the national convention if state after state pledged its support for him. The emotion of the moment could overcome not only the uncommitted, but also those with strong reservations about Seward. Ironically, Judd's mission for April and early May was to prevent at the Republican National Convention exactly what he wished to achieve at the Illinois Republican convention: a cascade of overwhelming support for the front-running candidate that would stifle any attempt for supporters of his competitors to upset him.

Making Lincoln's chance to upend Seward an even longer shot was that Lincoln was still not the second choice at the national level, nor the third- or even the fourth-ranked Republican candidate. His speeches and his message had garnered more national attention than he could have hoped for back in 1859, but the leading candidates either held positions of national prominence, had also received national exposure for their speeches and letters, or both. Perhaps as many as fifty thousand people outside of Illinois had attended a Lincoln speech between August 1859 and March 1860. A huge majority of them walked away with a favorable opinion of Lincoln, but this did not mean that they thought he would be the best Republican candidate for president. Very few of them would be selected at state conventions to cast ballots at the national convention, and none of them were going to sway a national delegate from his initial intent of voting for Seward, Chase, Cameron, Bates, or any other candidate the delegate was wed to by state allegiance or by influence from the national standing the front-runners enjoyed.

Lincoln was still the dark horse in this race, but Judd expected that a month of editorials in the wake of Lincoln's magnificent speaking tours, influenced by the spread of the pamphlets and books of his speeches, would magnify Lincoln's name and appeal as a feasible and safe middle-ground alternative to all the other Republican presidential candidates.

Ever the optimist, Judd still believed that the Seward train could be de-railed and that the passengers would flock to the Lincoln train, preferring its accommodations to those of the several other options available.

Judd explained all of this to Lincoln. Expecting several states to come to the convention committed to Seward, Judd realized that united opposition was required to stop him. What was needed was coordinated action by the swing states—Pennsylvania, Indiana, Illinois, and New Jersey—to control the convention by refusing to declare for Seward, and resisting any temptation to grasp at promises guaranteed to be offered by Seward's wily and seasoned campaign manager, Thurlow Weed. Realizing that New Jersey would be hyping its favorite son, William L. Dayton, and Pennsylvania would be strongly supporting Simon Cameron, Judd reasoned that it would be useless—and perhaps detrimental—to even attempt to persuade these states to drop their candidates and unite on Lincoln. That persuasion would wait until the convention. For now it was more important for these states to be committed not to go to Seward as their second or third choice, or even their ninth or tenth one.

To achieve this outcome required persuasion through the mails. Judd had six weeks to help spur this movement, which he began with an editorial in the *Chicago Press and Tribune*, and a letter to Senator Lyman Trumbull in Washington urging him to work with Republicans in the swing states to influence their delegates to stop Seward. "Nothing but a positive position will prevent Seward's nomination," Judd told Trumbull, adding his belief that the Lincoln boom "has neutralized to some extent the Bates movement in our state." Judd assured Trumbull that Illinois was prepared to take its part in stopping Seward by its expected commitment to Lincoln. "State pride will carry a resolution of instruction through our convention," predicted Judd, not needing to explain which candidate was the source of that state pride.[18]

All indications are that Lincoln understood the hurdles between him and the nomination. He had done all he could do to position himself as an alternative to radical candidates. Although his burgeoning popularity made it likely he would garner most if not all of Illinois's delegates, it was a sobering fact that his efforts on the speaking circuit would have virtually no influence on the first round of ballots at the national convention. No state outside of Illinois was expected to come to the convention entirely committed to Lincoln. And if Seward collected enough support to put him over the top on the first ballot, it would be nearly impossible to change the delegates' minds. The strategy Lincoln had adopted back in 1859—to acquire widespread support while representing the party as an inoffensive statesman—could propel him only if delegate votes deadlocked on the top-tier candidates short of the minimum needed to nominate.

Nevertheless, Judd's positive attitude was infectious, for he had convinced Lincoln that he had a solid chance to have all of the Illinois delegates sent to Chicago voting only for him. Throughout April and early May each Illinois county would hold a convention to select its delegates to send to Decatur on May 9. Most of these county delegates would come to Decatur carrying resolutions adopted in their home counties. Lincoln expected to be named more than any other candidate as the preferred presidential nominee, but he understood that Seward probably had broad appeal across the northern counties, while Bates had support spread throughout the southernmost eighteen counties of Illinois, a region collectively known as "Egypt." Ironically, Lincoln's chances to achieve unanimous statewide support at Decatur improved if Stephen A. Douglas won the Democratic nomination at the party's national convention in Charleston late in April.

Whether Douglas achieved his party's support or not, Lincoln also realized that Cook County would be sending forty-seven delegates to the Decatur convention, more than twice as many as any of the 101 other counties. It was imperative for those delegates to be dedicated to him and not to Seward or Chase. Working in Lincoln's favor was his manager, Norman Judd. But there was a wild card threatening the security of this necessary piece of the nomination puzzle: Long John Wentworth, the new mayor of Chicago, the seat of Cook County.

The problem for Lincoln was not that Wentworth did not like him, for he did, although his newspaper had neither endorsed Lincoln nor publicized him over any other candidate. Lincoln's quandary was that Long John still harbored a malignant hatred of Judd, an emotion that had not abated one iota despite Judd's overt support for his mayoral election in March and the apparent end to the libel suit. Judd's dual missions at the state convention were to obtain a unit vote for Lincoln and to be nominated for governor himself. Wentworth dedicated himself to derailing the

gubernatorial bid; claimed David Davis, "I think [Wentworth] insane almost on the subject." As mayor, Wentworth had the power to stop Judd by
refusing to let Judd get his preferred delegates in Cook County's April
convention. But Lincoln needed to be concerned that Judd's failure in
Cook County might result in delegates sent to Decatur not rock solid for
Lincoln. Wentworth informed Lincoln, "I do not intend that [Judd]
should be Governor *under any circumstances*." Those circumstances could
equate to the loss of Cook County for Lincoln.[19]

For the present, Lincoln's chief political confidant in northern Illinois
was Norman Judd. Perhaps to shore up his support with the Lake Michigan counties, Lincoln took advantage of a break in the Sand Bar case to
deliver a speech. After court duties ended on Monday afternoon, April 2,
Lincoln and Judd rode forty miles north to Waukegan, the seat of Lake
County. As the two entered Dickinson's Hall no one needed to point out
to either of them that this would be Lincoln's first speech as a recognized
candidate for the presidency of the United States.

Lincoln began his speech rather inauspiciously, much like the scores of
speeches delivered over the past three years. "When he began to speak he
did not impress me," recalled J. W. Hull, who complained of the squeaking
voice hitting him "like a dash of cold water." But Hull fell in line like most
other Republicans listening to Lincoln and warmed to the message. Lincoln
denounced the immorality of slavery, yet the United States held the dubious
distinction of reducing this immorality to "the standing of an institution."
In a conciliatory tone, Lincoln declared that current slaveholders were not
blameworthy, for most had inherited their slaves as property.

He was unable to continue. Twenty-five minutes into his speech, the
distinctive sound of the fire alarm rang out, loud enough for everyone inside Dickinson's Hall to hear it. One of the attendees stood up and declared it was a Democratic trick to break up the meeting. Others urged
people to ignore it, for it was a false alarm. After a few discordant moments, Lincoln said, "Well, gentlemen, let us all go, as there really seems to
be a fire, and help put it out." The fire destroyed warehouse buildings at
the north pier of Waukegan. It also put an end to Lincoln's speech. The
Waukegan Gazette made the best of it in its report: "Although disappointed in not hearing his speech through, yet we had the pleasure of seeing him, which really does one's soul good."[20]

Lincoln took time during a subsequent afternoon and rode the rails from Chicago to the northern suburb of Evanston, home to twelve hundred citizens and the six-year-old Northwestern University. Lincoln had arranged a visit to an influential friend, Julius White, a harbormaster and a member of the Chicago Board of Trade. Lincoln was treated like a celebrity, a common occurrence throughout Illinois since his return from Ohio in September. Well-wishers greeted him in White's home, while a throng gathered on the lawn and serenaded him with shouts, songs, and blowing horns. Lincoln stepped outside and delivered a short and gracious speech before reentering the home to shake hands and tell stories.

He exuded a full spectrum of humor, wit, and charm that evening, shining with a personality that left impressions on the minds of visitors to White's house that time could not erase. Lincoln pulled aside one of the serenading singers he heard on the lawn. "Young man," announced Lincoln, "I wish I could sing as well as you. Unfortunately I know only two tunes; one is 'Old Hundred,' and the other isn't." He also engaged in a habit he shared with tall men: sizing himself with them by a back-to-back measure. Lincoln discovered he was tied with the tallest man in Evanston, J. Watson Ludlam. "I remember as though it was but yesterday," recalled a Northwestern University student nearly half a century afterward, "the tall, lanky form of Lincoln and his expressive countenance as he stood shaking hands with admiring friends, while a stream of wit and humor, and story and laughter, came bubbling up from the great soul within."[21]

Lincoln's Chicago trip culminated with a victory in the courts. On April 4 the jury in the Sand Bar case deliberated for five hours before delivering a verdict in favor of the defendants. The next day Lincoln received $350 for his work on the case and trained back to Springfield. Dedicating his focus to his nomination, Lincoln ended his active law work for the season with this trial.[22]

Only one month from the Republican state convention, Lincoln was bombarded with out-of-state requests for public addresses, including queries to hear his "Discoveries and Inventions" presentation. In a candid moment, Lincoln confessed his shortcomings as a lyceum speaker. "I am not a professional lecturer," he admitted to the Harrison Literary Institute in Philadelphia. "Have never got up but one lecture, and that I think rather a poor one." Lincoln's moment of self-deprecation was short-lived, for later in April he delivered the "Discoveries and Inventions" lecture one final time in Springfield. His real reason for declining most offers for speeches in April—political and otherwise—was that he didn't have time to prepare his speeches and travel out of state to deliver them.[23]

He did agree to deliver a political speech in Bloomington, feeling obligated to satisfy the request of friends there. He appeared in Bloomington on Tuesday, April 10, and headed to Phoenix Hall. He chose to speak about current topics of the day. This included a long discussion of polygamy by the Mormons in Utah Territory. Lincoln highlighted the Democrats' denunciation of the practice and their proposal to solve the problem by dividing up Utah Territory and attaching pieces of it to neighboring territories. While not endorsing the practice of polygamy, Lincoln juxtaposed the Democrats' attitude here with their lack of desire to interfere with slavery in the territories. Lincoln dared to speak the paradoxical thoughts of those who espoused popular sovereignty: polygamy was a moral wrong repugnant enough to speak out against, while slavery was greeted with silence, thus leaving the impression that it was right in their minds.[24]

The *Bloomington Pantagraph* offered nothing but praise for Lincoln's speech. "While he convinces the understanding by arriving at legitimate and unavoidable sequences, he wins the hearts of his hearers by the utmost fairness and good humor," praised the report in the following morning's edition. "Several of his home thrusts, last night, went through the sophisms and duplicities of the Shamocracy with a terribly damaging effect."[25]

Lincoln spent four more days away from Springfield without revealing where he went and what he did after the Bloomington speech. Chances are he met with top Illinois political operatives. These would have included David Davis, particularly if he was home in Bloomington at the time of Lincoln's trip to the judge's town. Davis took a train to Chicago during the third week of April, about the same time that Lincoln returned to Springfield. During his Chicago trip, Davis met with Mayor Wentworth. Long John already commanded an unusual degree of influence on Judge Davis, perhaps the only Lincoln associate still hanging on Wentworth's every thought.

Impetuous as ever, Wentworth usually felt compelled to contact Lincoln whenever he met with Davis, perhaps buoyed by sharing the same mind-set with the normally discerning judge. Wentworth wrote Lincoln on April 21 in his typical blunt and grating style. Long John displayed his ignorance by opening the letter warning Lincoln that Trumbull was competing with him for the vice-presidential nomination (still unable to tout Lincoln consistently at the top of the ticket). He then went on a typical anti-Judd rant, mockingly asserting that "Judd is crying & whining" over Wentworth's attempt to thwart his gubernatorial bid. Without restraint and characteristically self-centered, Wentworth explained to Lincoln that Judd should not be governor because this "would be as calamitous to me personally as to the state at large." Wentworth took another swipe at Judd and his unsuccessful record as Lincoln's campaign manager. "Davis & I shall not call until you are beaten once more," he teased.[26]

Including Judge Davis in the provocative line must have disappointed Lincoln, as did Long John's assurance that "Davis is here. He agrees with me in all things." More distressing to Lincoln was Davis's confirmation of Wentworth's claims two days later. "I have just returned from Chicago," wrote Davis to Lincoln on April 23, shocking him by proclaiming, "I am more & more Convinced of the wonderful power of John Wentworth." Davis parroted nearly everything espoused by Wentworth. "If he had managed the campaign in this State in 1858," claimed Davis, "I w[oul]d have bet half I am worth that you would have been successful." Davis rambled on about several of Wentworth's opinions: his hatred of Judd, his distrust of Lyman Trumbull and Gustave Koerner, and his desire to be appointed as one of the four at-large delegates to head to the national convention.

Davis had clearly fallen under Long John's spell. He relayed Wentworth's belief that the *Press and Tribune*'s endorsement of Lincoln was "a mere blind" to hide its true advocacy for Trumbull's nomination. "He believes this," declared Davis of Wentworth's conspiracy theory. "There is no mistake about it, & I must confess to sharing his opinion a good deal." As it turned out, representatives of the *Press and Tribune* did contact Trumbull in April about his interest in the vice presidency, second on a ticket featuring a recently hyped candidate, the venerable Supreme Court justice John McLean. Although he celebrated his seventy-fifth birthday in 1860, a growing movement for McLean could not be overlooked. Joseph Medill reasoned through several scenarios and decided that if McLean somehow became the fallback choice of a deadlocked convention, then "a young, fresh, *reliable*" vice president should balance his ticket: "The judge is old and may not live thro' a term." Medill's musings, however, could hardly be called a conspiracy against Lincoln. He considered Trumbull for the second slot mainly because he understood Lincoln's disdain for that position on the ticket, and he made sure Trumbull understood that the paper was not advocating McLean's nomination, but wished to balance it with an Illinois man if Lincoln's supporters were unable to push Lincoln through at the top of the ticket.[27]

Everything that Davis revealed in this letter lowered Lincoln's opinion of Wentworth, whom Lincoln mocked, disregarded, and avoided as tenaciously as Davis clung to the mayor. The point of Davis's communication was to notify Lincoln that four of the twenty-two delegates sent by Illinois to the national convention would be at-large choices of Lincoln, and Lincoln should choose wisely:

> *No matter what [Wentworth's] motive, you could not have a more Effective or efficient friend—He will not desert you until I do— . . . I am not only Satisfied that Wentworth wd if in the Convention be for you—but I am Satisfied that he can really do more to advance your interests than any man in Illinois, or out of it. . . . Wentworth must be appointed one of the delegates at large—I will vouch for his faithfulness—When Wentworth is trusted, he is true—abuse & distrust don't help the matter with him. The appointment of him as a delegate, & the fact that you had confidence enough in him to select him, Makes him your friend—He thinks the State is for you—You ought to have got him long ago to "run you."[28]*

David Davis had cast his lot with Wentworth and in doing so risked alienating himself from the circle of Lincoln's friends. The teaming up against Judd made matters worse for Wentworth—and by extension, Davis. Lincoln would neither heed their warnings nor act on any of their suggestions. No better evidence for Lincoln's mistrust of Wentworth and his disappointment in Davis exists than his refusal to respond to any of the six letters they sent to him in the three weeks before the state convention. In fact, Lincoln disregarded Davis's written instructions to burn his letter. No doubt, Lincoln's silence irritated Davis, who may have referred to this period when he candidly complained six years later, "He never thanked me for any thing I did—never as I before said asked my advice about anything—never took my advice."[29]

Lincoln and his supporters expected to know who the Democratic Party's nominee was before the Republican state convention was held. The Democratic National Convention convened in Charleston, South Carolina, on April 23, with Stephen A. Douglas expected to be nominated, although a growing opposition within the Southern wing of the party was determined to prevent his nomination. The Southerners succeeded, many of them bolting the convention after they failed to get a resolution endorsing a federal slave code for the territories added to the party platform. The remaining delegates proceeded to ballot among the candidates; Douglas was favored by the majority, but he failed to clear the two-thirds of Democrats required to nominate. Fifty-seven fruitless ballots forced the convention to dissolve with hopes of settling the differences by the time it reconvened in Baltimore on June 18.

The new date placed the Democratic convention one month after the Republican National Convention, guaranteeing an air of uncertainty over whom the Democrats would nominate. The uncertainty stirred up hope among the Republican faithful, for if they remained a united party, whoever they nominated had an improved chance to win the election in November. Each camp of the Republicans could claim a benefit from the lack of conclusion in Charleston. Seward's supporters saw gold in the inconclusive results. They knew that many Republicans were uneasy with Seward as their likely candidate; the potential elimination of Stephen A. Douglas from the race buoyed their hopes. One of them predicted that Douglas would not win the Democratic nomination, and he assured Thurlow Weed—Seward's manager—that if this occurred, "you can *walk* over the course."[30]

Notwithstanding these eruptions, Lincoln saw positive signs for his own nomination and became convinced, as he told an Ohio supporter a week before the state convention at Decatur, that "the Illinois delegation will be unanimous for me" at the national convention. This is what Judd had maintained a month earlier, and what Lincoln had thought essential the previous winter. He made this sanguine forecast based at least partially on county-convention resolutions published in Lincoln-supporting newspapers. Oddly, the reports he read in the *Chicago Press and Tribune* and the

Illinois State Journal, although uplifting, were far from decisive on the matter. Nearly two-thirds of the 102 county-convention resolutions had been published. Although this strong sample indicated that he was the overwhelming choice of the counties for president, Bates also received some support. More troublesome was that support for Lincoln was offset by counties that chose no candidate at all. These noncommittal counties—at least thirty of them—would send their delegates to Decatur with no mission to send delegates to Chicago committed to Lincoln's nomination.[31]

Although more than one hundred counties would be represented at the Republican state convention, one county's delegates would hold more sway than any other's. This was Cook County, which would send forty-seven delegates to Decatur, three times more than the next most populous county and at least ten times more than most of the counties in the state. Although several towns would have one or two delegates at the county convention, Chicago would run this show. Each of the city's ten wards would flood the county convention with between four and ten delegates.

Those city delegates were determined by a primary election on Saturday, April 28. This was Judd versus Wentworth, political powerhouses waging war on each other for control of the county by getting their men elected as delegates. It was a make-or-break outcome for Judd, who claimed earlier in the month, "I shall not ask any one to nominate me unless I have Cook." Whereas Judd sought delegates that would support his gubernatorial nomination in Decatur, Wentworth was determined to generate an anti-Judd movement in his city. The mayor used the full brunt of his power and influence, including turning out the police force who, by "zealous activity," peddled the anti-Judd candidates in every ward. Although Wentworth had promised that his slate of preferred candidates would be pro-Lincoln delegates, no one could ever be sure with Long John.[32]

It turned out to be hardly a contest at all. The Judd men prevailed by overwhelming numbers, the average being five to one for the slate of delegates in every single ward. Two days later, in the supervisor's room in the courthouse, the county convention commenced. Judd got what he needed, forty-seven delegates heading to Decatur committed to electing him governor at the state Republican convention. Judd entered the room near the end of the afternoon and took the stand to thunderous applause. Judd briefly acknowledged the honor, basking in a rare triumphant moment over Mayor Wentworth. "A great many men are afraid of the elephant," Judd said, employing his sobriquet for Wentworth; "I can pull his teeth." Indeed, Judd removed a few of Long John's teeth at the Cook County convention.[33]

But the elephant had plenty of fight left in him, and Judd knew it. Wentworth prepared to be at Decatur to do all he could to end Judd's gubernatorial bid at the state convention. He wrote Lincoln the day of the county convention to urge Lincoln to be there as well. Still consumed with the Trumbull conspiracy, Wentworth warned Lincoln, "The Convention will instruct & the delegates will play for Trumbull." Long John felt compelled to advise Lincoln but conceded that Judd's presence within Lincoln's inner circle was problematic for him. "I am anxious to post you now," he wrote Lincoln on April 30, "as the possible nomination of Judd may place us at loggerheads during the campaign."[34]

Wentworth headed south to Springfield shortly after the county convention to make a personal plea with Lincoln, one he obviously had discussed with Davis a few weeks earlier. Wentworth found Lincoln at breakfast and, after bringing up his Trumbull conspiracy, attempted to upend Judd once again. According to Lincoln, Wentworth blurted, "I tell you what, Lincoln. You must do like Seward does—get a feller to run you." Lincoln never revealed his response, but he thought so little of Wentworth that he turned the meeting into a comical anecdote to add to his repertoire. The phrase "run you" must have struck him because it was the exact phrase Davis had used to endorse Wentworth barely one week earlier.[35]

By the first week of May, David Davis had, to his credit, successfully divorced himself from Wentworth's conspiracy theory concerning Trumbull, but he continued to urge Lincoln to bring the acerbic mayor in as one of the four at-large delegates sent to Chicago. "There ought to be no mistake about Wentworth as one of the delegates," advised Davis four days before the state convention. "He will help you—if he is—& if he is not could hurt you more than any man in the state. . . . it would be suicide now not to appoint him."[36]

Lincoln had no intention of taking Davis's wayward advice about Wentworth. Judd was confident that when Wentworth "whispered his poison" to Lincoln, it would fall on deaf ears. Regardless, Judd felt compelled to communicate his concern that Wentworth's Springfield visit would affect weaker minds. "[O]ur friends in the State house must not listen to his suggestions," he told Lincoln.[37]

Lincoln displayed no concern about Wentworth spreading his wild theories about Trumbull and his supporters, for he had been corresponding with the senator since he returned from the East, as had Judd and others working for Lincoln's nomination. But Lincoln and his supporters did not know that Trumbull was so pessimistic about Lincoln's chances that he had begun to look for advantages for himself as vice president on another ticket. Trumbull had easily been swayed by Medill's suggestion that he be McLean's running mate. In fact, the senator wrote McLean as soon as he read Medill's letter. Trumbull assured McLean that he was "the only person who can be nominated in Chicago in opposition to Governor Seward." Without suggesting himself as McLean's potential running mate, Trumbull claimed to believe that the old judge was in the unique position to obtain united opposition support from the key states of Ohio and Pennsylvania—ostensibly referring to the second ballot. "I think we could also give you Illinois," postulated Trumbull, believing that support for Lincoln would disintegrate after the first ballot.[38]

To Trumbull's credit, he never hid his thoughts about presidential prospects from Abraham Lincoln. Trumbull's last letter to Lincoln before the state convention arrived late in April, an eight-page communication discussing all the possibilities between the Republican candidates in head-to-head matchups at the national convention. Three days had passed since he wrote McLean, time for Trumbull to consider the judge's advanced age and lack of vigor as a huge detriment. So although he believed Seward could not carry Illinois in a national election, Trumbull calculated that Lincoln would lose at the convention if the Republican contest was reduced to only him against Seward, but still believed McLean was the strongest fallback candidate for Republicans to support if the balloting failed to put Lincoln over the top against Seward. Regardless of this prediction, Trumbull had become a Lincoln man and asserted his support for him. "I wish to be distinctly understood as first & foremost for you," declared the senator. "I want our State to send delegates not only instructed for you, but your friends who will stand by & nominate you if possible, never faltering unless you yourself shall so advise."[39]

Trumbull's candid remarks reached Lincoln before Wentworth's anti-Trumbull letter did, helping reduce Long John to a caricature in Lincoln's hierarchy of political prognosticators. On the eve of the state convention, Lincoln was confident—regardless of who would be nominated governor—that he had garnered as much support as he could expect from the selected delegates. But he also believed that it would be difficult to keep the twenty-two delegates in his camp. Judd had already admitted, "A majority of our delegation are for Seward with the proviso that he can be elected—but every man is a Lincoln as a first choice."[40] There was a glimmer of hope for Lincoln that his delegates could make waves at the national convention, but those same delegates could leave him and marry any other candidate once they concluded they could not win with Lincoln. As slim as the hopes and possibilities were, they were real enough for Lincoln to hide them no longer. Lincoln opened up to Trumbull on the eve of the state and national conventions with an admission he expressed in his telltale understated style: "The taste *is* in my mouth a little."[41]

Nine

THE RAIL SPLITTER

DECATUR MARKED THE place where Abraham Lincoln's life in Illinois began. Back in the middle of March 1830, the extended Lincoln family (including Lincolns, Johnsons, and Hanks family members) rode into the fledgling town. Abraham, twenty-one years old, had accompanied his father, Thomas; his stepmother, Sarah Bush Johnson Lincoln; three of his cousins and step-siblings; and his dog on a two-week journey as they escorted an oxcart full of all the family belongings from Spencer County, Indiana, two hundred miles away. Decatur was then the new seat of Macon County—so new in fact that the finishing touches were still being applied to the log courthouse in the town square the day the Lincolns rode in from the southeast.

One of the men completing the court building was John Hanks, a cousin of Lincoln's birth mother. Hanks had settled in Decatur a year earlier and convinced Tom Lincoln to move his family there. Six years Abraham's senior, Hanks took on the role of the older brother. He escorted the family ten miles west of the town square to the small patch of farmland he had already cleared just off the north bank of the Sangamon River. After erecting a cabin from logs previously cut by Hanks, the Lincoln men cleared fifteen acres that spring and summer and started a farm. Throughout the summer of 1830, Abraham Lincoln and John Hanks paired up in rail-splitting ventures for the Lincoln farm and their Decatur neighbors. Several thousand rails (most of them oak and walnut) were produced by the ax-holding hands of the two cousins during their first year there.

Lincoln made sure there was no second year at Decatur. After surviving the feverish prairie plague known as ague that autumn, the Lincolns huddled in their cabin during one of the most brutal winters in Illinois history. The family survived what was forever dubbed "the Winter of the Deep Snow," enduring the thirty-one heavy snowfalls that paralyzed the state for the first two months of 1831. To no one's surprise, Thomas Lincoln decided against risking another such hit on the open prairies and chose to return to Indiana that spring (he stopped short of the border and spent the remaining twenty years of his life in Coles County, Illinois, sixty miles east of Decatur). Abraham Lincoln went the other way. Separating from his family, Lincoln ventured down the Sangamon, eventually making a life and career of his own in Springfield, forty-five miles west of Decatur.

Thirty years after living there, Lincoln found that he could never completely part from Decatur. He had visited there at least twice a year since the 1840s: it was a stop on the Eighth Judicial Circuit. In May 1860 he rode there again, strictly for the convention and not for court duties, as he had temporarily suspended his law work since April. The visit must have conjured up bittersweet memories from the time he skirted north of his father's old farm on the Sangamon. He may have been amused to see the property lines as he approached the town, for many of the thirty-year-old rails he had split with John Hanks remained wedged in the fence posts on those Macon County farms. It was starkly ironic that those oak rails survived in and near Decatur, a reminder of the type of work he detested at a place where he escaped the hard-living farm life his father had predetermined for him.

The town presented a different image. Decatur certainly had changed since the days Lincoln lived in Macon County. Although he still practiced law in the original log courthouse, most of the primitive cabins had given away to more stately homes. Businesses sprouted and grew, but had still not supplanted agriculture as the major occupation of the prairie. The town square was an unusual mix of old and new for Lincoln. The old courthouse dominated the square, presenting the same image to Lincoln viewing it from the northern sector of the square as it had when he mounted a stump back in 1830 and delivered an extemporaneous defense of his principles to a small gathering who had been subjected to the rants of two politicians who spoke before him. That happened to be Lincoln's first political speech. Thirty years and a few hundred speeches later, he was no longer viewed as the new barefoot neighbor of the town, but as a favorite son of Illinois, seeking unanimous delegation support of his bid for the presidency of the United States of America.

That endorsement, if it came to fruition, would do so in the newest and most unusual structure in Decatur. It was a political meeting hall of a type fairly common in frontier politics, called a wigwam. The Decatur wigwam was erected during the first week of May in the heart of Decatur, just east of the town square, on State Street near the intersection of South Park Street. Wedged between two brick buildings, the wigwam was one hundred feet by seventy feet; its platform was surrounded on three sides by five sections of seats, seventy-three rows of them, to accommodate 2,500 attendees.[1] This anticipated flood would swell Decatur's population by over 60 percent.

Richard J. Oglesby took charge of convention preparations. A thirty-five-year-old Decatur resident, Oglesby had known Lincoln since the middle of the decade. (Both men were born in Kentucky and toiled as lawyers in Illinois.) Oglesby was a Mexican War veteran and had participated in the California gold rush. He had failed to win a congressional seat in 1858 but, undeterred, was in 1860 making his first bid as a Republican candidate for the state senate. He seems to have appointed himself leader of the Decatur preparations, for he was not a delegate to the convention, nor was he charged with a specific function there by the Illinois Republican State Central Committee.[2]

Oglesby raised the $250 necessary for the wigwam construction and oversaw the project. The original concept called for more lumber in the construction, but Oglesby improvised by procuring a canvas (perhaps from a circus tent) and stretching it over the top of the wood-framed structure. The finished wigwam looked more like a tent than a meeting hall. It completely blocked State Street. Oglesby also made sure that each of the nine congressional districts of Illinois was accommodated with headquarters space in the various hotels of the city.

Oglesby was determined to see the convention run smoothly, in no small part for the benefit of Lincoln, whom he expected to win the large majority of delegates. Having known John Hanks for many years, Oglesby called upon Lincoln's elder cousin and questioned him about the old Lincoln homestead he and Lincoln had helped build and clear back in 1830. Oglesby asked Hanks if he and Lincoln had split rails out there. Pleased by Hanks's confirmation, Oglesby asked Hanks to ride with him down to the site of the old homestead.

Early in May the two Decatur men took the buggy ride ten miles outside of Decatur to the original clearing. Hanks inspected fencing and found the rails he was sure had been split by Lincoln and him thirty years before. They even inspected the stumps of the trees from which the rails had been created. Oglesby chose two of the best rails and tied them under the rear axle of his buggy, and he and Hanks rode back to Decatur. Oglesby planned to put the rails to good use by creating a new image for Abraham Lincoln, one that would replace the stale and uninspiring nicknames of "Old Abe" and "Honest Abe."[3]

"Before the convention met I talked with several Republicans about my plan," declared Oglesby. He apparently talked to too many party members, for one of them nearly revealed what was about to happen to thousands of readers of the *Illinois State Journal*. On May 4, a Republican correspondent closed his preconvention report to the *Journal* with the following teaser:

> *Among the sights which will greet your eyes will be a lot of rails mauled out of Burr Oak and Walnut, thirty years ago by Old Abe Lincoln and John Hanks of this county. They are still sound and firm, like the men that made them. Shall we not elect the Rail Mauler President? His rails, like his political record, are straight, sound, and out of good timber.*[4]

The reporter's revealing letter was published in the May 8 issue of the *Journal*. Lincoln may not have seen it that Tuesday, for he was on his way to Decatur. It rained hard and heavily that day, and when Lincoln arrived he immediately sought shelter at the Junction House, where he registered and shared a room with two delegates from Scott County. Lincoln was one of more than four thousand Republicans to swell Decatur's population for the convention. Delegates and conventioneers packed the trains; Springfield alone had sent hundreds of Republicans to Decatur, most of them making the forty-five-mile trip on the Great Western Railroad. Hotels, boardinghouses, and private residences took in the travelers for this anticipated two-day event.

The two most important items of business to be accomplished by the convention were to select the twenty-two delegates that would head to Chicago for the Republican National Convention the following week, and to officially nominate the candidates for the state offices of Illinois. Of the latter, the most intriguing was the gubernatorial nomination, for it not only pitted Norman Judd against two other candidates (Bloomington lawyer Leonard Swett and Jacksonville's Richard Yates), but it also added another round to the contest between Judd and Long John Wentworth. Most important for Lincoln was to secure a unit vote from the delegates chosen for the national convention—an outcome he was confident he would secure.

The rains and wind dissipated, and Wednesday morning was clear and cool. The convention opened in the wigwam at ten A.M. Several hours were required to appoint convention officers and to fill committee. By early afternoon the wigwam was standing room only with three thousand Republicans wedged inside it and another two thousand crowding outside. Lincoln barely found space in the makeshift structure, sitting on his heels at the opposite end from the platform, just inside the door.[5]

John M. Palmer, the temporary chairman of the event, turned over his duties to the newly selected president of the convention, Joseph Gillespie, lawyer and politician as well as a good friend of Lincoln's from the time he volunteered in the same militia company in the Black Hawk War in 1832. But neither Palmer nor Gillespie would direct the next course of action. Dick Oglesby now took it upon himself to spring his convention surprise.

Oglesby made his way up to the platform, got the attention of the conventioneers, and announced that "a distinguished citizen of Illinois—and one whom Illinois would ever delight to honor—was present." Oglesby made a motion that the convention allow this citizen to have a seat on the platform. Oglesby withheld naming him; according to a witness, he seemed to do so "as if to tease expectation to the verge of desperation." Finally, Oglesby blurted out his name: "Abraham Lincoln."

The wigwam responded in applause upon hearing Lincoln's name.

The conventioneers redirected their gazes from the platform to the back of the room, where Lincoln had been sitting. "Everybody in that vicinity, seemed inspired with a new born desire to get close to him—to take hold of him," observed another spectator near the door. Take hold of him they did, and more. Unable to push through the dense crowd, Lincoln was literally lifted from his feet and hoisted over the heads of the crowd. With cheers exploding near his ears, he negotiated toward the platform by clambering and crawling over the heads and outstretched hands of the packed wigwam while uplifted hands pushed him toward the front. "Lincoln was a mighty long man," remembered one who was there, "but they carried him down over their heads right over everybody in the crowd. I have heard of that sort of thing, but never before nor since have I seen a long fellow like Lincoln passed hand over hand over a solid mass of people." Lincoln reached the stage greeted by the roaring of the sea of people and the tossing of hats—"as if hats were no longer useful." Lincoln was overwhelmed and a little embarrassed by it all, but he still managed a polite bow. Once the applause subsided, he smiled and thanked the participants "for their Manifestations of Esteem." He then sat in a chair on the stage as the proceedings continued.[6]

Oglesby really knew how to milk a moment, and he had more in store for this crowd. Lincoln was seated on the platform with the convention officers as they began a preliminary vote for the gubernatorial nominee. But before the official balloting commenced, Oglesby interrupted the proceedings again. He announced that "an old Democrat of Macon county, who had grown gray in the service of that party," desired to give the convention a present. Many in the crowd affirmed the offer by hollering "Receive it!" while others yelled "What is it?" The unknown offer was accepted amid this great commotion.[7]

The commotion turned to pandemonium as the door in the back of the wigwam opened. Lincoln appeared as puzzled as everyone else in the hall about what Oglesby had in store for them. As he strained to see what was happening near the door, an incredible burst of enthusiasm rippled toward the platform. "Whenever that crowd cheered," wrote one who was in the wigwam that day, "one had to anchor himself to the ground to prevent being raised off his feet." This moment it appeared that even anchors would fail to keep the men grounded.[8]

John Hanks and a Decatur carpenter named Isaac Jennings entered the wigwam carrying Oglesby's surprise. Each man held upright one of the two rails that Hanks had identified for Oglesby as ones Lincoln had split. At the top of the parallel rails, attached to a board that adjoined them over the men's heads, was a handmade banner evoking a new image for Lincoln supporters to embrace:[9]

ABE LINCOLN

THE RAIL CANDIDATE

OF THE PEOPLE FOR 1860

TWO RAILS FROM A LOT OF 3,000

MADE BY

ABE LINCOLN AND JOHN HANKS

IN 1830, TEN MILES WEST OF DECATUR.

THE FATHER OF ABE LINCOLN,

THE FIRST SQUATTER

IN MACON COUNTY.

Oglesby had performed perfectly. Although "Old Abe" and "Honest Abe" would remain embedded in the lexicon of the Sucker State, this new symbol for Lincoln was one that would tantalize the eastern states—the tall, rough-hewn, ax-wielding Western candidate.[10] And the convention crowd absolutely loved it. Everybody was on their feet, waving their hats and chanting Lincoln's name. As Hanks and Jennings slowly paraded the rails and banner seventy feet to the front of the platform, a stunned convention-eer noted that "the tempest of enthusiasm burst forth, wilder—Stronger and more furious than before. The Chicago and Central Illinois folks seemed perfectly besides themselves." The same witness studied Lincoln and claimed that he "seemed to shake with inward laughter" as chants to make a speech rang in his ears.[11]

What could Lincoln say? The surprising moment was exhilarating but also so ironic that it left him temporarily speechless. The banner was somewhat inaccurate in its claim, for his father had not been nearly the first pioneer of the area (and he'd left Macon County after only one year to resettle sixty miles east of it). More striking was the largely fictitious message it portrayed. Lincoln grew up hating the idea of living life splitting rails and toiling on a farm—the life his father had been resolved to live. He preferred reading to manual labor, and had been so ashamed of his humble past that back in December 1858 he'd refused to reveal it in a short autobiography. But he had warmed to the idea over the following year, showing some pride in his wilderness upbringing in his Indianapolis speech and in the autobiography he wrote in December 1859.

But Oglesby had shown Lincoln right then and there in the Decatur wigwam that he should embrace the image he had been running away from. Back in 1840 Lincoln had been extremely active as a state campaign manager for the election of William Henry Harrison as the ninth president of the United States. No one could fault him if images of the "Hard Cider and Log Cabin Campaign" flashed in front of him when he saw those rails and that banner. As the delegates and other convention members chanted for him to speak, Lincoln must have realized that Oglesby's coup guaranteed a unit vote for him by the Illinois delegates to the national convention—even though that resolution would not be introduced in the state convention for another day.

Yet, Lincoln still could not embrace the image, choosing instead to stay at arm's length from it. With his hands folded in front of him, Lincoln walked to the front end of the platform, "looking very much amused." He spoke in a more reserved tone than the moment called for. "Gentlemen," Lincoln announced as he pointed to the rails, "I suppose you want to know something about those things." He went on to claim that he and John Hanks had indeed made rails in the Sangamon Bottoms thirty years earlier, although he could not confirm that those two rails were authentically his creations. He then mocked the quality of the rails and proclaimed, "I can make better ones than these now." Not willing to hold up the convention proceedings any longer, Lincoln ended the speech there and sat back down in his chair on the platform.[12]

The crowd soaked up Lincoln's brief acknowledgment, but some of the most perceptive ones saw right through him. "After it was all over with I began to think I could smell a very large mouse," insisted a man surnamed Johnson, who caught on to the notion that "this whole thing, was a cunningly devised thing of knowing ones, to make Mr. Lincoln, President, and that banner was to be the 'Battle flag.' "[13] Johnson was in the minority, for most in the wigwam were consumed by the apparent spontaneity of the moment. Few sensed Lincoln's trepidation about being defined by the inscription on Oglesby's sign. Instead, they looked forward to converting that banner into the battle flag for Illinois Republicans, and turning it into the national standard for the party.

Norman Judd witnessed the transformation of Lincoln from a practitioner of law to a mauler of rails, but he could not relish the moment. Immediately after Lincoln sat down, the official balloting to select the Republican nominee for governor began. The very nature of a three-man contest heightened the uncertainty over who would win the nod. Judd could count on a slew of delegates, but informal preliminary balloting revealed he did not have the majority required to win on the first ballot. That Long John Wentworth was pressing for his downfall intensified the moment. Three successive ballots failed to push Judd over the threshold of 318; he was stuck at 255, then 263, then 252. Leonard Swett progressively lost votes, and Richard Yates rose from 197 to 238. Realizing they could not win, all but 36 of Swett's supporters voted for Dick Yates, who upended Judd on the fourth ballot and became the nominee of the Republican Party for governor of Illinois.[14]

Judd's crushing defeat became Wentworth's triumph. He had withstood a libel suit to cut Judd down, and on Wednesday afternoon he finally succeeded. He had been highly visible in Decatur for two days, his height elevating him a head above most others in the wigwam, where he had delivered a rousing speech against Norman Judd the previous evening. With Judd's loss and David Davis's support, Wentworth hoped and perhaps expected to be given a major role in the national convention in Chicago. As mayor of the host city, he expected Lincoln to choose him as one of the at-large delegates, one who would cast Judd aside as a less important Chicagoan.[15]

Wentworth's unbridled joy was short-lived. Immediately after Richard Yates addressed the wigwam on his nomination victory, the crowd chanted for Judd. There had been rumors floating about that if Judd did not win the nomination, he and his supporters would bolt from the party. According to a reporter, Judd appeared "somewhat excited at first." But he calmed down as he pledged his devotion to the Republican cause. He denounced all the wild rumors about his dissatisfaction and his threats to fractionate the party. He personally ratified Yates's nomination and exhorted that the delegates fight the Democrats with the same spirit and zeal that his enemies had fought him. His composure and conciliation won over the crowd, who cheered him repeatedly during his short speech and extended their hearty applause for him when he finished it.[16]

He also won over the reporters and editors of the Republican papers that supported other candidates. The *Chicago Journal* had rarely credited Judd for any of his accomplishments in the past but was moved by his "eloquent speech." The *Bloomington Pantagraph*—an obviously pro-Swett paper—hailed Judd for "his gallant, noble and manly bearing after his defeat," and characterized his speech as "earnest, judicious, and well timed, to say nothing of its honest, practical character."[17]

That is the way that Lincoln considered Judd, much to Wentworth's dismay. After the first day's proceedings ended that afternoon, Lincoln rounded up Judd, David Davis, Leonard Swett, and members of the committee appointed to select delegates to the Chicago convention. They exited the wigwam and isolated themselves in a nearby grove—likely the one-year-old square later named Central Park—in front of the building. The men lay down in the grass and studied the committee's list of delegates to be submitted to the convention for adoption the next day. According to Burton C. Cook of the committee, Lincoln and the others revised the list prior to its submission. The list included two delegates for each district (eighteen in all) with alternates. This left Lincoln with four at-large delegates to complete the slate of twenty-two.[18]

Lincoln revealed the names of the four delegates he preferred. One was Gustave Koerner, a solid choice who could rally the Germans in Chicago to support him in the balloting in Chicago. Lincoln also selected Orville

H. Browning, perhaps surprising Judd because of his outspoken support for Bates over Lincoln. But Lincoln wanted the Old Whig element well represented, and he had known Browning since the 1830s and considered him experienced enough to handle the duties. Lincoln also named Judd, rewarding him for his sacrifices, support, dedication, and experience. Judd's Chicago connections would also help at the convention, a factor that must have weighed in Lincoln's decision.

David Davis would have been the only member of the conference to be disappointed in Judd's selection. This meant that Lincoln would not select Long John Wentworth. Once again Lincoln had ignored Davis's advice. But Lincoln found a way to satisfy Davis with a happy surprise. Lincoln chose *him* as a delegate at large, to round out the slate.

There is no indication that Davis expected this honor. He had likely conferred with Lincoln in March or April and agreed to help out at the national convention by making sure he was present in Chicago. Lincoln had written to others in April, placing Davis's name at the top of his list of confidential friends, and instructing a correspondent to meet with the judge in Chicago when he went there to attend the convention. Lincoln had disregarded Davis's advice, but in doing so he disregarded Davis's unexplainable devotion to Wentworth and the poorly hidden animus he had held against Norman Judd.

The committee took the revised list with it into the wigwam on Thursday morning, May 10, and the delegates accepted the report. Other state nominees were chosen by ballot, and the presidential electors were named. Then John M. Palmer offered up a resolution that had been rendered something of a formality by what had happened in the building the previous day: "That Hon. Abraham Lincoln is the first choice of the Republican party of Illinois for the Presidency, and that our delegates are instructed to use all honorable means to secure his nomination by the Chicago Convention, and to vote as a unit for him." A Chicago delegate attempted to strike the final words "for him," ostensibly to leave the door open to vote as a unit for Seward or another candidate if "all honorable means" had been exhausted for Lincoln. The amendment failed, and—as Lincoln and Judd had expected—Palmer's resolution passed unanimously.[19]

The convention closed Thursday afternoon with many winners, including gubernatorial candidate Richard Yates. But in defeat Norman

Judd came out a winner after his affecting speech. Not only was he a delegate at large, but the positive impression he made cleared any opposition to his being selected to head the State Central Committee for another term, this one with new members such as David Davis on it. Never before had he received universally positive press as he did for his performance in the wigwam, an effort that considerably weakened the influence of Long John Wentworth. Judd left the state convention a party hero. The *Illinois State Journal* hailed him: "There is probably no man in the State to whom the Republicans of Illinois are under greater obligations for the present commanding position of their party, than the Hon. Norman B. Judd, of Cook County." The *Bloomington Pantagraph* went further: "All honor to Norman B. Judd of Cook County," it crowed.[20]

The biggest winner, of course, was Abraham Lincoln. He left the convention with the unit vote he had sought, a slate of supporting delegates that met his approval, and a vibrant campaign image that could only enhance his presidential prospects. The immediate and automatic outcome to this could be seen in most the Republican-biased papers of Illinois with their first issues published after the convention. "For President, Abraham Lincoln of Illinois," blared their headlines (though many added a parenthetical disclaimer: "subject to the decision of the Republican National Convention").

Lincoln and his supporters were buoyed by the fact that the candidate was booming so perfectly. But Illinois was not the benchmark for the country. The task before Lincoln's delegates was to carry the momentum of the state convention into Chicago, develop a strategy to keep undecided delegates away from William H. Seward and place them in Lincoln's camp, and somehow convince other delegates more friendly to Seward to switch their allegiances to Lincoln as well.

Lincoln would not be joining them. No announced candidate had ever attended the national convention to see his team work to win his nomination; it was considered as undignified in 1860 America as was openly campaigning for the nomination. The political decorum was to leave this business to one's handlers. But the practice did not sit well with Lincoln. He had adopted a pat response to the question of whether he would attend the convention, one he used at least three times in the week between the Decatur convention and the national one: "I am too much of a candidate to go and not quite enough to stay at home."[21]

Nationally, Lincoln was not considered a major candidate. The day after he returned to Springfield, the country's widest-circulating illustrated periodical, *Harper's Weekly Illustrated Newspaper*, displayed the faces of what it considered to be the top eleven Republican candidates for the presidential nomination in Chicago. The centerfold collage consisted of all Brady images. To no one's surprise, William Henry Seward's visage occupied the center, flanked on either side by sets of five other faces of presidential hopefuls, each quintet designed like a house with two images stacked upon each other with the fifth on top forming the roof. Lincoln's face made it onto the page, his image taken from Brady's studio photograph the day of his Cooper Union address. Brady's remarkable photograph—he somehow made Lincoln appear handsome—appears to have been displayed for the first time in this May 12 centerfold, but the face was on the lower right corner of the left side of the collage, surrounded by Salmon P. Chase and John C. Frémont, as well as by a panoramic view of Washington; thus, it failed to grab attention. Biographical sketches of these candidates filled another page. Not only was Lincoln's biographical paragraph the shortest of the eleven, but it was one of the last ones presented. At least *Harper's* mentioned him; two campaign handbooks published at the same time failed to include Lincoln in their biographical sketches of Republican candidates.[22]

The less than prominent display spoke volumes about the uphill climb ahead for Lincoln's team to carry their man over the top. Any strategy he discussed with his managers, particularly the at-large delegates, took place in Decatur. He had done all that he could to carry his message as far and wide as he could, to wipe out any radicalism associated with his two-year-old "House Divided" speech, and to get all who took in any of his speeches in person or in print to consider the messenger as well as the message. From this point on Lincoln was forced to endure several days of uncertainty. He would receive news from the convention in the newspapers (one day delayed from the actual event), and telegrams would transmit personal messages to him in the office of the *Illinois State Journal*. His letter to his Kansas friend Mark Delahay, who was already in Chicago as a member of the Lincoln team, contained the same message he wished to convey to all his supporters: "[B]e careful to give no offence, and keep cool under all circumstances."[23]

The rest was up to them.

Ten

CONVENTION WEEK

DAVID DAVIS STEPPED off the train in Chicago on Saturday morning, May 12, dedicated to winning the nomination of Abraham Lincoln. He was much more optimistic about Lincoln's chances than he had been three months earlier. "Lincoln can be elected President," proclaimed Davis earlier that month. "If he is not nominated at Chicago, the Republican party will regret it." Now he found himself in charge of preventing those regrets. The convention was set to begin on Wednesday, May 16, but Davis wanted to have the Lincoln machine up and running before Monday, the day when Chicago was expected to be flooded by delegates, supporters, and journalists.[1]

It appears that Davis and Lincoln had communicated in April, with Davis agreeing to be in Chicago for the convention. He was never appointed the chairman of Lincoln's team, but the fact that he oversaw the operation without dissent from the other delegates indicates that it was an assumed role that everyone else understood. It appears Lincoln's decision to make Davis an at-large delegate was an afterthought, one that materialized at the time of the state convention in Decatur. The decision strengthened Davis's role in Chicago, but it cannot be ruled out that Lincoln chose Davis as a delegate to leave the impression that the judge was taking the position Davis had earlier suggested for Long John Wentworth to fill. Regardless of the reasons behind the move, Lincoln deemed it imperative to have Davis there where his organizational and leadership skills could dominate. But Davis's abilities could not completely mask his lack of experience. Not only had he never been part of a delegation at a national convention, but he had never even attended one.

Davis was blessed with the interpersonal skills necessary to negotiate with the most obstinate delegations. Those attributes were sharpened and honed from his decades of dedicated service on the Eighth Judicial Circuit. He was as good a listener as he was a conversationalist, and his genial nature could only help him in Chicago. His obesity would handicap lesser people, but Davis's more pleasant features balanced his corpulence. The judge was a tall, light-haired man with small and delicate hands and feet and a fair complexion. A friend of his insisted that Davis "was in spite of his heaviness rather attractive."[2]

Judge Davis was dismayed to learn that every candidate had headquarters established in the city—everybody except Lincoln, that is. No one had bothered to reserve rooms, an oversight that led to finger-pointing at Norman Judd, Lincoln's Chicago man, who appears to have disregarded this function. Davis made his way to the Tremont House, the ten-year-old, 260-room hotel on the corner of Lake and Dearborn streets, five blocks from the convention site. Bates's managers had rooms reserved there for several months, and apparently all the other candidate teams had reserved space for weeks. Fortunately for Davis (and Lincoln), there were still available rooms. The judge rented two of them and got to work.[3]

Other Lincoln supporters, like Mark Delahay, were already in the Tremont House and wooing delegates. Once they learned that the Lincoln headquarters were established, Delahay and other supporters escorted other state delegates to Davis's rooms. No one who was in the Tremont House supporting Lincoln rested that weekend. Discussions continued in earnest on Sunday. Minnesota's and Kansas's delegations were not swayed from their rock-solid devotion to Seward, but some of Iowa's delegation appeared to warm somewhat to Lincoln, although they had only seven men and not all of them were going to commit to the "Rail Candidate."

Davis counted on much greater support from Indiana's delegation. The Hoosier State had indicated since the winter that it would not commit to Seward, but it had not completely committed to Lincoln either, for some delegates were still Bates men. Still, this was a state that was completely winnable for the Lincoln team. Davis was also encouraged by Ohio's delegation. Eight of its forty-six members declared their commitment to Lincoln and were urging the others to do so as well. Others in the delegation were strongly for Judge McLean, a fellow Buckeye, while all sensed an undercurrent for Senator Benjamin F. Wade as a potential dark horse Ohioan. None of this boded well for Salmon P. Chase. He could no longer be considered a top-tier candidate, a fact spelled out for him by one of his managers in Chicago, who compared notes with other delegates and decided to deliver the bad news even before the start of convention week. "I have never deceived you and shall not begin now," wrote Edward L. Pierce to Chase on Sunday; "I do not believe from present indications that Seward or yourself will be nominated."[4]

Pierce's pessimistic prediction for Chase was an accurate one, but it was premature for Seward. The primary reason for this was the skills and influence of Thurlow Weed, the first Republican boss of New York State and Seward's manager, and arguably the ablest political tactician in the country. Weed was a savvy veteran of rough-and-tumble politics, and he was not one to be worried about emotional perceptions, particularly concerning his candidate, for William H. Seward was still the front-runner and the odds-on favorite to win the nomination within the first two ballots. Although it is unlikely that Weed entirely perceived the early accomplishments of Lincoln's team, he knew his man was an inviting target for his critics to strike, and he was prepared to do everything possible to neutralize the opposition and get Seward nominated—hopefully on the first ballot. Weed was respected by all of Seward's opponents, although one of them firmly believed that "One hundred Thurlow Weeds cannot nominate Seward if he does not suit the fancy of the hour."[5]

Weed arrived in Chicago early and was already in place with his headquarters at the Richmond House before the delegates had begun to flow into the city by rail. With headquarters established and an efficient team in place, Weed could keep a delegate count of firm versus lukewarm support for Seward. He also benefited from the presence of Governor Edwin Morgan, the chairman of the Republican National Committee, who set up a secondary headquarters for Seward at the Tremont House. Weed had arrived in Chicago with five states and Kansas Territory firmly in his corner,

assuring Seward nearly half the delegates he needed to win on the first ballot. In addition, Weed could count on most of the delegates from the New
England states and some of the delegates from the central states to edge
him closer to the total.[6]

Yet on Sunday, before the start of the convention, Weed had to be aware
that Seward's chances to win on the first ballot were not as strong as they
had been during the winter. Too many "favorite sons" were bound to receive first-ballot recognition from their respective states. This left Weed
with the task of wooing those delegates on the second ballot. The most
prized state in this category was Pennsylvania, whose huge cadre of delegates would likely guarantee Seward's nomination if Weed's team could
unite them for Seward after they registered their complimentary vote for Simon Cameron on the first ballot. Weed also eyed New Jersey (committed to
native William Dayton, the Republican Party's first vice-presidential candidate in 1856, on the first ballot); he also looked westward with hopes of
hooking Chase's Ohio and even Lincoln's Illinois.

With Weed firmly planted at the Richmond House and Morgan too
close for comfort at the Tremont House, the Lincoln team intensified its
efforts. Jesse Dubois was awed at Davis's energy that weekend, claiming he
"never saw him work so hard and so quick in his life." What had encouraged Davis was a strong response for Lincoln and some wavering from Seward. Most of the states would not be registering a unit vote for the
presidential nomination. This was a huge benefit for Lincoln, for he could
receive a few votes from several other states on the first ballot. This would
add to the twenty-two committed votes from Illinois and most—if not
all—of the twenty-six from Indiana. The Lincoln camp also received a
positive response from the Massachusetts delegation. Lincoln was well
spoken of among a small contingent, although this was still regarded as a
Seward state. Maine and New Hampshire also prepared to make a solid
front for Lincoln.[7]

So two and a half days before the convention, the Lincoln team had
overcome the handicap of a late start to achieve a preliminary goal for
their candidate. The value of a delegate's vote would be determined during the convention. Since 2 delegates represented one electoral vote for
each state, there would be 465 delegates representing twenty-four states
and territories present. It was still unknown if each delegate vote would

be counted, or if two from each state were required for one electoral vote. Regardless, Davis went to bed Sunday night likely believing he had a good shot at securing one of his two goals—obtaining a hundred delegate votes for Lincoln on the first ballot. Most important was to make sure that the voting did not end after one ballot. This required an effort to prevent Seward from gaining the majority of ballots required to win the nomination.[8]

The Lincoln managers awoke on Monday morning to news that New York and Pennsylvania delegates had been verbally sparring with one another. This dispute improved Lincoln's chances, for if Seward was unable to obtain the necessary votes on the first ballot, he could not count on the neighboring state of Pennsylvania—with the second-highest delegate votes at fifty-four—on subsequent balloting. William Butler, a Springfield friend, kept Lincoln apprised of the goings-on with daily letters from Chicago; he was quite pleased about the eastern rivalry, for each feuding state told the Illinois men not to go for the rival candidate under any circumstances, thus playing into the Illinois plan. But each of the states thought it was throwing Illinois a bone by proposing to run Lincoln as vice president. Butler assured Lincoln, "We have persistently refused to Suffer your name used for Vice President on any ticket."

That same Monday the Lincoln team added more space to their headquarters by securing a parlor at the Tremont House to carry out their discussions. They also firmed up Indiana's support with the help of Gustave Koerner. The German at-large delegate convinced the Indiana delegation that the Germans would bolt from the party if any of their delegates stayed with Bates, a renowned supporter of Know Nothing principles. The mission was to have Indiana secured as a unit vote for Lincoln. The objective appeared met that Monday. "Indiana is all right," proclaimed Mark Delahay to Lincoln that day; Nathan Knapp reported, "Things are working; keep a good nerve."[9]

Davis and the Lincoln team steeled themselves to confront the irrepressible force of the Seward machine. The New York barrage stormed into Chicago on Monday in thirteen packed cars on the rail line—nearly two thousand Seward men arriving at once. Whereas the Lincoln team scraped and clawed for rooms and a parlor at one hotel for headquarters, the Seward organization seemingly had rooms in every major hotel in

Chicago—and there were more than forty of them. Weed's skills at organization yielded an overwhelming product by the end of Monday, two
days before the convention was scheduled to begin.[10]

Notwithstanding the bull rush of Seward's "Irrepressibles" and Weed's
looming presence, the Lincoln team remained guardedly confident. They
completed their first day of convention week with Indiana completely in
their corner and with votes from several other states committed to Lincoln. The century goal was well within reach. They also believed by
Monday night that all the other candidates were taking votes away from
Seward on the first ballot, preventing the front-runner from claiming the
nomination in the first round. Seward's people also sensed the resistance to
their candidate and understood that more than one ballot would be
needed to achieve the 233 delegate votes (more than half of the 465 delegates expected to ballot) necessary to seal the bid. What Seward's team did
not grasp by Monday night was the strength of Lincoln's first-ballot support. All indications suggested that Lincoln had home-state commitment,
just as William Dayton had in New Jersey. They were also aware that Indiana would give him votes as well. But Seward's supporters had a solid grip
on Wisconsin—Illinois's northern neighbor—and Bates of course had a
lock on Missouri, preventing a regional spread of Lincoln's influence. The
"Sewardites" never conceived that Lincoln had anywhere near 100 delegates supporting him on the first ballot, nor could they fathom that he had
risen to second place in the crowded field of Republicans by the end of
the first day of convention week.

Lincoln's managers had their candidate close to the exact position they
wanted him to be on Monday, May 14. Newspaper correspondents sensed
the upsurge. "Lincoln's stock is on the rise," reported the newsman from
the *Philadelphia Press* that day. "Abe Lincoln is looming up to-night as a
compromise candidate and his friends are in high spirits," asserted the reporter for the *Boston Herald*. Murat Halstead of the *Cincinnati Daily Commercial* echoed this sentiment by informing his readers on Monday night
that Lincoln "seems to be gaining ground, and his Illinois friends are
greatly encouraged tonight at the prospect of his uniting on the doubtful
States and the North-West." The Democratic *New York Herald* winnowed
down the contest Monday night to one between Seward, Lincoln, and
Wade, an assessment repeated the next day by Halstead. These reports

clearly indicated that Abraham Lincoln could no longer be called a dark horse candidate.[11]

Incredibly, most of the Chicago press refused to raise Lincoln's status to the same high tier as did the out-of-state reporters. The *Chicago Journal* was a pro-Seward paper. It did not officially advocate his nomination as the *Press and Tribune* had done for Lincoln, but the *Journal* did routinely publish positive articles about Seward during convention week. The staff at the paper also hung a huge "Seward" banner outside their office—in plain view of the Illinois delegation at the Tremont House across the street. Feeling the pro-Lincoln sentiment pulsing throughout the city, the *Journal* did not fail to recognize Illinois's favorite son—"with either as our candidate, we feel sure of Illinois"—but editor Charles Wilson beat the drum louder and louder for the front-runner. His Seward advocacy ruffled the feathers of the Lincoln machine, inducing one to write Lincoln on May 15, "I feel much incouraged [*sic*] though you Must be prepared for defeat. Wentworth & Wilson are both against you."[12]

Wentworth posed a more troublesome obstacle for the Lincoln machine. Perhaps smarting over the snub at not being chosen as an at-large delegate to the convention or as a member of the retooled State Central Committee, Wentworth chose to highlight Seward in his paper as the man to nominate. Rumors swirled that he was in cahoots with Thurlow Weed to advertise Seward's candidacy in the *Democrat*. As mayor, Wentworth flexed his muscles, ordering a raid upon the city's brothels—arrests that included many convention delegates.

But Wentworth's articles and editorials irritated Lincoln's team more than anything else he did. The paper launched convention week with biographies of thirteen candidates for the nomination, choosing to run the feature in alphabetical order of each man's surname. Not only was his feature on Lincoln buried at the end of the piece; it was the shortest of the thirteen biographies, with a mere ten lines of column print dedicated to him (Chase received a hundred lines; even long-shot Nathaniel Banks of Massachusetts earned five times more ink than Lincoln). Joseph Medill at the *Press and Tribune* complained to Lincoln that Long John was wielding "all his power to defeat your nomination." Mark Delahay concurred. "I for one think he is a *dog*," he seethed of Wentworth, "and unworthy to be called a member of our party."[13]

Norman Judd told Lincoln that he considered Wentworth "politically ruined, unless resuscitated by your friend Judge Davis' like or fear of him and dislike of me." But Davis no longer was raving about the "wonderful power of John Wentworth" that he had espoused in April. Recognizing that Wentworth's grudge was harmful to Lincoln's nomination, Davis admitted, "I have reluctantly come to the conclusion that he wants to beat" Lincoln. Wentworth had taken his destructive act into the hotel lobbies, proclaiming boisterously for Seward with the stentorian voice expected of a giant. Davis's only recourse against the ostentatious mayor was to detail a Lincoln supporter to follow Wentworth wherever he went and to counter him every time he made remarks damaging to Lincoln.[14]

The *Press and Tribune* was the only Chicago paper pressing for Lincoln's nomination. Not only did the paper hoist Lincoln's name "for President," it also ran daily supporting articles of him throughout convention week. The paper stressed that Lincoln was the only candidate who could beat Douglas in Illinois, calculating that he had actually received 4,000 more votes "from the people" in the 1858 U.S. Senate race, in which 250,000 votes were cast. "These figures," ran an editorial, "show to our friends from distant States the delicate, yet hopeful ground on which we stand." The Democratic press in Springfield, in a position to objectively compare the three chief Republican organs of Chicago, acknowledged that the *Press and Tribune* exclusively "makes a loud appeal for Lincoln as the man for success."[15]

Charles Ray, the proprietor of the *Chicago Press and Tribune*, had concluded that the ground was too delicate to stand upon for Lincoln supporters in Chicago. He firmly believed that some backroom dealing—normal for political conventions—had to be conducted. Although these bargains were sometimes considered essential, it was an unattractive necessity and one that the public had frowned upon ever since the "corrupt bargain" of 1824 between Henry Clay and John Quincy Adams secured the presidential election for the latter and the powerful position of secretary of state for the former. Ray felt it equally imperative to obtain the blessing of the candidate to conduct the necessary negotiations. In a letter he marked "profoundly private," Ray laid out the case to Lincoln:

> *Your friends are at work for you hard, and with great success. Your show on the first ballot will not be confined to Illinois, and after that it will be*

strongly developed. But you need a few trusty friends here to say words for
you that may be necessary to be said. . . . A pledge or two may be neces-
sary when the pinch comes. Don't be too sanguine. Matters now look well
and as things stand to-day I had rather have your chances than those of any
other man. But don't get excited.[16]

Despite Ray's plea, no specific bargains had been necessary by the close
of Monday. Indiana's delegation was easily wooed to Lincoln without exchanging its support for a cabinet position, but still with an implicit understanding that the Hoosiers would get high consideration for their
votes. Pulling Indiana over to Lincoln's side without concrete promises
was a coup for the Illinois team. Jesse Fell afterward explained that "a dis-
position of favors was a good deal spoken of at Chicago, in a quiet way,
though of course no improper pledges . . . were asked . . . and [they]
could not be given." Although Fell's assertion was challenged later in the
convention, Caleb B. Smith, a high-ranking Indiana delegate in Chicago,
confirmed the tactics of ambiguity employed by the Illinois team when he
stated, "The Republicans of [Indiana] *generally supposed* that Mr. L. would
select some man from this state for a place in his cabinet [emphasis
added]." Newspaper correspondents felt confident enough on Tuesday,
May 15—the day before the official proceedings—to report: "Illinois and
Indiana are for Abe Lincoln." But no other state was willing to commit its
delegates to Lincoln by a unit vote, so the task ahead for Davis and the Illinois men at the Tremont House was to fractionate state delegations to ac-
crue votes for Lincoln wherever possible.[17]

"The nomination at present lies between Seward and Lincoln," proclaimed an Illinois insider on May 15. In a mere three days the Lincoln
machine in Chicago had made giant strides in its uphill climb to overcome the lack of unified support from the Chicago press, the incredible
power of Weed and the Seward machine, and the insufficient manpower
in Lincoln's camp. Their success behind the scenes was no longer a secret,
for the press had already begun to report on Lincoln's ascension from also-
ran to top-tier candidate by Tuesday morning, twenty-four hours before
the convention officially began. Obviously cued in to the best inside information at the hotel headquarters, Murat Halstead correctly informed
his readers of the *Cincinnati Daily Commercial* at noon on Tuesday that

Salmon Chase had no chance and that the nomination contest had been whittled down to two people. "My present impression is that the test fight will come between Seward and Lincoln," he reported.[18]

Lincoln's team strengthened that Tuesday when Orville H. Browning and the remaining Lincoln delegates finally arrived in Chicago and appeared at the Tremont House headquarters. Browning arrived before breakfast, and Davis immediately put him to work. Davis and Browning met with the Maine and Massachusetts delegations. Browning delivered short speeches and apprised them of "the aspect of political affairs in Illinois." Fortunately for Davis, these were not the first visits to these delegations, for Davis had overseen visits to these statesmen since Saturday. Browning's late arrival was never explained, although his notorious support for Edward Bates prior to the convention had concerned the Illinois men all along. Davis was so concerned about Browning that he felt compelled to take him aside and assure him that there was "no earthly chance for Bates to win the nomination," even considering the efforts of Horace Greeley to promote the Missouri Whig. Davis was swiftly satisfied that Browning was a dedicated advocate of Abraham Lincoln and no one else.[19]

Davis had no reason to complain about Browning's work, but one delegate caught his ire. This was Stephen T. Logan, Lincoln's law partner prior to Billy Herndon, one of two delegates representing Illinois's Sixth Congressional District. What Davis needed, in the absence of money, was a team of influential men—cajolers. He was disappointed to find out quickly that Logan was not up to this task. Davis complained in an interview six years later that this necessary trait was not part of Logan's nature, and it showed in Chicago. "Logan did nothing much," Davis reportedly told his interviewer; "[he] was not the kind of man to go to men and order—Command or Coax men to do what he wanted them to do."[20]

Logan appears to have been the lone exception on the Lincoln team. Not only were all of the twenty-two delegates dedicated to their task, so were editors Ray and Medill of the *Chicago Press and Tribune*. Davis also depended on fellow Bloomingtonians Jesse Fell and Leonard Swett, members of the Illinois Republican State Central Committee (old and new), gubernatorial nominee Richard Yates, and Illinois men chosen as alternates to the delegation. Adding out-of-state supporters like Mark Delahay made the Lincoln machine a small but efficient force of perhaps thirty-five total operatives working for a common cause.

These operators of the Lincoln machine delivered a fairly consistent message to the Republican delegates. Not only did they hype Lincoln's middle-ground position and his attractive but disingenuous "railsplitter" background, they also focused on toppling Seward from the mantel of choices. By linking Seward with his "Irrepressible Conflict" speech to present him as too radical to win a general election against any Democrat who should eventually win the opposing party's nomination, Lincoln's team coaxed the delegates to their man as the best available choice for Republicans. In most cases, the Illinois men worked the other state delegates as if this were a contest between Lincoln and Seward, paying the other ten to twelve potential candidates little heed. Their mission was to forecast the Electoral College's totals in November, and to convince the undeclared delegates that even if Seward could sweep through several states north of the Mason-Dixon Line (no Republican was going to win a Southern state in 1860) he could not win the majority of states that Frémont had lost four years earlier. Thus, the Lincoln men turned this into a contest to win Illinois, Indiana, Pennsylvania, and New Jersey. And with Indiana locked in with Lincoln's delegation, and Pennsylvania's and New York's delegations sparring with each other, the pitch for Lincoln and against Seward not only was a focused message, but became a more plausible one during convention week.

The sales pitch the Lincoln team delivered to state delegates had to be tailored to the demands of the occasion. The New Jersey team, for example, presented a problem that David Davis could not solve alone. Despite his entreaties, the Garden State delegation still insisted on Seward as the top of its ticket with Lincoln as his vice president. Unable to sway the delegates from this seemingly fixed decision, Davis returned to the New Jersey men accompanied by John Palmer, selected in Decatur as an Illinois member of the Electoral College. Together, they found a unique way to split the Seward–Lincoln ticket in the minds of this delegation. Palmer insisted that this ticket was a surefire loser because both Seward and Lincoln were former Whigs, and there were forty thousand Illinois Democrats who were strongly leaning Republican in 1860 but would never vote for a ticket with two ex-Whigs and no former Democrat on it. "You must take a Democrat for one of these offices," insisted Palmer—meaning, of course, an anti-Nebraska Democrat who had joined the new Republican Party after 1854. The ploy was risky, for Lincoln could be dropped from consideration because of his former-Whig status, but Palmer and Davis believed it imperative to cease any further discussions of a Seward-Lincoln ticket (discussions that rarely put Lincoln's name ahead of Seward's). Palmer's conclusion was that "Mr. Lincoln and Mr. Seward were brought face to face," returning the New Jersey deliberations to a decision between the two rather than a pairing of them.[21]

The anti-Seward campaign run by the Illinois men was made easier by Horace Greeley's much-celebrated vendetta against Seward and Weed. Back in the early 1850s they were formidable Whig allies in New York, but Greeley insisted that Seward had deceived him and that Weed had ignored him, and he dissolved the relationship at the end of 1854. Greeley's festering hatred, particularly of Senator Seward, swelled over the next five years. Greeley came to the convention not only as the *New York Tribune* editor and reporter, but as a replacement member of the Oregon delegation in support of Edward Bates's nomination.

But Greeley appeared as dedicated to upending Seward as to promoting Bates. He was a constant and unmistakable presence in the Tremont House, moving about with his short-stepped gait and commanding attention with his cherubic look and falsetto voice. "The way Greeley is stared at as he shuffles about, looking as innocent as ever, is a sight," noted a fellow reporter, who was awestruck at how Greeley attracted the densest crowds at the hotel, "and there is a most eager desire to hear the words of wisdom that are supposed to fall on such occasion."

But Greeley appeared to lack wisdom when he overstepped in his mission to promote Bates, circulating a condescending handbill promoting Bates as the best available Republican around whom to rally. The problem was that Bates was not a member of the Republican Party but a Whig. Greeley's history of supporting non-Republicans for Republican causes (including his ardor for Stephen A. Douglas in 1858) grated on the conventioneers. He appeared to hold court longer in his denunciations of Seward at Chicago, but his unorthodox alliances weakened his punch. Other prominent anti-Seward men in Chicago, like gubernatorial candidates Henry S. Lane of Indiana and Andrew G. Curtin of Pennsylvania, delivered speeches that were more effective than Greeley's erratic rants, for these respected Republicans based their messages on the concern that Seward could not carry their states in November's election.[22]

Greeley's ostentatious anti-Seward campaign and the more clandestine ones orchestrated by the Illinois delegation and those from other states did not sway those delegates committed to Seward. But they did convince the uncommitted delegates—even those leaning toward Seward—to reconsider. The strongest factor working against Seward was the growing conviction that he could not win a general election, even with a split Democratic field, because he was unlikely to improve upon Frémont's total in 1856. Not one of the Republican delegations in the key Northern states that Frémont had lost—Illinois, Indiana, Pennsylvania, and New Jersey—was supporting Seward in 1860, and these states' delegates were convincing all the others that he could not win there. The collective desire running against Seward was for the convention to nominate a candidate who offended no one and had a chance to take those states in a general election, regardless of who was the chief Democrat running against them.

Thurlow Weed was hardly unaware of the voices of dissent concerning his candidate, but he remained focused and undeterred by the anti-Seward campaign swirling around him. Aided by his congenial personality, Weed ran his operation smoothly, inviting delegates over to the Richmond House to chat while sipping his champagne and chomping on his cigars, or sending out his workers—armed with cigars and promises—to welcome undeclared delegates into the Seward camp. Weed's good-natured approach rubbed off on his subordinates, who carried out his mission with a soft-spoken zeal that disarmed the camps of the opposition. "We were not troubled so much by their antagonism as by the overtures they were constantly making to us," remarked a member of the Illinois delegation of Seward's team. "They literally overwhelmed us with kindness."[23]

Seward's machine ran on a fuel alien to Lincoln's men—money. The New Yorkers had an astounding amount of it—"oceans of money" insisted a reporter—and they were not shy about flaunting it. In an effort to buy off the Illinois delegation, Weed sent his roommate, Senator Preston King, to the Tremont House with permission to open his war chest to the Illinois men. King brought another New Yorker as his conduit, offering $100,000 "placed in the proper hands" to carry Illinois and Indiana for

Seward if Lincoln could be placed on his ticket as Seward's vice president. The Illinois men held firm; they refused to have Lincoln's name connected in any way to the vice presidency. Although successful in spurning the New Yorkers' advances, some in the Illinois delegation rightfully worried that other states' delegates—particularly those who had promised never to shift to Seward's camp—would be blandished by Weed's riches. "I am a little afraid of this eliment [*sic*]," reported William Butler to Lincoln after the New York men left his room; "to extent it may be used I Cant say." Money had the potential to overturn the most logical arguments and to negate the most skillful discussions made by state delegations like Illinois's, which had no money to offer.[24]

The Tremont House became progressively more awkward as the headquarters of Lincoln's team. By Tuesday, May 15, this hotel hosted more conventioneers than any of the other forty-one establishments in Chicago. Greeley was a major attraction there, as was Frank Blair, the distinguished Missouri Republican running the Bates machine. "The Tremont House is so crammed that it is with much difficulty people get about in it from one room to another," wrote a reporter for the *Cincinnati Daily Commercial*. The newsman estimated that "fifteen hundred people will sleep in it to-night." Other hotels overflowed with conventioneers. One observer claimed that 130 people in the hotel in which he was quartered were "glad" to find space to sleep upon billiard tables. Estimates of the number of convention visitors went as high as forty thousand, although twenty-five thousand to thirty thousand appeared more accurate. It was undoubtedly the greatest attraction in the thirty-year history of political conventions.[25]

The building that would attract most of the delegates, reporters, and onlookers was not the Tremont or any other hotel. The official proceedings, slated to commence at noon on Wednesday, May 16, and to run through Friday, May 18, were scheduled to take place five blocks away from the Tremont House at a building called "the Great Wigwam." Like Decatur's, the Chicago Wigwam was constructed specifically as a convention hall, but it was a much larger and sturdier complex than the makeshift canvased structure Dick Oglesby had overseen. The Chicago Wigwam was constructed near the corner of Lake and Market streets, on the site where a popular hotel had stood before burning down years before. Begun early in April and completed barely in time for the convention, the two-story

Wigwam was 180 by 100 feet and designed to house up to ten thousand conventioneers.

There was nothing apparent about the exterior of the Wigwam to justify its five-thousand-dollar price tag; in fact, to some it looked like an oversized barn. But inside, it was a most impressive convention hall, not so much for the carpentry but for the spectacular decor. Immediately greeting the visitor was a dazzling combination of colors and shapes consistent with a festive convention. Across the front of the galleries were painted the coats of arms of all the states. Flags, wreaths, and bunting emitted red, white and blue throughout the hall, more pronounced when illuminated by the gaslights fitted for the occasion. Miniature busts and portraits of distinguished Americans captured the eye, as did paintings representing Liberty and Justice. Equally mesmerizing was the incomplete enormous banner "For President . . . For Vice President . . ." Evergreens and flowers added a natural beauty, a telltale calling card left by the women who decorated the interior. One reporter considered it a "small edition of the New York Crystal Palace."[26]

The hall was constructed to conduct business. Approximately one-third of the floor space was set aside as a platform for the delegates, complete with comfortable settees arranged across its five thousand square feet. The platform was wide and deep, designed to hold six hundred people and equipped with a speaker's chair in the front that overlooked the entire national delegation. Each side of the platform was bookended by committee rooms, and a small enclosed space in front was built to hold a musical band. The three-sided galleries were pitched perfectly to overlook the platform. They were spacious enough to accommodate the thousands of men and women expected to crowd into them. The Wigwam dazzled everyone at its dedication ceremony on May 12, an appropriate christening for the largest convention to date in American history.[27]

The Lincoln machine had a skilled operative in place to control the action at the Wigwam. While David Davis ran the show at the Tremont House, Norman B. Judd stationed himself at the Wigwam. The astute John M. Palmer would recognize Judd's work ethic in Chicago that mid-May. "Undoubtedly, Judge David Davis and Norman Judd contributed most," insisted Palmer, who continued to feel obligated to pair these two rivals in the same accolade; "they were indefatigable in their efforts to secure [Lincoln's] nomination." Judd would likely have had few qualms about being recognized equally with Davis in his efforts. He would, however, have been vexed at the continued rumors regarding his lack of loyalty to Lincoln during the convention. One well-placed Illinoisan misfired when he wrote his congressman claiming that Judd was prepared to convince the Illinois delegation to vote for Ohio dark horse Benjamin Wade after the first ballot. The rumor gained an audience, notwithstanding the logic-defying premise that Judd would derail eighteen months of time, money, and energy spent on behalf of Abraham Lincoln. Wade now represented the third candidate Judd was rumored to support instead of Abraham Lincoln (he had earlier been accused of supporting Bates and Seward). This rumor mill reflected the hangover that had throbbed in the heads of pro-Lincoln politicians since February 1855, when Judd (then a Democrat) voted for Lyman Trumbull (also a Democrat) instead of Lincoln (a Whig) for U.S. Senator.[28]

If Judd heard any of these rumors during convention week in Chicago he shook them off to focus on the business of nominating Abraham Lincoln. Judd took advantage of his original coup of landing the convention in Chicago by converting the Wigwam into a hall set up to the advantage of Abraham Lincoln, but doing it in a way that was not readily apparent to the other candidates' delegates, who, to this point, considered it a mere coincidence that Abraham Lincoln had emerged as a serious candidate on his home turf. Judd flexed his muscles as a railroad attorney and had the rail fares reduced by half on the Illinois Central Railroad and other Prairie State lines for the first days of convention week. The expected effect was exceeded: Ten thousand to twelve thousand passengers from all over the state took advantage of the cheap fares and went to Chicago, guaranteeing that nearly one-third of the conventioneers called Illinois home.[29]

Next on Judd's agenda was to subtly arrange the seating of delegates to put the Seward supporters at the worst possible advantage. Without raising suspicion, he was able to finagle the responsibility for superintending the seating. "I put New York about the centre on the right hand side," Judd later explained, "and grouped New England, Wisconsin, Minnesota, and all the strong Seward States immediately around her." To the left side of the presiding officer's chair Judd placed the Illinois delegation, and next to it Indiana's (he knew the Hoosiers would go for Lincoln). Most important, on the far side of these two states Judd placed pro-Cameron Pennsylvania, with the pro–Bates Missouri delegation nearby; and he surrounded this entire side with the border state delegates and those from the smaller doubtful states.

The seating was marked by placards and would hold for all three days of the convention. Judd explained, "The advantage of the arrangement was, that when the active excitement and canvassing in the Convention came on, the Seward men couldn't get over among the doubtful delegations at all to log-roll with them, being absolutely hemmed in by their own followers who were not likely to be swerved from their set preference for Seward." Implicit in Judd's preconvention plan was to group the Pennsylvanians well away from Seward, but close to Illinois—"within a handshaking distance," he explained to his wife before the convention began. This suggests that Judd had checked in enough times at the Tremont House to understand that the Pennsylvania and New York delegates were quarreling and that the Lincoln team hoped to capture Pennsylvania after its delegates registered their complimentary vote for Cameron on the first ballot. His arrangements also revealed that he (and by extension the entire Lincoln team) had little concern about the logrolling abilities of Bates's supporters, who were also adequately separated from Seward's influence on the convention floor. Most important about Judd's strategic seating plan was that no one outside of the Illinois delegation caught on to the advantage this provided Lincoln.[30]

By Tuesday night, the evening before the official proceedings commenced, the Lincoln team could claim pride in their efforts and the results obtained from them. They revealed their confidence to Lincoln in the letters and telegrams sent down to Springfield from Chicago. "Prospects very good," reported Jesse Dubois by telegram. Judd sent a telegram too, employing his ungrammatical catchphrase: "Don't be frightened. Keep cool; things is working." Even the usually reserved David Davis found time to wire Lincoln a very positive outlook; he and Dubois informed Lincoln that they were "moving heaven & Earth. Nothing will beat us but old fogy politicians. The heart [sic] of the delegates are with us."[31]

Davis hid any worries about the tactics employed by Weed, because he was sure Weed was the one who would be surprised when the balloting began. Nevertheless, Davis faced problems. First, he had to make sure Weed could not scrape up enough delegates to seal Seward's nomination;

second, he had to look over his shoulder to ensure that a true dark horse—like Benjamin Franklin Wade of Ohio—would not attract delegates after a multi-ballot stalemate between Seward and Lincoln, and most important, he had to make sure that Lincoln's team found enough additional delegates to win this for their man as fast as possible so that multi-balloting and a dark-horse compromise were avoided. Everyone in Lincoln's team understood as well as the savviest veterans of national conventions that the negotiations for delegates had to be completed before the balloting began, lest the emotions that breathed life into such a convention would take over the event and run it in an unpredictable direction.

The gavel pounded inside the Wigwam at 12:15 P.M. on Wednesday, May 16, to start the official proceedings. Ten thousand citizens packed the Wigwam to take in the event. The most anticipated agenda of the convention would be the nomination balloting, which was expected to occur by the afternoon of the second day. But before the balloting could begin, the convention conducted important business related to the anticipated nomination, including presenting and adopting the Republican platform.

The first day's proceedings presented a paradox for the Republicans. While bloated speech after speech acknowledged how momentous this event was—the word "solemn" was reportedly uttered more than any other adjective—the party sometimes refused to act in that manner. The proceedings were nearly interrupted to take up the offer of the Chicago Board of Trade to take an excursion by boats on Lake Michigan (after lengthy discussions this was put off until the evening hours). Speakers were hissed at and rudely cut short. Much hostility was shown to convention officials. Orville H. Browning, for example, dismissed temporary chairman David Wilmot as "a dull chuckle headed, booby looking man." A three-hour afternoon break and more long-winded speeches slowed down the pace of accomplishments; still, few who left the Wigwam were concerned that the nomination would not be held the following day.[32]

Lincoln's prospects looked even better that Wednesday. In addition to the proceedings on the floor, enough caucusing of delegations was occurring to keep the spirits of the Lincoln team uplifted. Mark Delahay reported to Lincoln, "Your chances have greatly increased to day, and we can easily perceive it & it is not less than second best in my opinion." The Illinois delegation and the other members of the Lincoln team seemed to agree with this sentiment. The stock for Salmon P. Chase and Judge McLean had plummeted, and the German delegates did indeed frighten off support for Bates—eclipsing the presence of the powerful Blair family and Horace Greeley to promote his candidacy. The teams of Cameron, Hickman, and Dayton had garnered little support for their candidates outside their own home states—and that support was likely to disappear after the first or second ballot. The Ohio dark horse, Benjamin Wade, also lost steam. The Ohio delegation caucused and when the staunchest Chase men were threatened by defections to other Ohioans, the Chase supporters threatened to throw their support to Seward; thus ended the discussion. This caucus seemed to guarantee two important results: that Ohio would not switch from Chase to a more agreeable Buckeye, and the door was left open to transfer the Ohioans' vote to an inoffensive middle-ground candidate outside of Chase's home state.[33]

Behind the scenes was a strong current of acceptance that Seward's chief opponent was Abraham Lincoln. Most of Lincoln's men remained optimistic and calm about his improved chances. But signs that members of the Lincoln headquarters were overconfident on May 16 ended up in Lincoln's mail. William Butler had reported to Lincoln daily since the previous weekend, but no letter was more sanguine than what Butler penned that Wednesday. He assured Lincoln that not only Indiana but also Iowa and New Hampshire would deliver a unit vote for him. Butler also insisted that Ohio and Pennsylvania would go to him by the third round of balloting. He was equally confident that Massachusetts would vote for Lincoln on the first ballot and that even Long John Wentworth "has changed his feet and is now for you."[34]

It was a letter bubbling with optimism and it likely reflected an opinion that was shared by other members of Lincoln's team. But it was almost entirely untrue. The only solid fact Butler delivered was Indiana's support for Lincoln. No other state was prepared to give him a unit vote, a vote of the majority of delegates, or a guarantee of any delegates at all. By the nature of conventions all was still in flux. So while Butler was unreasonably confident that Lincoln had more than twice as many unit votes outside of Illinois as he actually had, he also was confident that Seward did not have enough votes to win on the first, second, or even the third ballot.

At least the latter conclusion by Butler had some merit. Chipping away at the tough enamel that encased the Seward machine was Horace Greeley. As the chief delegate at large for Oregon, Greeley went far beyond representing that state at the convention. His first and primary task was to derail the Seward steam engine, and Greeley apparently expended an incredible amount of energy with his anti-Seward rants and rallies. But it seems Greeley's power was overcredited in Chicago. He came in as Bates's most influential supporter (even more so than the Blair family), but few insiders gave Bates a chance on the eve of the balloting. And although Seward's stock was sinking by Wednesday night, this had less to do with Greeley's influence than with the growing opinion that Seward was unelectable.

This opinion was evidenced by two new agenda items planned for Thursday, May 17. One was to require the nominee to achieve not only a majority of the convention ballots, but 103 electoral votes (a test of unit votes by states to determine the viability of the candidate in a general election). The other was an effort to exclude several territorial and Southern delegations from balloting. These were pro-Seward delegations. If both measures succeeded, or at least parts of the second along with the first, Lincoln's team thought, this would "terminate the struggle" for Seward and leave Lincoln as the last man standing.

That optimism disintegrated on Thursday. Both anti-Seward measures failed to pass, leaving the Seward-rich delegations eligible. Seward gained even more momentum when the fourth rule presented by the Committee on the Order of Business failed to pass. The committee had recommended that a two-thirds majority (310 out of 466 official delegates) be balloted for one candidate before he won the nomination. This rule was detrimental to Seward because it was almost certain that several ballots would be needed to achieve that mark. The New York delegation killed off this rule by invoking a key theme the Republican Party: the party wanted to foster the majority rule, but the two-thirds rule would guarantee minority rule. After all, this is what had tied up the Democrats in Charleston and forced the convention to adjourn without a candidate, even though Douglas had won the majority of ballots. To counter, the Sewardites submitted an alternative to the rule allowing a simple majority. After heated debate, it passed, requiring that the threshold number of delegate ballots to nominate be placed at 233 votes—one vote past the halfway mark out of 465 official delegates.[35]

These lengthy proceedings, including the contentious presentation and adoption of the seventeen-plank platform, dragged the session deep into the afternoon. When the motion to begin the balloting was finally presented, the secretary informed the chair that the necessary papers to log the ballots were not yet at hand. Rather than delay the proceedings for the delivery of the papers, it was agreed upon to adjourn for the day and proceed with the balloting on Friday morning.[36]

Thursday was a dream day for Thurlow Weed and the Seward forces. Not only did all of the anti-Seward measures fail, but the extra time afforded them to entice delegates improved their chances. It became apparent that the Massachusetts and New Hampshire delegates were leaning much stronger to Seward than to Lincoln, the antithesis of William Butler's earlier prediction. Weed was so confident that the momentum had turned to Seward that he claimed, "Lincoln's Friends started him only for the second place, for which I immediately accepted him." Weed never identified which of "Lincoln's Friends" made the offer; it appears to have been a ruse to keep Lincoln in the background. This hardly seemed to matter by Thursday night. At half past ten additional news thrilled the Seward camp. New Hampshire was reportedly ready to vote as a unit for Seward by the second ballot, and Cameron's confidant, Alexander Cummings, promised Weed that after the first ballot, Pennsylvania would be open for him to attempt another interview with its delegation.[37]

"The Seward feeling to-night runs like a spring flood," telegraphed Murat Halstead to the *Cincinnati Daily Commercial*. Halstead's daily convention reports show that he had the rare talent and access to be able to provide the most accurate and detailed descriptions of what was happening behind the scenes as well as at center stage. He went on to predict, "There cannot be any combination formed that may possibly beat Seward, unless upon Lincoln, and the Cameron men are not now disposed to enter it." Furthermore, Halstead received inside information from the Seward camp that Weed was more confident of getting Pennsylvania on his side, primarily by touting Seward's "good Tariff record" and promising to empty his war chest into the state to carry it for Seward against any Democrat in the autumn election. "The indications now are that Seward will be nominated to-morrow," concluded Halstead; "I do not doubt that he will be. . . . The Sewardites now claim his nomination on the first ballot, and say that the only question remaining is whether he shall be nominated by acclamation."[38]

Seward's "Irrepressibles" could hardly control themselves. The victory celebration began that night at the Richmond House with delegations joining the New Yorkers for a huge champagne supper. Three hundred bottles of the bubbly were expended for the festivities. Greeley, of course, was not in attendance to hear his name frequently linked with the moniker "damned old ass." The celebrations spilled out the hotel doors and onto the streets, and a late-evening rain failed to dampen the spirits of the Sewardites. Two New York bands paraded through the streets and serenaded all the onlookers, followed by a raucous procession of revelers on foot and in carriage, flaunting the inevitable nomination of their home-state candidate. At the previctory celebration, Greeley was described as both terrified and defeated, but he could hardly argue with the consensus. "He gave up the ship," noted a reporter, who submitted Greeley's *New York Tribune* dispatch as his evidence: "My conclusion, from all that I can gather to-night, is that the opposition to . . . Seward cannot concentrate on any candidate, and that he will be nominated."[39]

Some of Lincoln's confidants were equally stunned by the speed and force of the Seward train that careened into them on Thursday. "We have done all that Can be done," declared William Butler in his last letter to Lincoln before the balloting. "If whipped, we expect to meet defeat Knowing we have done all in our power." But not all Lincoln's men had surrendered. Mark Delahay also penned his final letter to Lincoln prior to the nomination vote. "We are still hopeful," he wrote Thursday evening, and he disagreed vehemently with Butler that all options had been explored. Nevertheless, he confidentially expressed to Lincoln—for the first and only time—his belief that the Lincoln men were not up to the task, and the huge momentum shift revealed that they were paying the price. "Davis is a good judge Doubtless and Duboise [sic] and Butler are honest & faithful," Delahay acknowledged, "but they are unacquainted with New York Polaticians [sic]." He went on to lament that Lincoln's team did not play by the same rules as Seward's team because he knew the New Yorkers as "desperate gamblers" whose tactics had withered him in the past—"I live among them & have suffered at their hands."

What Delahay had wanted was exactly what Charles Ray had intimated three days before in his letter to Lincoln. Patronage must be offered to win key delegations. "I know that you have no relish for such a Game," Delahay acknowledged to Lincoln. "But it is an old [maxim] that you must fight the devil with fire." He could sense that momentum for Lincoln had peaked twenty-four hours earlier and now had ebbed, while Seward's stock continued to soar even as he wrote. Delahay groaned at the prospect of Lincoln losing because of dealings behind closed doors in the smoke-filled rooms at the Richmond House. He assured Lincoln that "if we are beat this is the last time I shall be heard of in Polatics."[40]

Delahay folded the letter and sealed it in the envelope that night not knowing that David Davis was doing what Delahay had wanted to. Through Wednesday night, Davis had been satisfied that Lincoln could win without any promises, counting on momentum to boost Lincoln to the nomination on subsequent ballots. But by Thursday night Davis's perception had changed. Just as he deemed it important to land Indiana on the first ballot, Davis now looked to securing a delegate-rich state for Lincoln on the second ballot. He had been too busy to write or wire Lincoln on a regular basis; he may have sent only one telegram since the start of convention week. On Thursday night, as Seward's advocates sang, danced, and shouted in the streets, doled out cigars, and popped corks from champagne bottles, Davis and select teammates pressed their negotiations in the Tremont House.

One of the last messages Davis had received from Lincoln was an admonition that the judge received perhaps a day earlier: "Make no contracts that bind me." But Davis heeded it not. As dead tired as he was, Davis still was thinking clearly. He and all the other Lincoln men had come too far and had done too much to let the Seward men steal their hard-fought gains. He was not about to let Lincoln's accomplishments of the past eighteen months, and their tireless efforts over the past six days, go to waste simply because Lincoln clung to a naive notion. Lincoln was not in Chicago; he did not understand what needed to be done. Davis was here and knew what to do. He would "fight the devil with fire."[41]

After delivering a final four-hour sales pitch to the New Jersey delegation in a meeting that ended at ten P.M., Davis focused his attention on the most prized state at the convention: Pennsylvania. It was always known as the Keystone State, and the moniker could not have been more fitting than it was in Chicago, for its fifty-four delegates made it the second-largest state represented. But unlike New York, the largest state with seventy delegates committed to Senator Seward, Pennsylvania's delegation would likely decide this contest. It was common knowledge that Simon Cameron was going to receive the bulk of Pennsylvania's ballots in the first round, but if the senator was unable to generate momentum in his favor, those delegates were up for grabs in subsequent rounds.

Several state delegations had been engaged in caucuses throughout the evening, both in combination with other states and by themselves. Members of Lincoln's team had representatives in place in many of these meetings to hype the Rail Candidate. Pennsylvania had caucused for first-, second-, and third-round candidates on Wednesday. Lincoln was the preferred choice of the delegates in the third round, but by only six votes over Bates. Despite the heated efforts of pro-Lincoln supporter David Wilmot and the vehement anti-Seward man Andrew G. Curtin (who came to the convention for Bates but was pro-Lincoln by Thursday), the Pennsylvania delegation was far from united on whom to support after the first ballot on Thursday night. One of Bates's managers was certain that he had "a large portion of the Pa. delegation" in *his* corner on the eve of the official ballot.[42]

Although it revealed an anti-Seward sentiment, this uncertainty was still unacceptable to the Lincoln team. Late on the night of May 17, Davis, Leonard Swett, and a few other Illinois men closed themselves in a room with a small Pennsylvania contingent headed by Judge Joseph Casey. Casey or another representative had apparently been present at the New Jersey meeting to witness the Garden State delegation agree to favor Lincoln after one or two complimentary ballots for its favorite son, William Dayton. Davis had convinced the Jersey men to consider Lincoln "for the general good and success of the party" and apparently achieved the agreement without any special bargains except for the understanding that the Pennsylvanians would also move to Lincoln before or at the same time that the New Jersey delegation did.[43]

But Pennsylvania would prove to be a much tougher nut to crack—and wherever Pennsylvania eventually shifted, so went New Jersey. Judge Casey refused to commit his delegates to Lincoln simply "for the general good and success of the party"; he demanded that a deal be made to exchange Pennsylvania's vote for a cabinet position for Simon Cameron, preferably as Lincoln's secretary of the treasury. Casey understood that if Pennsylvania went to Lincoln, so would New Jersey; and this combination with Illinois and Indiana already committed to him would mean that Lincoln could claim all four states considered the keys to the 1860 election. This would not guarantee that he would win those states against a Democrat in the fall election, but it would prove to the other delegates congregating at the Wigwam on Friday morning that these delegations considered Lincoln the best hope for the party to win those four states against Douglas or any other Democrat. Hedging his bets in favor of his friend, Simon Cameron, Casey sought the best possible reward that the Lincoln team had to offer.

Davis would have realized that Casey held the upper hand in this negotiation. It would have been inconceivable for Davis not to appreciate the heated efforts of Weed to woo the Pennsylvanians over to him on Thursday. If a reporter was cued in to the "oceans of money" Weed had promised to Pennsylvania to win the state for Seward over any Democrat, how could Davis not be aware of it? It was also within the realm of possibility that Davis had an inkling of Weed's attempt to bring Pennsylvania back to the negotiating table through another Cameron friend, Alexander Cummings. Prior to this day, Davis had been confident that Pennsylvania would eventually come over to Lincoln's side as the most available candidate to nominate. Weed and the Seward machine had changed the game and upped the ante. Davis now had to redefine the word "confident" to mean "certain" and the word "eventually" to mean "the second ballot." In addition, he needed enough Pennsylvania delegates committed to Lincoln on that ballot to attract other states to him, as well as to keep them from going to Seward.

Judge Davis agreed to Judge Casey's demand, but he did so in a way to claim some future deniability—at least in his mind. For his part Casey left the meeting convinced that he had exchanged Pennsylvania's commitment to Abraham Lincoln on the second ballot in return for the desired cabinet position for Simon Cameron. In response to the Lincoln deal, Casey wrote Cameron, "It was only done after everything was arranged carefully & unconditionally in reference to Yourself—to our satisfaction—and we *drove* the anti-Cameron men from this State into it." Davis saw it differently, claiming that he had agreed only to recommend Cameron to Lincoln, but he had assured Casey that Pennsylvania would most certainly be represented in Lincoln's cabinet. Swett, who was with Davis at the negotiations, also denied Casey's claim that the "Hon. Leonard Sweat [*sic*]" would meet with Cameron in Pennsylvania and "bring with him assurance" of the deal; Swett claimed that "no pledges have been made, no mortgages executed." Swett later acknowledged that Lincoln's team was battling Seward's team to win over the Keystone State's delegates, but insisted that Lincoln's team won because "our arguments prevailed, and the Cameron men agreed to come to us upon the second ballot." Evidently, the Pennsylvanians agreed to switch not only because the arguments for Lincoln prevailed but also because they firmly believed they had Illinois's pledge for a cabinet position for Simon Cameron should Lincoln win the general election in November.[44]

The negotiation ended near midnight when the portly form of David Davis descended the stairs to the lobby of the Tremont House. "Damned if we haven't got them," he declared to *Press and Tribune* reporters. When asked "how," Davis reportedly responded, "By paying their price." Absolutely worn out from six straight days of exhausting work, Davis wrote a short message to wire to Abraham Lincoln: "Am very hopeful. Don't be Excited. Nearly dead with fatigue. Telegraph or write here very little."[45]

Indeed he was hopeful, but everything depended on subsequent balloting in the next day's nomination vote. Based on the general feeling throughout the city, Lincoln's success was doubtful. According to Murat Halstead, "[E]very one of the forty thousand men in attendance upon the Chicago Convention will testify that at midnight of Thursday-Friday night the universal impression was that Seward's success was certain."[46]

David Davis knew better: he was sure that if the contest was not decided after the first ballot, Lincoln would win.

Eleven

THE WIGWAM

A BRAHAM LINCOLN WAS up early on Friday morning, May 18. He had returned to Springfield from the Decatur convention the previous weekend and had endured each day since then with a growing combination of uneasiness, anxiety, and anticipation. But nothing compared to the restlessness that discomfited him on Friday morning. The course of his future—and the future of the United States—would be determined in the Great Wigwam of Chicago.

He had left matters in Chicago to his most talented and trusted friends, but he never seemed comfortable delegating authority. He had twirled the idea in his head earlier in the week to go to Chicago, until a wire from Davis and Dubois put him in his place. Reading newspaper accounts and letters from his confidants at the convention, Lincoln grew concerned that Judge Davis and other members of his team were making promises in his name, but without his consent. To put a stop to this he sent to Davis an admonition to "make no contracts that will bind me." But this was about the extent of his involvement in the national convention—the event that might nominate him as *the* Republican candidate for president of the United States.[1]

Shortly after the Decatur convention, Lincoln answered a question about his chances, "I reckon I'll get about a hundred votes at Chicago, and

I have a notion that will be the high water mark for me." The response reflected Lincoln's pessimism about his overall prospects at that time, but
also his naïveté about how difficult it would be to get a quarter of the pie
with a dozen candidates vying for a large slice of it. Still, so many positive
reports had crossed the doorstep of his house over the past four days that
Lincoln knew he was a high-ranking candidate on the morning of the
nomination. Telegrams and letters from the Tremont House all conveyed
the same thoughts: the contest was between him and Seward, and if Seward
did not win on the first ballot, Lincoln's chances were better than any
other's. The last message received would have been the last one sent from
David Davis, who reiterated how "hopeful" he was at the prospects of
Lincoln's success. Lincoln was unaware of the negotiations, and to his credit,
he appears to have heeded Davis's advice not to write to them while they
were conducting business with the other delegations.[2]

Since he was not in Chicago to feel the surge of Seward's reinvigora-
tion on Thursday night, and since he had yet to receive Mark Delahay's
angst-filled letter concerning the successful tactics of the New Yorkers,
Lincoln walked toward Springfield's town square Friday morning free
from the depressing influences of Thurlow Weed and the Seward machine. Understandably, he was anxious for any views from those in the
know about the convention. The opportunity popped up when he made
a brief stop at the Lincoln-Herndon Law Office and learned that James C.
Conkling, a friend since the 1830s, had returned from the convention.

Lincoln traversed the west side of the square down Fifth Street and
greeted Conkling in his office. Conkling realized how desperate his friend
was to extract as much updated news from the convention as he could. He
tried to assure Lincoln that he would be nominated, but Lincoln was too
anxious to stay and hear him out. "Well, Conkling, I guess I'll go back to
my office and practice law," Lincoln blurted to end the conversation. And
with that, at 8:30 A.M., he departed. But he did not return to the office
right away, for he was too nervous. Instead, he chose to expend the energy
as he had all week long—he played handball.

The game was called "fives" although it was usually played with six
people, three to a side. The losing team routinely paid ten cents each for its
loss. The handball court in Springfield was known as the "Bull Ring"; it
was formed from vacant lots between the three-story Logan Building and

the equal-sized brick store of John Carmody on the east side of Sixth Street, off the upper right corner of the public square. The buildings enclosed the walls north and south, while board fences sealed off the east and west sides. Seats were aligned inside these fences for spectators and players waiting to compete in subsequent games.

Lincoln arrived on the court that morning and played some handball, swatting a buckskin-covered ball (inside were tightly wound old stockings) against the north wall of the Logan Building. "Mr. Lincoln was not a good player," said William Donnelly, the nephew of the store owner and the gatekeeper of the court, the young man who smoothed the walls, leveled the ground, and made the balls. He remarked that Lincoln was on the court "a good deal" throughout the week, and on this particular morning "he was plainly nervous and restless." Donnelly believed Lincoln's age handicapped him in a younger man's game, "but he liked to play."

A passerby would have been taken by the attempt of a fifty-one-year-old man—one who towered at least half a foot over his opponents—trying to compete in a contest against young men still in their twenties and early thirties. No one at the Bull Ring that morning remembered how long or how well Lincoln played, but the game succeeded in eating up time for him as he awaited news from the convention, set to reconvene at ten A.M. Lincoln left the handball court and walked up the north side of the square back to his law office.[3]

Lincoln was back in his office by 9:30 A.M., chatting with Charles Zane and Christopher Brown, two young Springfield lawyers and frequent handball opponents. Brown could see that the sporting event had failed to quiet Lincoln's nerves, noting that he was "intensely excited" and fidgeting. Lincoln chose a comfortable outlet for this restlessness in the office— anecdotes and vulgar stories. Brown recalled specifically that Lincoln told one of his favorite stories that morning: Shortly after the Revolutionary War one of its heroes, Ethan Allen, visited England. During his tour of the former mother country Allen was constantly harassed by the British, who teased him about the new Americans and even denigrated George Washington. One day one of his British hosts took the teasing to a new level by hanging a painting of General Washington in the privy in the back of the house where Allen was staying. Mockingly, they asked Allen if he had been to the outhouse and if he had seen the Washington painting there. Allen answered that he had yet to see it, but he commended his hosts for finding such an appropriate place to display Washington's image. The British in the house were shocked at Allen's response. When they asked why he thought so, Allen responded, "There is nothing that will make an Englishman shit so quick as the sight of General Washington."[4]

Lincoln enraptured his young friends with his funny and vulgar tales, told while sitting in his favorite chair in the office or lying on the sofa in the room. Perhaps an hour after he arrived, the editor of the *Illinois State Journal* entered the office to inform Lincoln that he had just received the news that the balloting was about to begin. "Let's go to the telegraph office," Brown remembered Lincoln saying. And with that everyone left the office and headed to the top center of the public square to receive the results of the first ballot. Lincoln and those with him hoped that for the sake of Lincoln's chances, the first ballot would not be the last.[5]

At about the same time Lincoln opened the door to his office the three twenty-foot doors of the Wigwam opened to the public on Market Street in Chicago. At least 25,000 people waited outside. The third day of the Republican National Convention would be the final one, and it was set to open with the most anticipated event of the entire proceedings—the nomination for president. On Thursday the crowd at the Wigwam had been noticeably larger than on Wednesday, for all had anticipated the nomination balloting to close that session. But the excessive haggling required to approve the national platform delayed the nomination and disappointed the throng awaiting it. It seems no one left Chicago between Thursday and Friday. If anything, more Republicans arrived in the city, swelling the population past 140,000.

But the Wigwam could hold no more than 10,000, and the composition of that crowd could sway the nomination proceedings by influencing the delegates on the grand stage. Norman Judd had organized the delegates on the platform to Lincoln's advantage, and their seating appears to have been unaltered and unquestioned throughout the convention. No attempt to tamper with the crowd observing the delegates had been made on Wednesday or Thursday, but Judd and the rest of Lincoln's team must have been alarmed at how large and vocal the contingent of Seward's supporters had been over the previous two days. This was a group that worried the Lincoln machine, for if the balloting did not go as predicted, the crowd could upset the best-laid plans to control the process by making the arena more chaotic and unpredictable. Rumors rippled through the Illinois ranks that the Seward supporters carried—"through some underhand work"—duplicated tickets to enhance their numbers inside the Wigwam. How could Seward's Irrepressibles be repressed on Friday morning?[6]

Lincoln's team found a way—aided by the overconfidence of the Sewardites. While the New Yorkers reveled overnight, paraded in the streets, and celebrated their impending victory, Lincoln's planners focused their attention on the Wigwam, and they took advantage of the host-state status. The Illinois Republican State Central Committee had been responsible for supplying admission tickets. The committee, apparently consisting of both former and new members, had met the day before. Jesse Fell, the former secretary, suggested that they oversee the printing of additional tickets—hundreds more—to distribute to the great influx of Illinoisans that came in on the low-fare trains. Those tickets were produced and distributed to Lincoln supporters, who were cautioned to arrive early on Market Street on Friday morning.[7]

All worked to perfection. The Lincolnites swarmed into the building in much greater numbers than any other candidate's rooters. By ten A.M. the floor and galleries were nearly full. At least two thousand Seward men were able to crowd into the Wigwam, but some of the best shouters from New York paid the price for their ostentatious approach to the building. Parading behind their distinctive and impressive band, they reached the Wigwam too late to enter as a unit. Many were unable to enter at all, and those who did were forced to mingle in the huge crowd, thus wiping away the advantage of concentrated lung power to shout for their candidate. By the time George Ashmun, the president of the convention, called the convention to order, the crowd of ten thousand inside was clearly top-heavy with Lincoln-supporting Illinoisans. Perhaps Seward's men dominated the thousands just outside the building, but that did not matter. Judd and the State Central Committee had tamed the beast. Their hope was that the balloting would go according to plan and would render the crowd influence moot.[8]

"Lincoln will be nominated," a confident supporter telegraphed shortly before the balloting began. The statement was premature. Unknown to the

Lincoln team was that their most reliable and most important first-ballot ally had been having second thoughts about the alliance. Indiana had been solidly in Lincoln's corner since the weekend before, assuring the Illinois delegation that all the Hoosier delegates would declare for Lincoln on the first ballot. But several hours earlier on Friday morning, a reporter at the Tremont House had noted that the Indiana delegation had been deliberating past midnight—an indication that it was second-guessing its support for Lincoln. Henry S. Lane, the head of the Indiana delegation and a passionate Lincoln supporter, was "pale and haggard" at one A.M. "He had been toiling with desperation to bring the Indiana delegation to go as a unit for Lincoln," asserted the newsman. If the report was accurate (Lane had also spent his sleepless night working to bring Virginia and Vermont into Lincoln's camp), he apparently entered the Wigwam believing the Hoosiers were back in line for Lincoln—at least for the first ballot.[9]

But in a committee room of the Wigwam that morning, an Indiana delegate named Cyrus M. Allen made a motion to his delegation that threatened to destroy the entire plan laid out by David Davis and the Lincolnites. Allen tried to persuade the Indiana delegation to reconsider in an effort to make one of its own a candidate for the presidency. He urged the Indiana men to split from the Lincoln camp and vote as a unit for Caleb Smith on the first ballot. If Allen succeeded in generating a dark-horse movement, the result would be catastrophic for Lincoln's chances, for it would prevent him from reaching the one-hundred-vote goal expected and needed at the end of the first ballot in order to stand out as the leading alternative to William Seward.

Caleb Smith had been excused from the committee room prior to Allen's surprise maneuver. But he somehow learned about what was going on behind closed doors in time to try to stop it. Smith reentered the committee room and interrupted the proceedings, pleading that the only way to beat Seward was to unite with the Illinois men on Lincoln and not to muddy the waters with another candidate. Since Smith was squelching his own potential nomination, his protest was powerful and affecting. The delegation voted down Allen's motion, thus salvaging the alliance made with David Davis three days earlier. The Indiana delegates left the committee room and took their seats on the platform as the crowd settled down to take in the dramatically awaited convention finale.[10]

Minutes after President Ashmun called the proceedings to order, another preballoting procedure went Seward's way. The Maryland delegation was three men short, and Montgomery Blair—a powerful anti-Seward Marylander and part of the Bates-supporting Blair family—moved to allow three more Bates delegates to complete the shorthanded delegation. The Seward delegation swatted this away by insisting on adherence to a rule that no more votes could be cast beyond the delegation present at the balloting. Their objections prevailed and the Marylanders remained shorthanded. This procedure finally closed all the preliminaries, and the official nomination process began.

The first test of crowd influence would be displayed as each candidate was officially presented to the national delegation. William M. Evarts, a prominent New York lawyer and a leader of the Seward delegation, held the honor of placing his candidate's name in nomination. The disadvantaged Seward crowd was still able to assert its presence inside. According to Leonard Swett, Seward's nomination "was greeted with a deafening shout, which, I confess, appalled us a little." Had Seward's full contingent been allowed to assemble within the Wigwam, the effect would have been more than appalling to the Lincoln supporters.[11]

Norman Judd followed this display. "I desire," bellowed Judd, "on behalf of the delegation from Illinois, to put in nomination as a candidate for President of the United States, Abraham Lincoln of Illinois." What followed in the Wigwam would be remembered for decades. A reporter gauged that "the response was prodigious, rising and raising beyond the Seward shriek." When Caleb Smith seconded Lincoln's nomination on behalf of the Indiana delegation, "the response was absolutely terrific." One witness claimed that the panes of glass in the Wigwam windows rattled "as if they had been pelted with hail." What made those windows quake was the best shouters in the state, men recruited specifically for this moment. "Lincoln's friends were packing the house with men of good lungs," recalled one of the recruits, unabashedly adding: "Mine would carry the best part of a mile and I had a position within fifty feet of the platform." Another Chicagoan with a voice that reportedly "could drown the roar of Lake Michigan in its wildest fury" was also in the pro-Lincoln crowd. But even these men were topped by the best shouter in the lot. He was a doctor with the surname of Ames who lived on the Illinois River near the town of Ottawa (the site of the first Lincoln-Douglas debate of 1858). An Illinois delegate had telegraphed Dr. Ames to take the train to Chicago to aid the Lincoln delegation with his voice. The successful recruitment of leather-lunged Dr. Ames was a feat in itself—he was a Democrat. But he was there, and he was heard.[12]

Chase, McLean, Bates, Dayton, and Cameron were officially presented with considerably less noise. It was clear to all in the Wigwam by crowd reaction alone that this was a contest between Seward and Lincoln, a fact known to the insiders since Monday. When a Michigan delegate seconded Seward's nomination, the response was so raucous that it forced hundreds to cover their ears. "The shouting was absolutely frantic, shrill and wild," reported Murat Halstead; thousands waved their black hats "with the velocity of hornets over a mass of human heads." The galleries, crowded with ladies and their escorts, joined in the shouting contest to aid Seward.[13]

No one at that moment believed that this reaction could be topped. But the Ohio delegation stirred up the beast in the Wigwam with a bit of a surprise. After delegates in the Ohio section officially put up Chase and McLean, Columbus Delano—a former Whig congressman—stood up on behalf of a portion of the Buckeye delegation and seconded Lincoln's nomination again. He did so by invoking the new campaign slogan adopted a week earlier in Decatur: "I desire to second the nomination of a man who can split rails and maul Democrats, Abraham Lincoln."[14]

As soon as the Lincoln supporters heard this, and gleaned that their man was going to get votes even from Ohio on the first ballot, they exploded. Halstead was awestruck at what followed Delano's announcement. "Imagine all the hogs ever slaughtered in Cincinnati giving their death squeals together, a score of big steam whistles going together," he wrote, attempting to describe the scene to his readers, "and you conceive something of the same nature. I thought the Seward yell could not be surpassed; but the Lincoln boys were clearly ahead . . . they took deep breaths all round and gave a concentrated shriek that was positively awful, and accompanied it with stamping that made every plank in the building quiver." Leonard Swett crowed, "No mortal eye before saw such a scene. . . . Five thousand people at once leaped to their seats, women not wanting in the number, and the wild yell made soft whisper breathing of all that had preceded." Thirty years later a gentleman who was in that crowd still vividly remembered the decibel level of the response to Delano. "It was worse than a shout," he maintained. "It was an unbridled shriek such as I never heard before and have never heard since. It was almost unearthly."[15]

On the platform, the delegations of New York, Michigan, and Wisconsin—Seward men through and through—sat stunned to silence by the raging Lincoln sea surrounding them. It was a surreal moment. As the hurricane of sound swirled within the building, Henry Lane, the head of the Indiana delegation, was so caught up in the frenzy that he jumped upon a table and swung his hat and cane in an attempt to amplify the noise even more. A reporter wrote that the Hoosier "performed like an acrobat." It did not end, for an Iowa delegate also seconded Lincoln's nomination to renew the cheers and excitement again.

As the noise began to wane someone could distinctly be heard yelling, "Abe Lincoln has it by the sound now." The assessment drew some audible hisses mixed within the cheering. The hissing grew louder when Stephen T. Logan formally proposed to the convention that the audience give three cheers "for the man who is evidently their nominee." Logan had caught Davis's ire at the Tremont House for his muted effort, and he clearly did not redeem himself on the Wigwam platform. A reporter was unforgiving of Logan's ill-timed gesture, claiming it was "in excruciatingly bad taste" and noting that the "poor delegate felt ashamed of himself" after his request was voted down.[16]

After what seemed an eternity to the Seward supporters, the Lincoln crowd finally settled down and the balloting began shortly before eleven A.M. By an agreement made previously during the convention, the balloting would be recorded geographically, beginning with the New England and Atlantic states and proceeding toward the Mississippi River before ending in the territories. For Seward's and Lincoln's managers, the first states to announce their votes would be a gauge of whose political machine had most effectively aligned its forces. Maine started ominously for Thurlow Weed and the Sewardites. Seward got ten of its votes, but Lincoln took the other six. Next was New Hampshire; it awarded Lincoln seven of its ten votes, with the other three split among Seward, Chase, and Frémont. Vermont, to no one's surprise, gave its full ten votes to Senator

Jacob Collamer—its complimentary gesture to a native son who had no chance to win. Massachusetts perhaps disappointed some in the Lincoln team who expected more than the four votes for Lincoln on the first ballot (Seward received the remaining twenty-one). Lincoln received only two more votes from Connecticut's and Rhode Island's combined twenty—but Seward received none. All interested parties were running their totals and could conclude very early in the first ballot that Seward had an uphill climb to achieve the necessary 233 votes; he tallied only thirty-two votes out of the first seventy-one cast, with Lincoln accumulating seventeen delegates to put him in second place.[17]

New York righted Seward's ship by awarding the largest delegate total of seventy entirely to him. New Jersey fulfilled its promise to William Dayton and gave him its fourteen votes. Then came Pennsylvania. Pro-Cameron forces dominated to give their favorite son 47½ of its fifty-four delegate votes, but Lincoln still extracted four votes while Seward pulled in only 1½ (Bates got the other). Maryland and Delaware disappointed the Sewardites—but did not surprise them—by awarding fourteen votes to Bates and only three to Seward. This vote confirmed for Weed how adamant the anti-Seward movement was as the pro-Bates forces in Maryland made their presence known.

A first-ballot shock emanated from Virginia. So regarded as a "Seward state" as to spur an unsuccessful movement the previous day by anti-Seward forces to bar its delegation from voting, Virginia gave Lincoln nearly two-thirds of its votes (fourteen), while Seward captured the remaining eight. The Lincoln team had successfully won over the Virginians the night before, turning this into a Lincoln state. The tally near the halfway point showed that out of 248 votes, Seward led comfortably with 113, but he was not gaining delegates at a rate to win on the first ballot, Cameron was in second with 47½, and Lincoln was in third place with thirty-seven votes; all others trailed way behind.

The balloting continued. Lincoln's birth state of Kentucky weakly acknowledged him with six votes, while Seward pulled in five, and Wade received the other two. Ohio put an end to the Wade dark-horse movement by not giving the native any votes, but the state awarded Lincoln eight of its delegates (Chase and McLean received the other thirty-eight). Lincoln picked up the forty-eight unit votes from Illinois and Indiana (the Lincoln delegates did not know how close Indiana had come to abandoning their cause), while Seward claimed all of Minnesota's, Michigan's, and Wisconsin's votes—a total of thirty ballots. Seward also pulled in all the votes of Kansas Territory, California, and the District of Columbia; all but two from Texas; half from Nebraska; and a couple from Iowa's ballots, which split up between five candidates. But the Blairs kept Missouri from Seward and totally committed to Bates, while Greeley succeeded in keeping any votes in Oregon from Seward as well; its five votes went to Bates.

The first ballot concluded with the announcement of the territorial votes shortly before noon. Before the secretary announced the official total, scratching pencils on paper had already calculated that Seward had not achieved the 233-vote threshold. The announcement caused no huge surprise, but disappointment and some worry in the Seward camp. He led all candidates with 173½ votes—sixty votes shy of victory. Lincoln's team had achieved all three of its goals: it had kept Seward from winning on the first ballot; it had acquired the minimal goal of 100 votes for Lincoln (he had 102); and it had presented Lincoln as the lone significant contender in a race against Seward. Of the remaining ten candidates who received votes on the first ballot, no one had more than fifty, meaning Lincoln had more than double the total of Chase, Cameron, or Bates, who essentially shared third place, with a margin of one and a half votes between the three. This was important, for the anti-Seward forces could now focus on Lincoln as the man to rally around, a man with a middle-ground message whose team adroitly had offended no one. The behind-the-scenes negotiations made by the Lincoln team the previous day were expected to close the gap between Lincoln and Seward and enhance Lincoln's momentum. But—as the Indiana delegation had demonstrated earlier that morning— no one could be sure of assurances.

The results of the first ballot were immediately telegraphed down to Springfield. Lincoln was at the telegraph office on the north side of Washington Street (directly north of the capitol building), awaiting the news. Lincoln said nothing after reading the results, but he failed to conceal how he felt about it. Charlie Zane observed him and noted, "From the manner in which Mr. Lincoln received this dispatch, it was my impression that it was as favorable as he expected."[18]

It certainly was, but it guaranteed nothing. Thurlow Weed certainly was not panicking, for he knew that his man could win on the second ballot merely by having two or three states that had given complimentary votes to their native candidates move to the front-runner. Weed must have been surprised that Lincoln had cleared the remainder of the field on the first ballot to achieve a hundred votes, and it must have alarmed him to see Lincoln ballot well in the eastern states. But at the same time there was ample reason for him to believe that Seward's seventy-vote lead should grow even larger during the second ballot—large enough to put him over the top even if none of Lincoln's adherents moved in Seward's direction.

The realization that a second ballot was in the offing electrified the crowd. Cries of "Call the roll" rent the air, and even some of the delegates of trailing candidates nursed the slightest of hopes that their man would surge forward on this ballot. As some state delegations huddled between the first and second ballots, the Pennsylvania delegation was permitted to "retire for consultation," probably in one of the side committee rooms. This move alerted the convention that Cameron might be withdrawn for another candidate in the second round. Most concerned was Lincoln's team—Lincoln's chances rested upon the second-ballot vote of the Pennsylvanians, an outcome that was supposed to be a fait accompli based on negotiations completed at midnight. Yet they found the need to meet alone. Could they be changing their mind at the last minute?[19]

Twelve candidates split up the 465 ballots in the first round, including three who received one vote apiece and one who received three. The number of candidates was expected to shrink considerably in the second round, yet there was a possibility that a dark horse could emerge. But within minutes of the start of the second round of ballots, this was clearly a Seward-versus-Lincoln race. New Hampshire initiated the trend. After registering ballots for four candidates the first time around, it announced nine votes for Lincoln and only one for Seward. Vermont was the first state to abandon its native candidate, Senator Collamer. The third state to announce on the second ballot, it stirred the Wigwam by declaring that all ten of its delegates now voted for Abraham Lincoln, fulfilling an agreement made with Lincoln's managers before Friday. "This was a blighting blow upon the Seward interests," reported Murat Halstead, who likened the Sewardites' reaction to an exploding bomb.[20]

The New York delegation should have felt more at ease after it pulled four votes from New Jersey (although the state still clung to Dayton with ten votes). Then all eyes trained on the Pennsylvania delegation, recently returned from its private deliberation. The Pennsylvanians' chairman said they had "sought divine guidance" and informed the convention that Cameron's name had been withdrawn by all but one of his delegates. Seward picked up one more delegate from the Keystone State (as did Judge McLean), but the remaining former pro-Cameron delegates—44 of them—followed Vermont's cue and switched to Lincoln. The near-complete transfer of these prized delegates to Lincoln (plus the four Pennsylvanians who clung to Lincoln from the first round) not only relieved the Illinois team by showing that their man was strengthening and not fading in this round; it also guaranteed that Seward could not haul in enough support to win the nomination on the second ballot.[21]

Anyone in the know at that moment would have realized that the abrupt switch must have been made through a bargain. Simon Cameron was in third place after the first ballot with nine others trailing him, yet his supporters withdrew his name before the halfway point of the second round—right after New Jersey's votes indicated that its delegates remained committed to their man, William Dayton, even though he was never a serious candidate. As the second round continued it became evident that had Pennsylvania remained with Cameron, he would have remained in third place, slightly outdistancing the candidates who were immediately behind him after the first round, and near enough to Lincoln to motivate his most ardent supporters. But instead the Pennsylvanians had removed him from further consideration. When Ohio balloted for the second time and remained 80 percent committed to Chase, and Missouri refused to abandon Bates on its second ballot, the surprising shift from Cameron to Lincoln appeared to be based on something more than doing what was good for the party.

As the states announced their totals, it was clear that Seward was picking up votes as well, but not nearly as many as Lincoln and not nearly enough to reach 200. After the completion of the ballot, Seward maintained his lead with 184½ votes, a pickup of only eleven delegates. Lincoln was right on his tail with 181 votes. Six other candidates received votes; none got more than forty-two. It was a neck-and-neck race between Lincoln and Seward, and the momentum lay with the team devoted to the Rail Candidate.

Now was the time to logroll, the moment for Seward's committed delegation to wheel and deal, to coax and cajole nearby uncommitted delegates in an attempt to slow down Lincoln's momentum while picking up
enough non-Lincoln delegates to win this thing on the third ballot. But
Judd's masterful work on the platform prevented this from happening.
The Seward delegation was locked in, an island within a raging sea of Lincoln. The delegations of Ohio, Missouri, and New Jersey—where the
bulk of those prized delegates rested—were seated too far away from the
New Yorkers for them to negotiate on the platform between the second
and third ballots. The crescendo and cacophony emanating from ten
thousand throats in front of them and above them in the galleries rendered useless any attempt to logroll to get the forty-two Chase votes, the
thirty-five Bates votes, the 10 Dayton votes, or even the eight McLean
votes from the states and territories that had committed to these also-rans
on the first and second ballots.

Amid this roar from the excited crowd, the call for the third ballot was
placed as state delegations huddled to deliberate prior to their respective
roll calls. More defections from Seward in the Eastern states at the start of
the round further excited the Wigwam. Massachusetts transferred four
from Seward to Lincoln. New Jersey was the next anticipated change. As
expected, all but one of them abandoned Dayton, and Lincoln's team was
awarded with eight of the defections; Seward picked up another one—
five total—to help offset his defections from Massachusetts. This had to
have been a disappointment for David Davis and the Illinois delegation;
based on the previous evening's negotiation, Lincoln was expected to gain
nearly all of New Jersey's ballots after Pennsylvania came his way; instead,
Lincoln barely exceeded half of those potential delegates.

Although New Jersey's support for Lincoln was more anemic than the
Illinoisans had wished for, the state did indeed award him most of Dayton's defections. While Seward's total remained stagnant throughout the
remainder of the third ballot, Lincoln picked up small numbers in several
states like Pennsylvania, Maryland, and Kentucky to nudge him closer to
the threshold of victory. The Lincoln team was confident that their
friends in Ohio would fulfill the agreement to switch from Chase to the
Rail Candidate. Ohio did not disappoint, awarding Lincoln fifteen additional delegates, the most by any single state on the third ballot.

Everything was working to the script of the Lincoln team. The Lincolnites had prayed that Seward lacked the support to win on the first ballot, and the commitments to favorite sons by several states had assured this. From that point on the anti-Seward demonstration by New Hampshire on the second ballot, followed by the prearranged switch to Lincoln by Vermont and especially Pennsylvania, prohibited the Sewardites from culling the delegate riches from New York's geographic neighbors. But more important, these new pro-Lincoln states generated the momentum to roll him ahead of Seward to the top as other states glommed on to Lincoln in bits and pieces throughout the third ballot.

But it did not appear to be enough. As the final states and territories registered their ballot results, the only significant gain for Lincoln was in Oregon, where he picked up 4 out of the 5 votes transferred from Bates. Hundreds were keeping their own tallies and realized at the end of the third ballot that Lincoln was close, but had not seized the majority required. He stood at 231½—only 1½ votes from victory. Seward wallowed at 180.

A surreal pause overtook the Wigwam the moment the ballot totals were announced just before one P.M. "The stillness was so effective," claimed a participant, "that the flutter of fans by the ladies and the scratching of pencils by reporters could be heard distinctly." All gazed at the great platform to see who would provide the decisive vote necessary to prevent another round of balloting. Ten seconds elapsed before one of the delegates stood. It was David K. Cartter, the chairman of the Ohio delegation. The collective attention in the Wigwam converged upon Cartter, a big and imposing man whose large shining eyes and bristling black hair helped distract attention from the pocked skin scarring his face. Cartter had placed Salmon Chase's name in nomination two hours earlier. His delegation of Chase supporters had dwindled from thirty-four votes on the first ballot to fifteen after the third ballot.

Just before the fourth ballot was set to begin, Cartter was about to shrink Chase's total even more and put an end to the nomination process. Cartter had just been informed by four members of his delegation that they wanted to rush ahead with an announcement that they had changed their votes. Normally afflicted with a stuttering problem, Cartter spoke clearly and concisely, with only a small hint of his impediment. He declared, "I rise Mr.

Chairman to announce the change of four votes to Ohio from Mr. Chase to Mr. Lincoln."[22]

The four Ohio delegates immediately began to whoop and holler, but their switch came so fast that their jubilation was initially confined to them alone. Cartter's declaration was met with seconds of silence from the convention hall. It took a breathless moment for all in the Wigwam to grasp the meaning of Cartter's words—he had officially completed a nomination that would have been considered impossible one year before. He had assured that the Republican nominee for the November election was Abraham Lincoln.

The moment of breathless silence ended abruptly when—seemingly in unison—the packed conventioneers took a deep breath, described by a reporter as "like the rush of a great wind, in the van of a storm." Then came the deluge. Wild cheering, hat waving, and stomping of feet ensued. A cannon had been placed on the roof of the Wigwam; those atop the building with it had been fed the results of each ballot through a skylight, and they conveyed the results to the crowd of more than ten thousand surrounding the building. When Cartter transferred his four votes, the man stationed at the skylight could be seen gesturing to find out what had just happened. An official shouted up to him, "Fire the salute! Abe Lincoln is nominated!" In less than a minute the distinctive boom of the cannon could be heard both inside and out, followed by the sulfurous smell of gunpowder, which drifted into the building.

On the platform other delegates were on their feet and on their chairs to get the attention of the convention president so they could change their third-ballot votes. Within minutes Lincoln's tally reached 354—more than 100 votes above the threshold. Lincoln's picture—likely the Brady photograph—was pulled from one of the committee rooms and held aloft center stage for the cheering masses. Each of the state flags was pulled off its staff and waved overhead—all except for New York's flag. Defiantly, the Seward forces had not partaken in the celebration or acknowledged Lincoln's victory. They had come from New York with the conviction that Seward, not Lincoln, would be nominated, and for them these proceedings had been a wicked nightmare. "I saw people in the galleries wipe their eyes as if they were at a funeral," reported a witness to the New York crowd.

Another observer watched a band of delegates prevent the removal of their flag, noting that they "were wrathful at the suggestion."[23]

William Evarts, the New York chairman and a passionate Seward devotee, mounted the table on the platform to address the delegation and the newly hushed crowd that strained to hear him. He expressed his disappointment that the convention had not nominated William H. Seward. He then said that New York would follow the decision and the will of the delegates. He closed his short, melancholy speech by announcing that this momentous day would have no dissension, that the Republicans were united at a time when the Democrats clearly were not: "I move, Sir, as I do now that the nomination of Abraham Lincoln of Illinois as the Republican candidate for the suffrages of the whole country for the office of Chief Magistrate of the American Union be made unanimous."[24]

After Evarts was rewarded with three hearty cheers for New York, his motion was seconded and voted upon, and at one P.M. on Friday, May 18, 1860, Abraham Lincoln had completed the seventeen-month transformation from a two-time Senate loser to the unanimous nominee of a united Republican Party. Although Lincoln was not there to accept the congratulations, his surrogates basked in his triumph. David Davis was so overcome with emotion at what he was able to witness that he "wept like a child" as he grasped the hands of congratulating friends.[25]

Jesse Fell was also overcome with awe and emotion. He felt privileged to be there, and was one of a rare few to appreciate the metamorphosis in the fortunes of the man he'd practically had to console in his brother's law office in Bloomington back in December 1858. He was not the first to get a message wired to the nominee, but his would have a special meaning both for him and for Lincoln: "City wild with excitement. From my inmost heart I congratulate you."[26]

Twelve

THE NOMINEE

S HORTLY AFTER NOON on Friday, May 18, Abraham Lincoln
stood in the telegraph office on the north side of the public square,
awaiting the results of the second ballot in the Great Wigwam of Chicago.
The first-ballot results must have been a relief to him, for although he was
well behind William Seward, he cleared 100 votes to meet the expectations of himself and his team. He also was the clear second-place candidate in a field of twelve—another expectation of his managers that had
been relayed to him since the start of convention week.

The second-ballot result arrived within an hour of the first one. Lincoln
read the results handed to him: Seward 184½ votes, Lincoln 181. He said
nothing but was convinced at that moment that he was going to win. He
and the companions who had met him in his law office earlier that morning left the telegraph office and headed one block north of the northeast
corner of the public square, passing the handball game in the Bull Ring
along the way, and entered the three-story brick building that housed the
office of the *Illinois State Journal*. Lincoln had been a frequent visitor to the
pro-Republican newspaper since the late 1830s when it was called the
Sangamo Journal, then a popular Whig paper. Here is where Lincoln decided
he would be when the third-ballot results were wired in. Shortly after Lincoln made himself comfortable in the *Journal* office, Edward L. Baker (one

of the owners of the newspaper) and four others left him and headed back to the telegraph office to await the ballot results.

Charlie Zane was one of the quartet who joined Baker in the short excursion to the telegraph office. As the message from Chicago clicked off the wires, Zane studied the telegraph operator as he first threw down his pencil, then took it up again before writing out the message he interpreted and then handed it to Baker. The others crowded around Baker and asked him how it looked. Baker responded that it looked bad—for Mr. Seward and all the other defeated candidates, that is. Jubilant, all five scampered out of the telegraph office and returned to the *Journal* building to tell the new nominee the good news.[1]

The number of messengers grew as Baker and his followers passed the handball court. They entered the alley and climbed the stairway to the second floor, entered the office, and found Lincoln sitting there. Baker did not tease Lincoln as he had the four in the telegraph office. Instead, he proposed three cheers "for the next president" and read the winning results of the third ballot before handing the wire to Lincoln. Lincoln read it aloud again; handshaking and jubilant backslapping followed. According to Zane, Lincoln revealed that he had expected to win after the second-ballot results came in. "He received all with apparent coolness from the expressions playing upon his Countenance," remembered Zane six years later; "however, a close observer Could detect Strong emotions within."[2]

Everyone in the cramped office followed Lincoln to the streets, where the celebration magnified, particularly when they reached the side of the handball court. All the players surrounded Lincoln to congratulate him, pledging their support. Aside from the *Journal* staff, there was only one other newspaper correspondent known to be in Springfield to follow Lincoln. He was a newsman for the *Aurora Beacon* who had reported on the state convention in Decatur and then taken the train directly to Springfield. He was taken by Lincoln's understated reason to get away from the impromptu celebration. In his "usual odd way," Lincoln excused himself and said, "Well, I guess I will go and tell my wife about it; she cares more about it than I do." He then hustled southward toward his home. "I can see him now as he went away," vividly remembered John Carmody. "He leaned forward and walked mighty fast. The boy that went with him had to run almost to keep up with him." Lincoln shook a few hands as he shot down the east side of Sixth Street and disappeared from view. He would never play another game in the Bull Ring.[3]

As Lincoln elated his wife with the news, the town of Springfield celebrated his nomination. The Stars and Stripes was displayed at the capitol and in front of the stately houses in the town. Church bells chimed as Lincoln banners were hung out in every shape and style. A one-hundred-gun salute was fired in his honor, and, according to a witness, "one universal shout for Lincoln rent the city from one end to the other." The most fitting and ironic display was rolling out El Cyclope, the cannon captured at Cerro Gordo more than a dozen years before, from its storage site in the capitol and firing the big gun in Lincoln's honor. This was the same cannon that had signaled Douglas's victory over Lincoln in January 1859. The Republicans in Springfield hoped to wheel out the gun again in Lincoln's honor in November.[4]

The celebrations continued unabated into the night. A crowd gathered at the rotunda, and at nine P.M. they paraded to Lincoln's house to serenade him. This was reminiscent of the honor bestowed upon him the previous October, right after the city learned of the triumphant effects his Ohio speeches had had in their elections. Lincoln stepped out of his house and appeared in front of the revelers. In a brief and humble speech he thanked them for the display and suggested it was more in honor of the Republican Party than for him. Right before he closed his speech, Lincoln stated that he would invite the entire crowd into his house if it were only large enough to hold them. A voice within the throng referred to inauguration day when he assured Lincoln, "We will give you a larger house on the fourth of March."

After the speech, much of the crowd invaded the Lincoln home to shake his right hand. They dispersed afterward, but they were not through, for they kept up the shout for "Old Abe" as they passed by beautifully illuminated houses while accompanied by loud bands. The celebrations on the streets continued past the midnight hour. "It would be useless for me to attempt to describe to you the enthusiasm that prevailed," remarked an awestruck out-of-towner. "But you must be assured that Springfield never saw such a demonstration before."[5]

Those who could not be there in person that day to congratulate the nominee did so by letter and telegram. This was particularly true for members of the Illinois delegation and other pro-Lincoln men in Chicago, wrapping up the convention. Nathan M. Knapp, the Scott County delegate who had advocated Lincoln's nomination since April 1859, wired Lincoln, "We did it. Glory to God." Mark Delahay was never able to convince the Kansas Territory delegation to switch from Seward to Lincoln until William Evart's call for a unanimous vote. But, like Knapp, he could not conceal his emotion in his letter to Lincoln: "It is the happiest day of my checkquered [sic] life." Even Long John Wentworth got into the act, making sure he was the first to inform Lincoln that Hannibal Hamlin of Maine (a former Democrat) had been chosen as the Republican vice-presidential nominee to balance Lincoln's ticket. Lincoln got a strong inkling of what had been done to get him nominated from David Davis's telegram. "Write no letters and make no promises till You see me," Davis instructed—a strong indication that he had made some assurances to state delegations in order to get their votes at the convention.[6]

Aside from the congratulations offered, the message most frequently wired from Chicago to Lincoln was the admonishment "Don't come here." Rather than allow Lincoln to travel up to the Wigwam to greet and address the delegates who had nominated him, a contingent headed by the Republican National Central Committee would travel by train down to Springfield the following day to meet Lincoln at his home and formally tender his nomination to him. Posters went up all over Springfield to advertise the committeemen's planned 6:30 P.M. arrival at the depot on a special train.[7]

Gustave Koerner and Ebenezer Peck arrived in Springfield on an earlier train Saturday afternoon than the one transporting the Republican committee. Preceding the distinguished contingent by a few hours, Koerner and Peck entered Lincoln's house and were horrified to see that Mrs. Lincoln had arranged the reception to include brandy and champagne. Worse, when the two Illinois delegates tried to explain to Mary Lincoln that this "festive" arrangement was not appropriate for a luncheon designed for solemn business with a committee that included temperance advocates, she protested in her usual animated way. It took Mr. Lincoln's intervention to finally settle her down; he compromised with his wife that after the formal business was completed, the alcohol could reappear for those who "may stay and have a good time."[8]

The alcohol was put away, and in the late afternoon the committee arrived for its first meeting with Abraham Lincoln. Amid tremendous fanfare offered by the Springfield citizenry, the committee was escorted by a fine cornet band from Philadelphia and surrounded by two hundred visiting delegates—all carrying rails.

The impromptu parade marched to the Chenery House, one of the finest hotels in the city, then to the state capitol to hear some speeches. About two hours after its arrival, the committee entered Lincoln's square frame house, where Chairman Ashmun read the official nomination to Lincoln in his parlor. Lincoln accepted, promising to write a formal response. To break the ice with his important guests, Lincoln proudly sized himself up with the tallest committee member, Judge William D. Kelley of Pennsylvania. After he learned that Lincoln beat his six-foot-three stature by an inch, Kelley conceded, "Then, Pennsylvania bows to Illinois. My dear man, for years my heart had been aching for a President that I could *look up to*, and I've found him at last in the land where we thought there was none but *little* giants."[9]

This day marked the official start of the Republican campaign for the election of 1860, a campaign of high hopes for the party faithful. Not only had they nominated the candidate most able to claim states that Frémont had lost in 1856 (and to keep a hold on the states he had won), but the undecided outcome in the Democratic Party enhanced the likelihood of its splintering into two or more factions, each with its own candidate. The Republican National Convention had selected a man they believed would win in November in a two-man race—particularly against Stephen A. Douglas—but they were absolutely convinced Lincoln would win in a race where he was pitted against more than one Democrat. The Baltimore reconvention of the Democratic Party was slated for the last week of June to determine what man or men Lincoln would face.

But even before this outcome was determined, the Republican Party began to celebrate and hype Lincoln's nomination in a manner not seen in American politics since the "Log Cabin and Hard Cider" campaign of 1840, when the Whig ticket of William Henry Harrison and John Tyler (dubbed "Tippecanoe and Tyler Too") was displayed in dazzling parades and special campaign events throughout the country, leading to their victory over the incumbent Martin Van Buren. Lincoln was presented to the public as "Old Abe" and "Honest Abe," the two monikers that had defined him for the past six years (even though he detested the shortened version of his first name). Mixed with these sobriquets and soon overtaking both of them was the one masterminded by Richard Oglesby in Decatur on May 9. The nickname the "Rail Candidate" had been little used in the buildup to the national convention, although Ohio delegate Columbus Delano wowed the Wigwam with a version of it when he seconded Lincoln's nomination there. The name quickly faded into oblivion, replaced by a new one, worn on the lapels of the coats of the Philadelphians accompanying the committee: "Rail Splitters."[10]

Lincoln now embraced the name he had seemed to keep at arm's length in Decatur. Within a few weeks, two campaign newspapers, one in Chicago and the other in Cincinnati and both with the title the *Rail Splitter* would begin circulation to Republicans across the North. Next to Lincoln, had the greatest beneficiary of the name was John Hanks, who made a cottage industry out of selling the rails he claimed he and Lincoln had split back in 1830. Within two weeks of the convention, Hanks had mailed out forty rails to buyers in Illinois, Ohio, Kentucky, and Massachusetts, devoted Republicans who paid up to $2.50 for a thirty-year-old piece of cut wood.[11]

Lincoln aided his own cause not with speeches, but with new photographs and autobiographies. By this time, his Cooper Union address and the Mathew Brady image taken the same day as the New York speech had also been reproduced and recirculated. His friends also kept up the momentum they had carried into Chicago in May to magnify Lincoln throughout the country. Even Illinois delegates lukewarm to Lincoln, like Orville Hickman Browning, dedicated themselves to the Republican Party and dropped their "first loves" to promote Lincoln's candidacy. Biographies of Lincoln appeared in newspapers and campaign books. Throughout the North and West, Lincoln's name and his rail-splitting image resonated in a way not seen in presidential politics in twenty years.

In Springfield on June 1, the Republican State Central Committee held its first meeting with the membership elected at Decatur during the Republican state convention three weeks earlier. Members of the previous committee were also present in Springfield, as were other prominent state Republicans like gubernatorial nominee Richard Yates. After completing their official duties in their meeting, the committee members joined the other prominent politicians at the house on the corner of Eighth and Jackson streets for a celebratory dinner.

Close to twenty of them dined with the Lincolns that evening; most had been active at the national convention in Chicago two weeks earlier; all had aided Lincoln's nomination. It was a fitting and appropriate event for the Lincoln team. They gathered without fanfare, much like Lincoln's entire campaign for the nomination. It was a group of ambitious, talented, and energetic politicians celebrating the victory of their candidate and working to put him in the White House. Despite the animosities they held for one another, grudges and ill feelings that had not been washed away by Lincoln's nomination, they had demonstrated clearly how they could put aside their differences for a common cause.[12]

No doubt the celebrants waxed eloquent over the past events that had made them all triumphant. Based on the party platform created at the convention, their victory was also a victory for the Republican Party because Lincoln was a perfect match for the most important planks of the platform adopted on May 17, the day before the balloting commenced. Among the many planks were key ones that (1) called for maintaining the principles of the Founding Fathers; (2) denied the authority of Congress to allow slavery to enter the territories; (3) supported suppressing the reopening of the African slave trade; and (4) opposed state legislatures that impaired citizenship rights of all their residents, whether they were native or naturalized. These were all ideals linked to Lincoln in his private letters and his very public presentations. Those planks dovetailed with Lincoln's ideals so tightly that those sharing supper with him could easily imagine him authoring those parts of the platform himself.

The familiarity of Lincoln's message allowed his team in Chicago to espouse those ideals to the other state delegations even before the platform was adopted. In the six months leading up to the convention, Lincoln had been a very visible Republican, one who had resoundingly emerged from a yearlong absence after the 1858 debates against Stephen A. Douglas. By delivering speeches from September to March in Ohio, Indiana, Wisconsin, Kansas Territory, New York, New Hampshire, Rhode Island, and Connecticut, Lincoln had displayed his middle-ground, conservative principles, which were then promulgated by newspapers not only within the states where he delivered those speeches, but across the entire country. Lincoln's logical and consistent message, as well as his booming popularity over those six months, made him the most attractive candidate, the one who had the best chance for success in November. This is the most likely reason why even eight of Ohio's delegates were committed to Abraham Lincoln at the start of the convention, despite the fact that no fewer than three Buckeyes were considered presidential timber at the time.

Republican candidates with positions that deviated from the pivotal planks of the platform—like Chase and Bates—could also succeed in November, but the credibility of the fledgling party as well as of the candidate would easily be called into question, which would weaken their chances in the general election. This left Lincoln as the best fit for the platform and the party. Indeed, Abraham Lincoln was the most available candidate for Republicans in 1860.

The greatest reason for Lincoln to celebrate his victory with the prominent Illinois Republicans was that the best-fit candidates for the principles of a party did not always win the nomination, sometimes bowing to a more nationally popular and experienced politician, or one whose team dominated all others at the convention. Abraham Lincoln won the Republican nomination because he was a principled pragmatist, but also because he was the candidate agreed upon in the parlors of Chicago's hotels *before* the balloting commenced in the Great Wigwam. Lincoln's team controlled extraneous events that could damage Lincoln's prospects in Chicago, while convincing the state delegations that he was indeed the best-fit candidate for the party and its principles in 1860. Some of the delegations came to the convention attracted to Lincoln; others were convinced through hard-nosed persuasion by Lincoln's team that he was the only logical choice as the party's standard-bearer; and at least one state—Pennsylvania—had to be promised future representation in Lincoln's cabinet in order to win its delegates' votes. Indeed, as appropriate as Lincoln was for the Republican Party in 1860, there is little doubt that he won because of the result of negotiations conducted in smoke-filled rooms.

Most of the twenty Republicans who broke bread with Lincoln at his home that night could claim a role in winning the nomination, but David Davis and Norman Judd had been essential for Lincoln's victory. Judge Davis took charge of Lincoln's team in Chicago and could rightfully claim credit for scripting the balloting sequence that started Lincoln strong after the first ballot, and then built his momentum in each subsequent round. Norman Judd's role was crucial, and Lincoln recognized this, claiming that he "was more indebted to Judd than any other one man for his nomination." Judd's dedicated advocacy of Lincoln's nomination throughout 1859 and 1860—despite rumors to the contrary and his own personal political failure—bore fruit time and time again for Lincoln. The most obvious contributions from Judd were his masterful negotiation to land the convention in Chicago and his seating strategy for the delegates in the Wigwam, which helped control the events within the building so that the work done at Lincoln's headquarters in the Tremont House was not squandered by random events on the floor of the convention hall. Judd called those successes his "two great political feats." Few would argue with the claim.[13]

Together, Lincoln's personal efforts to emerge as a presidential candidate and the efforts of his team in Chicago were the ingredients for success. Not to be overlooked was the keen sense of timing shared by the nominee and his influential supporters. Lincoln, the Republican State Central Committee, and other informed Illinois politicians followed the same script beginning early in 1859. Their plan to keep Lincoln's presidential ambitions under wraps and enable him to emerge as a studious spokesman for the party allowed Lincoln to travel on extensive speaking tours appearing as a statesman rather than a candidate. Nobody outside of Lincoln's closest circle seemed to notice until the end of winter of 1860 that this lanky lawyer, who coyly denied that he was fit for the presidency and who had delivered only one speech outside of Illinois between his two Senate defeats, had suddenly ventured into eight states and a territory—beginning with Iowa in August 1859—and delivered thirty speeches while interest in the presidential campaign of 1860 was intensifying.

Looking at it in hindsight, it is difficult to imagine that this sequence of events was purely a coincidence. The possibility of happenstance further disintegrates when Lincoln's financial status is factored into the equation; he was jeopardizing his financial health by abandoning his law duties to embark on those out-of-state speaking tours at a time when he had not completely recouped his debts from the unsuccessful 1858 senatorial campaign. Lincoln's ability to subtly appear presidential late in 1859 without scrutiny from outsiders allowed his team to prepare his nomination by securing the national convention in Illinois, conducting a state convention with more than 650 delegates supporting Lincoln's presidential bid, and sending a picked team of delegates and other advocates to that convention dedicated to the victory they ultimately achieved.

The dinner celebrants undoubtedly discussed the hope of enjoying another triumphant moment together after the November elections. They soon learned they would not have to wait months for the outcome. The Democrats could not resolve the issues that divided the party between its Southern and Northern wings. After the convention in Charleston dissolved and adjourned after failing to select a nominee—after fifty-four ballots—at the end of April, the party reconvened in Baltimore on June 18. The polarized factions fought again, this time over the recognition of new delegates chosen to replace the ones who had walked out at Charleston. Once again some of the delegations walked out in protest, hampering the ability of Douglas to reach the two-thirds majority needed to win the nomination. This time the remaining Democrats changed the floor rules to allow the nominee to win with two-thirds of the delegates present. Douglas won the nomination under these new rules on June 23, but the fractured party would not heal. Instead, Southern Democrats held a third convention in Richmond, Virginia, a few days later and nominated John C. Breckinridge as their candidate, the second Democrat and fourth presidential candidate for November (John Bell of Kentucky had already been nominated as the Constitutional Union Party's candidate).

Republicans were hopeful with Lincoln in a two-man race. But with four men in the field, and two of them stealing votes from each other in the Democratic Party, those hopes now turned to expectations. It became clear that the Democratic split all but assured the Republicans that the election belonged to Lincoln. Normally cautious, Lincoln studied closely the events in Charleston, Baltimore, and Richmond. As June turned to July the outcome seemed certain even to him.

Lincoln celebrated the Fourth of July in Springfield. One year earlier he had delivered a nonpolitical speech in Logan County and had yet to launch his campaign for the presidency. But a year made all the difference. On this particular day in 1860—the nation's four-score-and-fourth birthday—Lincoln not only marked the anniversary of the Declaration of

Independence, but also was prepared to predict where he would be for the next four years. For the first time Lincoln was so convinced he would win the general election that he was ready to tell others in writing.

The recipient of this July 4 prediction was Dr. Anson Henry, Lincoln's friend since the 1830s who had taken up residence in Oregon. In the winter of 1859, shortly after Lincoln's Senate defeat, Henry had assured Lincoln that he had not become irrelevant: "The people—the great & glorious People, will bear you in their memories untill [sic] the time comes for putting you in possession of their House in Washington, which they are bound to do in their good time." No one will ever know if Lincoln was thinking of the physician's bold prediction when he wrote him as the presidential nominee of the Republican Party. But four months before the November election, Lincoln knew he had already won. He admitted this to Dr. Henry, choosing to do so by not referring to himself in the first person, the third person, or any person at all. "We know not what a day may bring forth," declared Lincoln in his Fourth of July letter, "but, to-day, it looks as if the Chicago ticket will be elected."[14]

With more than a little help from his friends, Lincoln placed his name at the top of that winning ticket.

ENDNOTE ABBREVIATIONS

ALPL   Abraham Lincoln Presidential Library, Springfield, Ill.

Browning diary   Theodore Calvin Pease and James G. Randall, eds., *The Diary of Orville Hickman Browning*, vol. 1, 1850–1864 (Springfield, Ill.: Illinois State Historical Library, 1925)

CPT   *Chicago Press and Tribune*

CW   Roy P. Basler, ed. *The Collected Works of Abraham Lincoln*. 8 vols. New Brunswick, N.J.: Rutgers University Press, 1953–1955.
Citation followed by volume number: page number.

HI   Douglas L. Wilson and Rodney O. Davis, eds. *Herndon's Informants: Letters, Interviews, and Statements about Abraham Lincoln* (Urbana and Chicago: University of Illinois Press, 1998)

ISJ   *Illinois State Journal*

ISR   *Illinois State Register*

LOC   Library of Congress, Washington, D.C.

LP   Abraham Lincoln Papers, Manuscript Division, Library of Congress, Washington, D.C.

NOTES

INTRODUCTION: BLOOMINGTON, ILLINOIS: DECEMBER 1858

1. David Davis, a Bloomington judge, dated Lincoln's first trip to Bloomington to 1837. See Davis interview, September 19, 1866, in *HI*, p. 346.

2. Lincoln to Eleazar A. Paine, November 19, 1858, in Roy B. Basler, ed., *The Collected Works of Abraham Lincoln* (New Brunswick, N.J.: Rutgers University Press, 1953), vol. 3, p. 340 (hereafter cited as *CW*); John Hay diary, November 8, 1864, in Michael Burlingame and John R. Turner Ettlinger, eds., *Inside Lincoln's White House: The Complete Civil War Diary of John Hay* (Carbondale: Southern Illinois University Press, 1997), p. 244.

3. Francis Fisher Browne, *The Every-day Life of Abraham Lincoln: A Narrative and Descriptive Biography with Pen-Pictures and Personal Recollections by Those Who Knew Him* (Chicago: Browne & Howell, 1913), pp. 209–10.

4. Fell's entire account of this postelection encounter in Osborn H. Oldroyd, ed., *The Lincoln Memorial: Album-Immortelles* (New York: G. W. Carleton, 1883), pp. 473–76. The exact date of this conversation cannot be pinpointed, for Lincoln made three trips to Bloomington after the Senate loss—all in December. He appeared in Bloomington December 15–16, and then returned the following week. "Hon. Abraham Lincoln," *Bloomington Daily Pantagraph*, December 17, 1858. He also was in the town on December 30. See "Opinion Concerning the Will of John Franklin," December 30, 1858, *CW* 3:347–48.

5. Douglas L. Wilson, *Honor's Voice: The Transformation of Abraham Lincoln* (New York: Vintage Books, 1999), pp. 210–231; David Herbert Donald, *Lincoln* (New York: Simon & Schuster, 1996), pp. 128, 153; Herndon to Jesse Weik, February 11, 1887, in Emanuel Hertz, *The Hidden Lincoln: From the Letters and Papers of William H. Herndon* (New York: Blue Ribbon Books, 1940), p. 172.

6. Oldroyd, *The Lincoln Memorial: Album-Immortelles*, p. 476.

ONE: RECOVERY

1. M. to the editor, January 6, 1859, *Blomington Pantagraph*, January 7, 1859.

2. "Douglas Re-Elected!" *ISR*, January 6, 1859; Arthur C. Cole, *Era of the Civil War: 1848–1870* (Springfield: Illinois Centennial Commission, 1919), p. 180.

3. "Senator Douglas," *ISR*, January 7, 1859; "The Voice of the People," *ISJ*, January 8, 1859; "Re-Election of Senator Douglas," *CPT*, January 6, 1859.

4. David Donald, *Lincoln's Herndon: A Biography* (New York: Alfred A. Knopf, 1948), pp. 22, 32; "Tablet Marks Site of Former Law Office," *ISR*, February 13, 1909.

5. Sunderine (Wilson) Temple and Wayne C. Temple, *Illinois' Fifth Capitol: The House That Lincoln Built and Caused to Be Rebuilt (1837–1865)* (Springfield, Ill.: Phillips Brothers, 1988), p. 148; "Springfield As It Is," *Cincinnati Daily Commercial*, January 12, 1859.

6. "Jubilant," *ISJ*, January 6, 1859; William E. Baringer, *Lincoln Day by Day: A Chronology, 1809–1865* (Washington, D.C.: Lincoln Sesquicentennial Commission, 1960), vol. 2, p. 239.

7. Charles S. Zane, "A Young Lawyer's Memories of Lincoln," in Rufus Rockwell Wilson, ed., *Lincoln Among His Friends: A Sheaf of Intimate Memories* (Caldwell, Idaho: Caxton Printers, 1942), p. 134.

8. Henry C. Whitney, *Life on the Circuit with Lincoln* (Boston: Estes & Lauriat, 1892), pp. 466–67. In a July 18, 1887, letter to Herndon, Whitney repeated Lincoln's desertion quote, but added "except Billy" (*HI*, p. 622).

9. "A Snow Storm," *ISJ*, January 7, 1859; "The Weather," *ISJ*, January 8, 1859; Penn to the editor, January 7, 1859, *Chicago Journal*, January 10, 1859.

10. Leonard Swett interview, *HI*, pp. 731–32.

11. Whitney, *Life on the Circuit*, p. 83.

12. G. W. Rives to O. M. Hatch, November 11, 1858, Hatch Papers, ALPL.

13. David Davis interview, September 20, 1866, *HI*, pp. 348–49; Willard L. King, *Lincoln's Manager: David Davis* (Cambridge, Mass.: Harvard University Press, 1960), pp. 59–60.

14. Whitney to Herndon, August 23, 1887, *HI*, p. 626; Davis interview, September 20, 1866, *HI*, p. 349; Lincoln's quotes in Emanuel Hertz, ed., *Lincoln Talks: A Biography in Anecdote* (New York: Viking Press, 1939), pp. 164–65, and Michael Burlingame, *The Inner World of Abraham Lincoln* (Urbana and Chicago: University of Illinois Press, 1994), pp. 249–50. In addition, three other sources refer to this informal meeting, although the authors may have parts of it confused with a more formal and conclusive meeting that transpired in February 1860. See Jeriah Bonham, *Fifty Years' Recollections with Observations and Reflections on Historical Events* (Peoria: J. W. Franks & Sons, 1883), p. 178, and Whitney, *Life on the Circuit with Lincoln*, pp. 82–84, 467–68.

15. Burlingame, *Inner World*, 250; Whitney, *Life on the Circuit*, pp. 83–84, 468. William E. Baringer (*Lincoln's Rise to Power*, p. 69) maintains that Whitney misapplied his reminiscences of an 1860 meeting to this 1859 one. Whitney's claim that it was held in the secretary of state's office and not the library evidences some confusion, but Whitney corrects any attempt to place the meeting in 1860: "Herndon fixes the date of this meeting as 'early in 1860.' In this he is in error; the occurrence was on the night succeeding the election of Douglas, on January 5th, 1859" (*Life on the Circuit*, p. 83). An as-

sessment of recollections of Lincoln rated both Whitney's and Davis's accounts as quotations "about whose authenticity there is more than average doubt" (Donald E. Fehrenbacher and Virginia Fehrenbacher, comps. and eds., *Recollected Words of Abraham Lincoln* (Stanford, Calif.: Stanford University Press, 1996), pp. liii, 131, 492–93. The agreement of these accounts with others stated above renders these plausible in the context presented here.

16. Henry Villard, *Memoirs of Henry Villard, Journalist and Financier, 1835–1900* (Boston: Houghton Mifflin, 1904), vol. 1, p. 96.

17. Ibid., p. 98; "Our Illinois Correspondence," January 7, 1859, published in the *Cincinnati Daily Commercial*, January, 12, 1859. The anecdote would be repeated often in Lincoln lore, but would change from the boy getting his finger squeezed to hurting his toe. The first use of this appears to be a misquote from Villard's interview by the *Alton Daily Courier*, on January 17, 1859. See Burlingame, *Inner World*, p. 247.

18. *ISJ*, January 27, 1859; Herndon and Weik, *Herndon's Life of Lincoln*, p. 304.

19. Herndon to Weik, November 24, 1882, in Emanuel Hertz, *The Hidden Lincoln*, pp. 88–89.

20. Only Orville Hickman Browning mentions the party. See Browning diary, February 2, 1859, p. 349.

21. Herndon to Weik, January 15, 1886, in Hertz, *The Hidden Lincoln*, p. 134; for claims of the abuse see *HI*, pp. 465, 467, 597, 722. Coffee incident described in Dale Carnegie, *Lincoln the Unknown* (New York: Century Company, 1932), p. 72; Davis assertion in *HI*, p. 349.

22. Gillespie to Herndon, January 31, 1866, *HI*, p. 181; Herndon to Weik, November 19, 1885, in Hertz, *The Hidden Lincoln*, pp. 104–5.

23. Gillespie to Herndon, January 31, 1866, *HI*, p. 181; Norman B. Judd to his wife, February 18, 1861, Judd Papers, ALPL.

24. Herndon to Weik, November 19, 1885, and February 18, 1887, in Hertz, *The Hidden Lincoln*, pp. 105, 176–77.

25. "Norman B. Judd," *Biographical Sketches of the Leading Men of Chicago* (Chicago: Wilson & St. Clair, 1868), pp. 659–70; King, *Lincoln's Manager*, 128; Michael Burlingame, ed., *Lincoln's Journalist: John Hay's Anonymous Writings for the Press, 1860–1864* (Carbondale: Southern Illinois University Press, 1998), pp. 18, 141; A. Sympson to O. M. Hatch, February 29, 1860, Hatch Papers, ALPL.

26. David Donald, *Lincoln's Herndon*, p. 78; King, *Lincoln's Manager*, pp. 128–29; David Davis to O. M. Hatch, August 18, 1858, Hatch Papers, ALPL.

27. "Conversation with Hon. N. B. Judd, Washington Feb 28 '76," in Michael Burlingame, ed., *An Oral History of Abraham Lincoln: John G. Nicolay's Interviews and Essays* (Carbondale: Southern Illinois University Press, 1996), p. 46. For a derogatory look at Judd, including a newspaper editor's claim that he favored three others in front of Lincoln, see Wilson, *Intimate Memories of Lincoln*, pp. 193–94.

28. Temple and Temple, *Illinois' Fifth Capitol*, pp. 148–49.

29. Quote in Browne, *The Every-Day Life of Abraham Lincoln*, p. 228.

30. Henry to Lincoln, February 16, 1859, LP.

31. "Second Lecture on Discoveries and Inventions," *CW* 3:356–63.

32. Professor David Zarefsky postulates this theory in "Lincoln's 1859 Speeches," *Abraham Lincoln in His Own Words* (The Great Courses, The Teaching Company Limited Partnership, 1999), part 2, lecture 17.

33. *CW* 3:356; Lamon, *The Life of Abraham Lincoln: From His Birth to His Inauguration as President* (Boston: James R. Osgood, 1872), p. 421; Herndon to Weik, February 21, 1891, in Hertz, *The Hidden Lincoln*, p. 262.

34. Caroline Kirkland, *Chicago Yesterdays: A Sheaf of Reminiscences* (Chicago: Daughaday and Company, 1919), p. 184; Jesse W. Weik, *The Real Lincoln: A Portrait* (Boston: Houghton Mifflin, 1922), pp. 73–74. The fastest trains in 1859, including stops, ran between thirty and thirty-five miles per hour to Chicago ("The Fast Train to Chicago," *Cincinnati Daily Gazette*, May 17, 1860). Lincoln's train likely averaged closer to twenty-five miles per hour and made at least ten stops. This would necessitate a ten-hour train ride from Springfield to Chicago.

35. Lincoln to Judd, November 15, 1858, and Judd to Lincoln, November 15 and 20, 1858, LP.

36. Lincoln to Judd, November 16, 1858, *CW* 3:337; Judd to Lincoln, May 16 and 28, 1860, LP.

37. "A Good Feeling Crowd," *CPT*, March 2, 1859.

38. Robert R. Hitt, "An Unpublished Speech of Abraham Lincoln," *North American Review* 157, issue 440 (July 1893), pp. 120–21.

39. Herndon to Bartlett, July 19, 1887, in Hertz, *The Hidden Lincoln*, pp. 191–92.

40. Hitt, "An Unpublished Speech of Abraham Lincoln," p. 120.

41. Ibid., "An pp. 120–21.

42. Lincoln to Trumbull, December 11, 1858, *CW* 3:344–45.

43. Hitt, "An Unpublished Speech of Abraham Lincoln," pp. 123–27.

44. Ibid., pp. 127–28.

45. "Local News," *Chicago Herald*, March 2, 1859.

46. Hitt, "An Unpublished Speech of Abraham Lincoln," pp. 120–21.

47. Drummond's recollection in Browne, *The Every-day Life of Abraham Lincoln*, p. 144.

TWO: DIVIDED HOUSE

1. Lincoln to William M. Morris, March 28, 1859, *CW* 3:374; "The Lecture," *Bloomington Pantagraph*, April 9, 1859; Harry E. Pratt, comp., *Concerning Mr. Lincoln, in Which Abraham Lincoln Is pictured As He Appeared to Letter Writers of His Time* (Springfield, Ill.: Abraham Lincoln Association, 1944), p. 22.

2. *CW* 3:372, 376–77.

3. William A. Ross to Lincoln, March 18 and April 2, 1859, LP; Lincoln to Ross, March 26, 1859, *CW* 3:372–73.

4. Lincoln to Henry L. Pierce and Others, April 6, 1859, *CW* 3:374–76.

5. Knapp to Hatch, May 12, 1859, O. M. Hatch Papers, ALPL.

6. "Very Proper," *Bloomington Pantagraph*, April 9, 1859; "The Tall Sucker," *Bloomington Pantagraph*, April 6, 1859.

7. Lincoln to Judd, November 16, 1858, *CW* 3:337; Lincoln, O. M. Hatch, and Jesse K. Dubois to Newton Bateman, November 20, 1858, *CW* 3:341; Donald, *Lincoln*, p. 231.

8. Donald E. Fehrenbacher, *Chicago Giant: A Biography of "Long John" Wentworth* (Madison, Wisc.: American History Research Center, 1957), pp. 162–66.

9. Ibid., p. 165; "Wentworth on Presidential Candidates," *CPT*, April 21, 1859; "Republican Mass Meeting at Metropolitan Hall," *CPT*, April 4, 1859; Wilson to Hatch, April 3, 1859, O. M. Hatch Papers, ALPL.

10. Lincoln to Judd, September 23, 1858, *CW* 3:202; Davis to Lincoln, January 1, [1859], LP.

11. Bissell to Hatch, n.d., O. M. Hatch Papers, ALPL. Although this is not dated, the letter is found in the January–April 1859 folder.

12. Donald, *Lincoln*, p. 242.

13. Judd to Lincoln, May 13, 1859, LP.

14. Thomas J. McCormack, ed., *Memoirs of Gustave Koerner, 1809–1896* (Cedar Rapids, Iowa: Torch Press, 1909), vol. 2, p. 80. Although Koerner's memoirs discuss the strategy toward the end of 1859, the genesis of it was likely at the April meeting of the central committee in Bloomington. It was the first formal meeting of Illinois Republicans in 1859, and it was held after Lincoln revealed his desire to run in January. Koerner discusses the strategy in his memoirs before his review of the Republican National Committee meeting in December, thus diminishing the possibility that this strategy was discussed the next time the committee met in the winter of 1860. The fact that Lincoln himself squelched an attempt to create a boom nine days after the Bloomington meeting (see Lincoln to Pickett, April 16, 1859, *CW* 3:377) is consistent and timely with the strategy being discussed and devised on April 7, 1859.

15. Cole, *The Era of the Civil War*, p. 23; Gustave P. Koerner to Lincoln, April 4, 1859, LP; Lincoln to Koerner, April 11, 1859, *CW* 3:376–77; McCormack, ed., *Memoirs of Gustave Koerner*, vol. 2, pp. 74–76.

16. Lincoln to Koerner, April 11, 1858, *CW* 3:376–77; Lincoln to Schuyler Colfax, July 6, 1859, *CW* 3:392.

17. "The Massachusetts Amendment: Letter from Hon. N. B. Judd," *CPT*, May 26, 1859.

18. Lincoln to Canisius, May 17, 1859, *CW* 3:380–81.

19. Judd to Lincoln, May 13, 1859, LP; "Contract with Theodore Canisius," May [30?], 1859, *CW* 3:383; Lincoln to Daniel A. Cheever, August 19, 1859, *CW* supplement: 41. For a translated excerpt of Lincoln's May 17, 1859, letter in German papers, see "Lincoln on the Rights of Foreign Born Citizens and on Fusion," *Cincinnati Daily Commercial*, May 25, 1860.

20. Pickett to Lincoln, April 13, 1859, LP.

21. Lincoln to Pickett, April 16, 1859, *CW* 3:377.

22. Scroggs to Herndon, October 3, 1866, *HI*, p. 365; *Central Illinois Gazette* article clipped into *ISJ*, May 12, 1859.

23. Lincoln to the editor of the *Central Transcript*, July 3, 1859, *CW* 3:389–90.

24. Lincoln's views on the law expressed in an August 24, 1855, letter to his friend, Joshua F. Speed. (See *CW* 2:320.)

25. Lincoln to Chase, June 9, 1859, *CW* 3:384.

26. Chase to Lincoln, June 13, 1859, LP.

27. Lincoln to Chase, June 20, 1859, *CW* 3:386.

28. John Niven, *Salmon P. Chase: A Biography* (New York: Oxford University Press, 1995), pp. 163, 213; Medill to Chase, April 26 and June 8, 1859, in John Niven, ed., *The Salmon P. Chase Papers* (Kent, Ohio: Kent State University Press, 1996), vol. 3, pp. 10–14.

29. J. M. Lucas to O. M. Hatch, July [1859], Hatch Papers, ALPL; Lincoln to Sargent, June 23, 1860, *CW* 3:387–88.

30. Lincoln to Samuel Galloway, July 28, 1859, *CW* 3:395.

31. Lincoln to Schuyler Colfax, July 6, 1859, *CW* 3:390–91; Lincoln to Sargent, June 23, 1859, *CW* 3:387–88.

32. Galloway to Lincoln, July 23, 1859, LP.

33. Lincoln to Samuel Galloway, July 28, 1859, *CW* 3:395.

34. Baringer, *Lincoln Day by Day*, vol. 2, p. 254.

35. *ISJ*, July 9, 1859; "The Fourth of July in Logan County," *Lincoln Herald*, July 6, 1859.

36. "Personal," *CPT*, July 20, 1859; "Mr. Lincoln in Iowa and Missouri," *CPT*, August 20, 1859.

37. "Abraham Lincoln at Council Bluffs," *Iowa City Citizen*, August 13, 1909.

38. Ibid.

39. Judd to Lincoln, August 28, 1859, LP; Grenville Dodge, *Personal Recollections of President Abraham Lincoln, General Ulysses S. Grant, and General William T. Sherman* (Council Bluffs, Iowa: Monarch Printing Company, 1914), p. 10; "Abe Lincoln," *Council Bluffs Nonpareil*, August 20, 1859; "Abe Lincoln on the Slope," *Council Bluffs Bugle*, August 17, 1859.

40. *St. Joseph Journal* excerpt republished under "Mr. Lincoln in Iowa and Missouri," *CPT*, August 20, 1859.

41. Lincoln to D. J. Powers, August 18, 1859, and Lincoln to Daniel Rohrer, August 19, 1859, *CW* 3:397.

42. "A House Divided," *CW* 2:461. In this famous and controversial speech, Lincoln completed the thought by claiming that either slavery advocates would succeed in spreading slavery throughout the land, or opponents would succeed in preventing the spread and thus allowing slavery to follow the "course of ultimate extinction."

43. Seward's speech in George Baker, ed., *The Works of William H. Seward* (Boston: Houghton Mifflin, 1884), vol. 4, pp. 289–302.

44. "A Word to the Adopted Citizens of the United States," *[Middletown, N.Y.] Banner of Liberty*, August 3, 1859.

45. Burlingame, *Inside Lincoln's White House*, p. 122; Swett to Herndon, January 17, 1866, *HI*, p. 163.

46. Greeley to Herndon, December 4, 1859, Greeley Papers, New York Public Library; *Bloomington Daily Pantagraph*, December 17, 18, and 23, 1858.

47. "Greeley in Kansas," *[Wellsborough, Pa.] Agitator*, June 9, 1859.

THREE: CHASE'S BACKYARD

1. *The People of Illinois v. Peachy Quinn Harrison*, 1859, trial transcript in ALPL.

2. Herndon and Weik, *Herndon's Life of Lincoln*, p. 264. Although Herndon's accounts claim teams of four for the prosecution and for the defense, the first page of the trial transcript lists only three attorneys for each side. All newspaper reports, along with the handwritten transcript, Hitt's printed court minutes, and grand jury records, are compiled in the Lincoln Legal Papers, CD-ROM at ALPL (hereafter cited as Harrison trial papers).

3. "The Harrison Case," *Springfield Daily Evening Independent*, August 31, 1859; trial transcript, p. 68, Harrison trial papers.

4. Trial transcript, Harrison trial papers, p. 60; Herndon to Weik, November 20, 1885, in Hertz, *The Hidden Lincoln*, p. 107; T. W. S. Kidd testimony in Ida M. Tarbell, *The Life of Abraham Lincoln*, pp. 45–46; Herndon quote reproduced in Burlingame, *Inner World*, p. 155.

5. Herndon and Weik, *Herndon's Life of Lincoln*, pp. 264–65; Herndon to Weik, November 20, 1885, in Hertz, *The Hidden Lincoln*, pp. 107–8.

6. Newspaper clippings, in Harrison trial papers; Herndon to Weik, November 20, 1885, in Hertz, *The Hidden Lincoln*, p 108.

7. Harrison trial papers; *ISJ*, September 5, 1859; Walter B. Stevens, *A Reporter's Lincoln* (Lincoln: University of Nebraska Press, 1998), p. 99.

8. Wilson, ed., *Intimate Memories of Lincoln*, pp. 89–90; Edward M. Pallette, "Abraham Lincoln and Quinn Harrison, Los Angeles. Reprint from the Bulletin of the California State Society, Sons of the Revolution December, 1937," ALPL; Harrison trial papers; Herndon to Weik, November 20, 1885, in Hertz, *The Hidden Lincoln*, p. 108.

9. Bascom to Lincoln, September 1, 1859, and Zinn to Lincoln, September 2, 1859, LP.

10. Stephen A. Douglas, "Popular Sovereignty in the Territories," *Harper's New Monthly Magazine*, September 1859, pp. 519–37.

11. Judd to Lincoln, September 10, 1859, LP; Lincoln to Zinn, September 6, 1859, *CW* 3:400.

12. "Fragments: Notes for Speeches," *CW* 3:397–99; Trumbull to Lincoln, August 29, 1859, LP.

13. "Fragments: Notes for Speeches," *CW* 3:397–99; Harry V. Jaffa and Robert W. Johannsen, eds., *In the Name of the People: Speeches and Writings of Lincoln and Douglas in the Ohio Campaign of 1859* (Columbus: Ohio State University Press, 1959), p. 3.

14. R. B. Hayes to Addison Peale Russell, September 14, 1859, reproduced in Daniel J. Ryan, *Lincoln and Ohio* (Columbus: Ohio State Archaeological and Historical Society, 1923), pp. 70–71.

15. Medill to Lincoln, September 10, 1859, LP.

16. Ibid.; "Mr. Lincoln in Ohio," *CPT*, September 19, 1859.

17. Ryan, *Lincoln and Ohio*, pp. 35–37; Jaffa and Johannsen, *In the Name of the People,* pp. 17–20.

18. Jaffa and Johannsen, *In the Name of the People,* p. 19; "Speech of the Hon. Abraham Lincoln at Columbus," *Ohio State Journal*, September 17, 1859.

19. Lloyd Ostendorf, *Mr. Lincoln Came to Dayton* (Dayton: Otterbein Press, 1959), pp. 7, 13–16.

20. Ibid., pp. 25–31; Daniel J. Kenny, *The American Newspaper Directory and the Record of the Press* (New York: Watson & Co., 1861), p. 121.

21. Ostendorf, *Mr. Lincoln Came to Dayton*, pp. 25–31; "The Republican Doctrine," *ISJ*, October 19, 1859; "Rob C. Schenck," *Janesville [Wisc.] Weekly Gazette and Free Press*, September 23, 1859.

22. Ostendorf, *Mr. Lincoln Came to Dayton*, p. 31.

23. W. M. Dickson, "Abraham Lincoln in Cincinnati," *Harper's New Monthly Magazine*, June 1884, p. 62.

24. Speech of the Hon. Abram Lincoln, of Illinois" and "Meteorological Observations," *Cincinnati Daily Commercial*, September 19, 1859; Kenny, *The American Newspaper Directory*, p. 121.

25. In part of his Cincinnati speech, Lincoln stated of Douglas, "At Columbus, and probably here, he undertook to compliment the people . . ." (Jaffa and Johannsen, *In the Name of the People*, p. 296). The definitive statement for Columbus and assumption for Cincinnati appears based on Lincoln's access to Douglas's remarks at the former, but not the latter.

26. Lincoln's speech, including parenthetical additions of the crowd reaction, are reproduced in Jaffa and Johannsen, *In the Name of the People*, pp. 271–307.

27. Ibid., pp. 274–76, 281.

28. Ibid., pp. 280, 284; Donald, *Lincoln*, p. 233.

29. Jaffa and Johannsen, *In the Name of the People*, p. 285.

30. Ibid., pp. 279, 284.

31. Ibid., pp. 286–90.

32. Ibid., pp. 294–95; Ryan, *Lincoln and Ohio*, pp. 98–101.

33. Jaffa and Johannsen, *In the Name of the People*, p. 295.

34. Ibid., p. 297.

35. Ibid., pp. 298–301.

36. Ibid., pp. 302–3.

37. Ibid., pp. 305–7.

FOUR: THE GIANT KILLER

1. "Republican Mass Meeting on Saturday Night," *Cincinnati Daily Commercial*, September 19, 1859.

2. Carter in "Abraham Lincoln," *Janesville [Wisc.] Gazette*, August 8, 1879; H. E. Dummer testimony, ca. 1865–66, in *HI*, p. 442; "Lincoln's Spectacles," *Washington Post*, August 4, 1883.

3. "Abraham Lincoln," *Janesville Gazette*, August 8, 1879.

4. Lincoln to Dickson, October 17, 1859, *CW* 3:490–91; "Lincoln and His Hotel," *Washington Post*, October 28, 1883; Mary Lincoln to Hannah Shearer, October 2, 1859, in Turner and Turner, *Mary Todd Lincoln: Her Life and Letters*, p. 59.

5. "Mr. Lincoln's Speech" and untitled editorial in *Cincinnati Daily Commercial*, September 19, 1859. For a broad array of editorials in Cincinnati papers, see Ryan, *Lincoln and Ohio*, pp. 98–99.

6. *Indianapolis Journal*, September 20, 1859; *Indianapolis Atlas*, September 20, 1859; *CW* 3:463–70.

7. Fletcher diary, September 19, 1859, in Gail Thornbrough, Dorothy L. Riker, and Paula Corpuz, eds., *The Diary of Calvin Fletcher* (Indianapolis: Indiana Historical Society, 1978), Vol. 6, p. 412.

8. Allen Thorndike Rice, ed. *Reminiscences of Abraham Lincoln by Distinguished Men of His Time.* (New York: North American Review, 1888), p. 414.

9. "Hon. Abraham Lincoln in Ohio," *CPT*, September 19, 1859; "Lincoln at Cincinnati," *CPT*, September 21, 1859; "Mr. Lincoln in Ohio," *Clinton Transcript*, September 22, 1859; "Lincoln in Ohio," *ISJ*, September 22, 1859.

10. *New York Times*, September 22, 1859; "Mr. Lincoln's Cincinnati Speech," *ISJ*, September 28, 1859 (mentions publication by *National Intelligencer* of September 22); "Items," *Portland Weekly Oregonian*, November 26, 1859; "Political," *CPT*, February 2, 1860 (mentions publication of speech by *Oregon Argus* of December 17); Bascom to Lincoln, September 20, 1859, LP.

11. "Abraham Lincoln in Ohio," *Aurora Weekly Beacon*, September 29, 1859.

12. Lincoln to Chase, September 21, 1859, *CW* 3:470–71.

13. E. Studly to "Cousin" O. M. Hatch, September 7, 1859, and J. M. Lucas to Hatch, October 7, 1859, Hatch Papers, ALPL.

14. *Chicago Times* article reprinted in "Douglas-Killing—Glorious Results," *Coshocton [Ohio] County Democrat*, November 9, 1859; "From the Chicago Press and Tribune,"

Whitewater [Wisc.] Register, February 25, 1860; "Mr. Lincoln's Speech," *Cincinnati Daily Commercial*, September 19, 1859.

15. "Speech at Cincinnati, Ohio," *CW* 3:438–62.

16. Lincoln to Powers, August 18, 1859, *CW* 3:397.

17. "The State Fair," *Milwaukee Sentinel*, October 1, 1859.

18. "Address Before the Wisconsin State Agricultural Society," *CW* 3:472–73; correspondence to the *Oeonto Pioneer* reproduced in "A Portrait of 'Abe' Lincoln," [*Platteville, Wisc.*] *Grant County Witness*, October 20, 1859.

19. *CW* 3:477–79.

20. Ibid., pp. 476–79; "Stiletto" quote in the *Appleton Motor*, October 27, 1859.

21. *CW* 3:479–81.

22. *Appleton Motor*, October 27, 1859; "The State Fair," *Lacrosse [Wisc.] Republican*, October 5, 1859.

23. *Milwaukee Wisconsin* editorial reproduced in *Lacrosse Republican*, October 12, 1859; *Free Democrat* editorial reproduced in "Abraham Lincoln—The Agricultural Address," *ISJ*, October 5, 1859.

24. *Rock County Chronicle* 3 (Janesville, Wisc.: Rock County Historical Society, 1957), p. 4; "The State Fair," *Lacrosse [Wisc.] Republican*, October 5, 1859.

25. "Beloit, Wis. Oct. 3d., 1859," *Prescott [Wisc.] Transcript*, October 8, 1859.

26. "Speech at Beloit, Wisconsin," *CW* 3:482–84.

27. "A Portrait of 'Abe' Lincoln," [*Platteville, Wisc.*] *Grant County Witness*, October 20, 1859.

28. "Of Course," *Janesville Weekly Gazette and Free Press*, October 14, 1859.

29. "Speech of Hon. A. Lincoln," *Janesville Weekly Gazette and Free Press*, October 7, 1859; *Lincoln Visits Beloit and Janesville, Wisconsin* (Madison: Lincoln Fellowship of Wisconsin, 1949), p. 9.

30. "Speech of Hon. A. Lincoln," *Janesville Gazette*, October 4, 1859.

31. "The Republican Doctrine," *ISJ*, October 19, 1859; "Items," *Portland Weekly Oregonian*, November 26, 1859.

FIVE: BIRTH OF A BOOM

1. "Republican Meeting," *Clinton Central Transcript*, October 20, 1859.

2. "De Witt Circuit Court," *Central Transcript*, October 6, 1859.

3. "Republican Meeting," *Clinton Central Transcript*, October 20, 1859; Miers, ed., *Lincoln Day by Day*, Vol. 2, p. 263.

4. "Republican Meeting" and "Lincoln for President," *Clinton Central Transcript*, October 20, 1859.

5. "Republican Meeting Saturday Night," *ISJ*, October 17, 1859; "Great Popular Demonstration," *ISJ*, October 18, 1859.

6. Bascom to Lincoln, October 13, 1859, LP.

7. Galloway to Lincoln, October 13, 1859, LP.

8. "A Presidential Ticket," *ISJ*, October 18, 1859.

9. Lincoln to William E. Frazer, November 1, 1859, *CW* 3:491.

10. Weed to Judd and Judd to Lincoln, October 20, 1859, LP.

11. Briggs to Lincoln, October 13, 1859, LP; Harold Holzer, *Lincoln at Cooper Union: The Speech That Made Abraham Lincoln President* (New York: Simon & Schuster, 2004), pp.

10–17. Lincoln was originally scheduled to speak in Kansas in May. See Mary Lincoln to Hannah Shearer, April 24, 1859, in Turner and Turner, *Mary Todd Lincoln*, p. 55.

12. Lincoln to Doctor——, November 2, and to P. Quinn Harrison, November 3, 1859, *CW* 3:492; Lincoln to Jesse A. Pickrell, November 3, 1859, *CW* 3:493; "Republican Torch Light Procession," *ISJ*, October 29, 1859; "Lincoln at Mechanicsburg," *ISJ*, November 7, 1859.

13. James M. McPherson, *Battle Cry of Freedom: The Civil War Era* (New York and Oxford: Oxford University Press, 1988), pp. 202–5.

14. Delahay to Lincoln, November 14 and 15, 1859, LP.

15. "From Chicago to St. Joseph by Railroad," *Chicago Daily Democrat*, October 29, 1859; Daniel W. Wilder, report of Lincoln in Kansas, July 4, 1884, Kansas Historical Society Papers; Alan W. Farley, "When Lincoln Came to Kansas Territory," address presented to Fort Leavenworth Historical Society, November 17, 1959; "Getting Scared," *St. Joseph Gazette* article excerpted in the *Leavenworth Daily Times*, December 3, 1859.

16. Wilder's account reproduced in Carol Dark Ayres, *Lincoln and Kansas: Partnership for Freedom* (Manhattan, Kans.: Sunflower University Press, 2001), pp. 78–80. The town of Elwood has since been moved a few miles inland from the riverbank it originally occupied.

17. "Speech at Elwood, Kansas," *CW* 3:495–97. Although the *Elwood Free Press* of December 3 suggests the speech was made on December 1, the subsequent timeline strongly suggests that this was impossible and that Lincoln's speech was actually delivered there on November 30.

18. Harold G. Villard and Oswald Garrison Villard, eds., *Lincoln on the Eve of '61: A Journalist's Story by Henry Villard* (Wesport, Conn.: Greenwood Press, 1940), pp. 8–9.

19. Albert D. Richardson, *The Secret Service, the Field, the Dungeon, and the Escape* (Hartford, Conn.: American Publishing Company, 1865), pp. 313–15.

20. "Killing Off 'Abe' Lincoln," *Iowa City Press-Citizen*, October 24, 1925.

21. Account of Frank A. Root, reproduced in Ayres, *Lincoln and Kansas*, pp. 88–89.

22. Ibid., pp. 89–95. Lincoln's joke spread through the press in slightly altered versions. See "Abe Lincoln's Wit," *Cincinnati Daily Commercial*, May 17, 1860.

23. "Great Gathering of Republicans!" *Leavenworth Daily Times*, December 5, 1859; "Old Abe Lincoln," *Leavenworth Weekly Herald*, December 10, 1859.

24. "Old Abe Lincoln," *Leavenworth Weekly Herald*, December 10, 1859.

25. "Great Gathering of Republicans!" *Leavenworth Daily Times*, December 5, 1859; "Old Abe Lincoln," *Leavenworth Weekly Herald*, December 10, 1859.

26. "Old Abe Lincoln," *Leavenworth Weekly Herald*, December 10, 1859.

27. "Mr. Lincoln's Speech," *Leavenworth Daily Times*, December 5, 1859.

28. Interview of Daniel R. Anthony published in the *Kansas City Star*, February 23, 1902; reproduced in Ayres, *Lincoln and Kansas*, pp. 119–20.

29. "Abram Lincoln Again," *Leavenworth Weekly Herald*, December 10, 1859.

30. "Second Speech of Hon. Abe Lincoln," *Leavenworth Daily Times*, December 6, 1859.

31. Ayres, *Lincoln and Kansas*, p. 121.

32. Inscription reproduced in Emanuel Hertz, *Abraham Lincoln: A New Portrait* (New York: Horace Liveright, 1931), Vol. 2, p. 761.

33. W. H. Gill to the *Leavenworth Weekly Herald*, December 7, 1859, published on December 10, 1859.

34. O. A. Benjamin to Lincoln, December 3, 1859, LP.

35. "Hon. A. Lincoln," *ISJ*, December 10, 1859.

SIX: WINTER HEAT

1. Donald E. Fehrenbacher, *Chicago Giant: A Biography of "Long John" Wentworth* (Madison, Wisc.: American History Research Center, 1957), p. 161.

2. For examples of these accusing editorials, see *Chicago Weekly Democrat*, November 12 and 26, and December 10, 1859.

3. Judd to Lincoln, December 1, 1859, LP.

4. Lincoln to Judd, December 9, 1859, LP.

5. Lincoln to Jesse W. Fell, December 20, 1859, *CW* 3:511–12.

6. Ibid.

7. "Mr. Lincoln and Mr. Judd," *ISJ*, February 9, 1860.

8. Lincoln to Judd, November 15, 1858 and December 14, 1859, *CW* 3:336, 509.

9. "National Committees," *New York Times*, December 22, 1859; "National Republican Committee," *New York Times*, December 23, 1859; "The Republican National Convention," *Milwaukee Sentinel*, December 26, 1859.

10. "The National Republican Convention," *CPT*, December 22, 1859; *Milwaukee Sentinel*, December 22, 1859.

11. "National Committees," *New York Times*, December 22, 1859; Reinhard H. Luthin, *The First Lincoln Campaign* (Cambridge, Mass.: Harvard University Press, 1944), p. 21.

12. "National Republican Convention to Be Held at Chicago," *Chicago Evening Journal*, December 22, 1859, "Republican National Convention at Chicago, June 13th," *Chicago Weekly Democrat*, December 31 1859.

13. Mark W. Delahay to Lincoln, December 23, 1859, LP. Assessment of necessary states for Republicans obtained from November 16 *Chicago Press and Tribune* editorial. See excerpt in Philip Kinsley, *The Chicago Tribune: Its First Hundred Years* (New York: Alfred A. Knopf, 1943), Vol. 1, p. 102.

14. "Secret Caucus of Leading Black Republicans," *New York Herald* report republished in *Dawson's Fort Wayne Times* on January 4, 1860.

15. "Mr. Lincoln and the Presidency," *ISJ*, January 14, 1860.

16. Baringer, *Lincoln's Rise to Power*, pp. 142–43. Grimshaw claimed that Lincoln took an additional day to consent (Grimshaw to Herndon, April 28, 1866, *HI*, pp. 247–48). Although possible, this seems unlikely, for it suggests that Lincoln was not anticipating this endorsement and needed to mull it over. The groundswell of support and endorsements, along with the 1859 State Central Committee plan, contradict any indecisiveness on Lincoln's part to agree to the backing of this all-important caucus.

17. George Browne to Hatch, February 21, 1860, Hatch Papers, ALPL.

18. Lincoln to Wentworth, February 9, 1860, *CW* second suppl.: 18–19; Fehrenbacher, *Chicago Giant*, pp. 171–72.

19. Wentworth to Lincoln, December 21, 1859, and Davis to Lincoln, February 21, 1860, LP.

20. *Chicago Weekly Democrat*, April 28, 1859; *Chicago Daily Democrat*, April 20, 1859; "Good News!" *Chicago Weekly Democrat*, December 31, 1859.

21. Lincoln to Judd, February 5, 1860, LP.

22. Ibid.; Judd to Lincoln, January 31, 1860, LP; Donald, *Lincoln's Herndon*, p. 135.

23. *ISJ*, January 25, 1860; "Republican State Convention," *CPT*, February 10, 1860; David L. Phillips to Lincoln, February 13, 1860, LP.

24. Browning to Charles Gibson, February 8, 1860, ALPL.

25. Ibid.; Browning diary, February 8, 1860, in *The Diary of Orville Hickman Browning*, vol. 1, p. 395.

26. Browning to Gibson, February 8, 1860, ALPL; George D. Prentice to Hatch, January 9, 1860, and E. M. Smith to Hatch, January 23, 1860, Hatch Papers, ALPL; Wentworth to Lincoln, February 7, 1860, LP; Greeley to Herndon, December 4, 1859, Greeley Papers, New York Public Library.

27. Davis to Henry E. Dummer, February 20, 1860, in Pratt, comp., *Concerning Mr. Lincoln*, pp. 22–23.

28. For Browning's discussion of Bates with Judd, see Browning diary, October 12, 1859, p. 382.

29. Lincoln to Judd, February 9, 1860, *CW* 3:517.

30. "Indiana," *CPT*, December 14, 1859; King, *Lincoln's Manager*, p. 127.

31. Horace White to Lincoln, February 10, 1860, LP; Lincoln to White, February 13, 1860, *CW* 3:519; *CPT*, February 16, 1860; Judd to Lincoln, February 21, 1860, LP.

32. Kinsley, *The Chicago Tribune*, pp. 107–8.

33. Newton MacMillan, "Recollections of Lincoln, Furnished by Joseph Medill," *Chicago Tribune*, April 21, 1895.

34. "Chicago," "From Washington," February 20, 1860, published in the *CPT* on February 27, 1860.

35. Number of Lincoln-endorsing papers determined by the *Clinton Transcript* and reproduced in *ISJ*, February 27, 1860. "Growth of U.S. Newspaper Publication, 1840–1860," in Allan R. Pred, *Urban Growth and City Systems in the United States, 1840–1860*, 2nd ed. (Cambridge, Mass.: Harvard University Press, 1973), table A 40. This table lists 3,725 newspapers for 1860, including 387 daily papers. It is assumed that at least a score of papers ran their first editions after February of that year.

36. *Reading Journal* editorial reproduced in *ISJ*, December 5, 1859; Harold K. Sage, *Jesse W. Fell and the Lincoln Autobiography* (Bloomington, Ill.: Smith Printing, 1971), copy in Fell Family Papers, LOC.

37. "Short Paragraphs," *Hartford Daily Courant*, February 6, 1860; *New York Herald* report reproduced in *ISJ*, January 18, 1860.

38. L. B. G. to the editor, January 8, 1860 published in both *ISJ* and *CPT*, January 12, 1860.

39. J. G. Paddock to Hatch, April 28, 1860, Hatch Papers, ALPL; John O. Johnson to Hatch, February 17, 1860, Hatch Papers, ALPL.

40. Lincoln to James A. Briggs, November 13, 1859, *CW* 3:494.

41. "The Hon. Abraham Lincoln," *Ohio State Journal* article excerpted in *CPT*, January 21, 1860; "Presidential. For Abraham Lincoln," Milwaukee newspaper article excerpted in *CPT*, January 9, 1860.

42. Pred, *Urban Growth and City Systems*, table A40; Kinsley, *The Chicago Tribune* p. 145.

43. Allen C. Guelzo, *Lincoln and Douglas: The Debates That Defined America* (New York: Simon & Schuster, 2008), pp. xxii, 97; Frederic Hudson, Alfred McClung Lee, and Frank Luther Mott, *American Journalism 1690–1940* (New York: Routledge, 2000), p. 251.

44. Horace White to Lincoln, February 10, 1860, LP; Lincoln to White, February 13, 1860, *CW* 3:519.

SEVEN: SEWARD'S BACKYARD

1. Holzer, *Lincoln at Cooper Union,* pp. 58–64. Joseph Medill claimed that Lincoln visited him at the *Press and Tribune* office on the first leg of his trip to give the editor an advance copy of the speech (Newton MacMillan, "Recollections of Lincoln, Furnished by Joseph Medill," *Chicago Tribune,* April 21, 1895). This is impossible for two reasons. His rail route never passed through Chicago (Holzer, *Lincoln at Cooper Union,* p. 60) and Medill was in Washington hyping Lincoln in his letters to the newspaper under the pseudonym "Chicago" (see "Chicago," "From Washington," February 20, 1860, published in the *CPT* on February 27, 1860).

2. Number of speeches obtained from James M. McPherson, *This Mighty Scourge: Perspectives on the Civil War* (Oxford and New York: Oxford University Press, 2007), p. 197.

3. *New York Tribune* article reproduced in "Mr. Lincoln in New York," *ISJ,* March 1, 1860.

4. Lincoln to Cornelius F. McNeill, April 6, 1860, *CW* 4:38; Holzer, *Lincoln at Cooper Union,* pp. 73–76; Charles C. Nott to Lincoln, February 9, 1860, LP.

5. Lincoln's letter to the committee is not extant but is acknowledged in a response likely received within the week he departed Springfield. See James A. Briggs to Lincoln, February 15, 1860, LP.

6. Ibid.; Henry C. Bowen, "Recollections of Abraham Lincoln," in William Hayes Ward, ed., *Abraham Lincoln: Tributes from His Associates* (New York: Thomas Y. Crowell, 1895), p. 27. Bowen states that Lincoln entered the office carrying his "comical-looking carpet-bag." If true, then the visit may have occurred before he checked into the Astor House.

7. Bowen, "Recollections of Abraham Lincoln," pp. 28–29.

8. *New York Herald,* February 27, 1860; "Mr. Lincoln in New York," *ISJ,* March 3, 1860.

9. Ralph Gary, *Following in Mr. Lincoln's Footsteps: A Historical Reference to Hundreds of Sites Visited by Abraham Lincoln* (New York: Carroll & Graf, 2001), p. 269; Roy Meredith, *Mr. Lincoln's Camera Man, Mathew B. Brady* (New York: Charles Scribner's Sons, 1946), p. 59.

10. Holzer, *Lincoln at Cooper Union,* p. 105.

11. "Republican Ratification Meeting: Speeches of Mr. William W. Evarts, Ex-Gov. Corwin, Senator Diven, and Others," *New York Times,* November 4, 1860.

12. Holzer, *Lincoln at Cooper Union,* pp. 108–9; George Haven Putnam, *Memories of My Youth, 1844–1865* (New York: Knickerbocker Press, 1914), p. 81.

13. "Address at Cooper Institute," *CW* 3:523–31.

14. See "National Policies," *New York Times,* September 8, 1859, for the text of the Douglas speech at Columbus, Ohio. Lincoln did not quote the Douglas line exactly, substituting "the Government" for "this Government."

15. "Address at Cooper Union," *CW* 3:523.

16. Ibid., pp. 523–32.

17. Ibid., p. 522.

18. Ibid., pp. 533–34.

19. Ibid., p. 535.

20. Ibid., pp. 535–37.

21. Ibid., pp. 537–41.

22. Gary Wills, *Negro President: Jefferson and Slave Power* (Boston: Mariner Books, 2005), pp. 8–9, 22–25, 120–22, 138–39; Jefferson to John Holmes, April 22, 1820, LOC; "Mr. Lincoln in New York," *ISR*, March 3, 1860.

23. "Address at Cooper Institute," *CW* 3:541–47.

24. Ibid., pp. 547–50.

25. Quote reproduced in Holzer, *Lincoln at Cooper Union*, p. 146.

26. Cummings written recollection reproduced in Henry B. Rankin, *Intimate Character Sketches of Abraham Lincoln* (New York: J. B. Lippincott, 1924), pp. 190–91.

27. It has been estimated that a minimum of 170,000 copies circulated in the four papers through February 28. See Holzer, *Lincoln at Cooper Union*, p. 149.

28. "Mr. Lincoln in New York," *ISR*, March 3, 1860.

29. *Providence Journal* report clipped into "Mr. Lincoln in Rhode Island," *ISJ*, March 7, 1860.

30. Frank J. Williams, "A Candidate Speaks in Rhode Island: Abraham Lincoln Visits Providence and Woonsocket, 1860," *Rhode Island History* 51, no. 4 (November 1993), pp. 114–15.

31. "Speech at Hartford, Connecticut, March 5, 1860," *CW* 4:5–6. At the March 5 speech Lincoln stated that he met Clay "in the cars at New Haven one day last week." It is not likely that he was actually in New Haven until after this speech; therefore, the exact date and place of the meeting cannot be determined.

32. William B. Morrill to Lincoln, February 28, 1860, LP; Holzer, *Lincoln at Cooper Union*, pp. 177, 183.

33. Edward L. Page, *Abraham Lincoln in New Hampshire* (Boston: Houghton Mifflin, 1929), pp. 26–102; Lincoln to his wife, March 4, 1860, LP; Stevens, *A Reporter's Lincoln*, pp. 95–96.

34. Lincoln to his wife, March 4, 1860, LP.

35. Ibid.; Lincoln to Briggs, March 4, 1860, *CW* second suppl.: 19–20; Holzer, *Lincoln at Cooper Union*, p. 191.

36. "Abe Lincoln at the City Hall," *Hartford Daily Courant*, March 6, 1860; " 'Old Abe' on Snakes," newspaper clipping, author's collection.

37. Francis B. Carpenter, *Six Months at the White House with President Lincoln: The Story of a Picture* (New York: Hurd & Houghton, 1866), pp. 310–11.

38. Gulliver's account in ibid., pp. 308–17. Although this recollection has enough factual errors in it to relegate it to a "pretended reminiscence" (see Fehrenbacher and Fehrenbacher, eds., *Recollected Words of Abraham Lincoln*, pp. 189–90), the fact that Lincoln received advance proofs of the reminiscence, had the option to suppress it, and chose not to indicates that he considered his conversation with Gulliver to be generally factual. (See Holzer, *Lincoln at Cooper Union*, pp. 200–201 for this contrary analysis.)

39. Holzer, *Lincoln at Cooper Union*, pp. 201–4.

EIGHT: THE CANDIDATE

1. Fehrenbacher, *Chicago Giant*, pp. 172–73.

2. Judd to Lincoln, February 21, 1860, LP.

3. Fehrenbacher, *Chicago Giant*, pp. 173–74.

4. Ibid.; Wentworth to Lincoln, February 22, 1860, and Davis to Lincoln, February 21 and 25, 1860, all three in LP.

5. *Chicago Journal*, March 22, 1860.

6. C. D. Hay to Lincoln, March 27, 1860, LP; Nathan M. Knapp to Hatch, March 12, 1860, Hatch Papers, ALPL; "A Bet Offered," *CPT*, March 15, 1860.

7. *Chicago Evening Journal*, March 31, 1860; unidentified newspaper clipping.

8. Galloway to Lincoln, March 15, 1860, LP; Trumbull to Lincoln, March 26, 1860, LP.

9. S. S. McClure, "Recollections of Lincoln, Furnished by Joseph Medill," *Chicago Tribune*, April 21, 1895; "Our Washington Letter," *CPT*, March 28, 1860.

10. Lincoln to Galloway, March 24, 1860, *CW* 4:33–34.

11. Holzer, *Lincoln at Cooper Union*, p. 213; Melvin L. Hayes, *Mr. Lincoln Runs for President* (New York: Citadel Press, 1960), p. 25; "Lincoln's Speeches," *Erie Observer*, March 31, 1860.

12. Lincoln to McNeill, April 6, 1860, *CW* 4:38; Miers, *Lincoln Day by Day*, vol. 2, p. 276.

13. Quote from Lincoln to McNeill, April 6, 1860, *CW* 4:38.

14. "The Sand Bar Cases," *CPT*, March 26, 1860.

15. "More Snow," *Chicago Evening Journal*, March 26, 1860; Lincoln to Lamon, March 28, 1860, *CW* 4:34–35.

16. Whitney, *Life on the Circuit*, pp. 53, 86–88. Whitney misidentified it as Rumsey and Newcomb's minstrels, but contemporary accounts identify the troupe as Hooley & Campbell's Minstrels, performing six days, March 21–27, 1860 (*CPT*, March 19 and 27, 1860).

17. "Personal," *Chicago Evening Journal*, March 29, 1860; Whitney, *Life on the Circuit*, pp. 539–45; "Art Matters in Chicago," *Chicago Tribune*, April 1, 1888.

18. "Gov. Seward, His Friends and His Enemies," *CPT*, April 2, 1860; Judd to Trumbull, April 2, 1860, Trumbull Papers, LOC.

19. Davis to Lincoln, May 5, 1860, and Wentworth to Lincoln, April 21, 1860, LP.

20. "Hon. Abraham Lincoln at Waukegan," *Waukegan Weekly Gazette*, April 7, 1860; J. Seymour Currey, *Chicago: Its History and Builders* (Chicago: S. J. Clarke Publishing, 1912), vol. 2, pp. 73–75.

21. J. Seymour Currey, *Abraham Lincoln's Visit to Evanston in 1860* (Evanston, Ill.: City National Bank, 1914), pp. 3–15.

22. "The Sand Bar Case," *CPT*, April 5, 1860.

23. Lincoln to John M. Carson, April 7, 1860, in *CW* 4:39; "Mr. Lincoln's Lecture," *ISJ*, April 28, 1860.

24. *Bloomington Statesman* report reproduced in *ISR*, April 17, 1860.

25. *Bloomington Pantagraph* report excerpted in "Mr. Lincoln at Bloomington," *CPT*, April 13, 1860.

26. Wentworth to Lincoln, April 21, 1860, LP.

27. Davis to Lincoln, April 27, 1860, LP; Medill to Trumbull, April 18, 1860, Lyman Trumbull Papers, LOC.

28. Davis to Lincoln, April 27, 1860, LP.

29. David Davis interview, September 20, 1866, *HI*, p. 348.

30. Wendell to Weed, April 18, 1860, Thurlow Weed Papers, LOC.

31. Lincoln to Richard M. Corwine, May 2, 1860, *CW* 4:47; Baringer, *Lincoln's Rise to Power*, p. 170 (n2).

32. "The County Convention," *CPT*, April 30, 1860; Judd to Hatch, April 10, 1860, Hatch Papers, ALPL.

33. "The County Convention," *CPT*, April 30, 1860; "Cook County Republican Convention," *CPT*, May 1, 1860; Judd to Hatch, April 10, 1860, Hatch Papers, ALPL.
34. Wentworth to Lincoln, [April] 30, 1860, LP.
35. John Hay diary, October 17, 1861, in Burlingame, *Inside Lincoln's White House*, p. 26. See also Judd to Lincoln, May 2, 1860, LP.
36. Davis to Lincoln, May 5, 1860, LP.
37. Judd to Lincoln, May 2, 1860, LP.
38. Trumbull to McLean, April 21, 1860, McLean Papers, LOC.
39. Trumbull to Lincoln, April 24, 1860, LP.
40. Judd to Lincoln, May 2, 1860, LP.
41. Lincoln to Trumbull, April 29, 1860, *CW* 4:45.

NINE: THE RAIL SPLITTER

1. Description of wigwam in "Appearance of 'Wigwam' of 1860," *Decatur Sunday Review*, June 13, 1915.
2. James T. Hickey, "Oglesby's Fence Rail Dealings and the 1860 Decatur Convention," *Journal of the Illinois State Historical Society* 54, no. 1 (Spring 1861): pp. 5–10. For the best modern study of Oglesby's career, see Mark A. Plummer, *Lincoln's Railsplitter: Governor Richard J. Oglesby* (Urbana and Chicago: University of Illinois Press, 2001).
3. Richard J. Oglesby, "Origin of the Rail-Splitter Legend," in Rufus Rockwell Wilson, *Lincoln Among His Friends: A Sheaf of Intimate Memories* (Caldwell, Idaho: Caxton Printers, 1942), pp. 191–94. John Hanks claimed that he originated the idea of securing the rails. See *ISJ*, July 16, 1860.
4. Oglesby, "Origin of the Rail-Splitter Legend," p. 192; "Viator" to the editor, May 4, 1860, *ISJ*, May 8, 1860.
5. Otto R. Kyle, *Abraham Lincoln in Decatur* (New York: Vantage Press, 1957), pp. 107–8.
6. Johnson to Herndon, 1865–66, in *HI*, pp. 462–63; "When Joe Cannon Met Lincoln," in Wilson, *Lincoln Among His Friends*, p. 186.
7. Oglesby, "Origin of the Rail-Splitter Legend," pp. 192–93; Johnson to Herndon, *HI*, pp. 462–63; "When Joe Cannon Met Lincoln," p. 186.
8. "Viator" to the editor, *ISJ*, May 10, 1860.
9. "Ex-Sheriff Jennings, 85 Years Old, Recalls Famous Bits of History," *Decatur Review*, October 23, 1910.
10. This version of the inscription agrees most closely with accounts published in the *[Macon] Illinois Gazette* on May 18, 1860, and the *Chicago Daily Journal* on May 10, 1860. A more frequently cited version of the banner inscription appears in *ISJ* on May 11, 1860, one that uses the phrase "For President" instead of "Of the People" and misnames Hanks as "Thos. Hanks," inverting the order of names on the banner. This version is rejected here for two reasons: it is extremely unlikely both that John Hanks's first name would be incorrectly placed on a banner that *he* was destined to carry into the Wigwam, and that his name would appear before Lincoln's in regards to the rails.
11. "Recollections of Judge Franklin Blades," in Paul M. Angle, ed., *Abraham Lincoln by Some Men Who Knew Him* (Freeport, N.Y.: Books for Libraries Press, 1969), p. 82. Johnson to Herndon, 1865–66, in *HI*, pp. 462–63.

12. "Recollections of Judge Franklin Blades," p. 82; "When Joe Cannon Met Lincoln," pp. 186–87. Although Joe Cannon claimed in 1907 that Lincoln was carried to the platform *after* the rails were brought into the Wigwam, contemporary accounts place him on the platform before this. See "Illinois Republican State Convention," *Chicago Daily Journal*, May 10, 1860.

13. Johnson to Herndon, 1865–66, in *HI*, p. 463.

14. "Republican Convention," *Carrollton Gazette*, May 12, 1860.

15. Fehrenbacher, *Chicago Giant*, p. 179; "State Convention," *Aurora Beacon*, May 10, 1860; "Two Notable Days in Decatur History: Anniversary of Lincoln-Yates Convention," *Decatur Semi-Weekly Herald*, May 10, 1903.

16. *Aurora Beacon*, May 17, 1860; *Waukegan Gazette*, May 12, 1860.

17. "Illinois Republican State Convention," *Chicago Daily Journal*, May 10, 1860; "The State Convention," *Bloomington Pantagraph*, May 16, 1860.

18. Isaac N. Arnold, *The Life of Abraham Lincoln* (Chicago: Jansen, McClurg, 1885), p. 163; Kyle, *Abraham Lincoln in Decatur*, p. 107.

19. "Illinois Republican State Convention," *Chicago Daily Journal*, May 11, 1860.

20. "Hon. N. B. Judd," *ISJ*, May 15, 1860; "The State Convention," *Bloomington Pantagraph*, May 16, 1860.

21. For three different sources of the quote, see Leonard Swett to Josiah H. Drummond, May 27, 1860, published in the *Bloomington Pantagraph*, January 8, 1909; Wilson, *Intimate Memories of Lincoln*, p. 294; Rice, *Reminiscences of Abraham Lincoln by Distinguished Men of His Time*, p. 209.

22. *Harper's Weekly Illustrated Newspaper*, May 12, 1860; Allen C. Guelzo, *Abraham Lincoln: Redeemer President* (Grand Rapids, Mich.: Eerdmans, 1999), p. 243.

23. Lincoln to Delahay, May 12, 1860, *CW* 4:49.

TEN: CONVENTION WEEK

1. Davis to Hatch, May 4, 1860, Hatch Papers, ALPL.

2. Quote from Gustave Koerner in David Davis biographical notes, Harry E. Pratt Collection, ALPL.

3. King, *Lincoln's Manager*, p. 135; Leonard Swett, "Lincoln and Weed," *CPT*, July 14, 1878.

4. Delahay to Lincoln, May 13, 1860, Dubois to Lincoln, May 13, 1860, and William Butler to Lincoln, May 14, 1860, LP; Pierce to Chase, May 13, 1860, in Niven, *The Papers of Salmon P. Chase*, vol. 3, p. 27.

5. Pierce to Chase, May 13, 1860, in Niven, *The Papers of Salmon P. Chase*, vol. 3, p. 27.

6. Perley Orman Ray, *The Convention That Nominated Lincoln* (Chicago: University of Chicago Press, 1916), p. 12.

7. Delahay to Lincoln, May 13, 1860, Dubois to Lincoln, May 13, 1860, and William Butler to Lincoln, May 14, 1860, LP.

8. "Electoral Vote of States Represented at Chicago," *Cincinnati Daily Commercial*, May 14, 1860; "The Chicago Convention," *Bloomington Pantagraph*, May 9, 1860. The one-hundred-vote goal was revealed in a letter written a little over a week after the convention by Leonard Swett. (See Osborn H. Oldroyd, *Lincoln's Campaign, or the Political Revolution of 1860* [Chicago: Laird and Lee, 1896], p. 71.) Although he did not specify, it is assumed Swett referred to one hundred delegate votes rather than one hundred electoral votes.

9. Oldroyd, *Lincoln's Campaign*, p. 71; Delahay to Lincoln, May 14, 1860, and Knapp to Lincoln, May 14, 1860, LP; Kenneth M. Stampp, *The Imperiled Union: Essays on the Background of the Civil War* (Oxford and New York: Oxford University Press, 1980), p. 158.

10. Ray, *The Convention That Nominated Lincoln*, p. 11.

11. "Chicago" to the editor, May 15, 1860, *Philadelphia Press*, May 16, 1860; M. H. to the editor, May 14, 1860, *Cincinnati Daily Commercial*, May 17, 1860; J. McCann Davis, *How Abraham Lincoln Became President* (Springfield, Ill.: Press of the Henry O. Shepard Co., 1908), pp. 63–64.

12. Baringer, *Lincoln's Rise to Power*, p. 213; "William H. Seward and the National Convention," *Chicago Daily Journal*, May 14, 1860; "William H. Seward," *Chicago Daily Journal*, May 15, 1860; Butler to Lincoln, May 15, 1860, LP.

13. *Chicago Weekly Democrat*, May 12 and 19, 1860; Fehrenbacher, *Chicago Giant*, pp. 178–79; Medill to Lincoln, August 9, 1860, LP; Delahay to Lincoln, May 15, 1860, LP.

14. Judd to Lincoln, May 28, 1860, and Davis to Lincoln, October 5, 1860, LP; Davis, *How Abraham Lincoln Became President*, p. 65.

15. "The Chicago Convention," *ISR*, May 17, 1860. Excerpt of *Press and Tribune* published in *Cincinnati Daily Gazette*, May 15, 1860.

16. Charles Ray to Lincoln, May 14, 1860, LP.

17. Donald, *Lincoln*, p. 249; Caleb B. Smith to David Davis, January 13 and February 5, 1861, David Davis Papers, ALPL. In the second letter, Smith reiterated, "The Republicans of Ind. would feel greatly agrieved [*sic*] by the neglect of the state." Both letters bear evidence of an expectation more than a pledge or a bargain made for their support of Lincoln.

18. Hermann Kreismann to Elihu Washburne, May 15, 1862, Washburne Papers, LOC; "Chicago" to the editor, May 15, 1860, *Philadelphia Press*, May 16, 1860; M. H. to the editor, *Cincinnati Daily Commercial*, May 17, 1860.

19. Browning diary, May 15, 1860, pp. 406–407; David Davis interview, September 20, 1866, *HI*, p. 348.

20. David Davis interview, September 20, 1866, *HI*, p. 348.

21. Palmer, *Personal Recollections*, p. 81.

22. Abram J. Dittenhoefer, *How We Elected Lincoln* (New York: Harper & Brothers, 1916), pp. 21–22; "The Greeley-Bates Circular," *Cincinnati Daily Commercial*, May 17, 1860; "On the Circuit of the Conventions," *Cincinnati Daily Commecial*, May 18, 1860; "Greeley at Chicago," *Cincinnati Daily Commercial*, May 25, 1860.

23. Davis, *How Abraham Lincoln Became President*, p. 67.

24. Baringer, *Lincoln's Rise to Power*, p. 222; Butler to Lincoln, May 15, 1860, LP; M. H. to the editor, May 17, 1860, *Cincinnati Daily Commercial*, May 19, 1860. The reporter was Murat Halstead, who had reported on the Charleston convention before the Democrats dissolved it at the end of April.

25. M. H. to the editor, May 15, 1860, *Cincinnati Daily Commercial*, May 18, 1860; Ray, *The Convention That Nominated Lincoln*, p. 11.

26. "The Great Wigwam," *CPT*, May 14, 1860; Currey, *Chicago: Its History and Its Builders*, p. 92; M. H. to the editor, May 15, 1860, *Cincinnati: Daily Commercial*, May 18, 1860; Ray, *The Convention That Nominated Lincoln*, p. 11.

27. "The Great Wigwam," *CPT*, May 14, 1860.

28. Palmer, *Personal Recollections*, p. 81; Hermann Kreismann to Elihu Washburne, May 13, 1860, Washburne Papers, LOC; Baringer, *Lincoln's Rise to Power*, p. 218.

29. "Half Fare," *Waukegan Gazette*, May 12, 1860; "Half Fare to Chicago," *ISJ*, May 12, 1860; Oldroyd, *Lincoln's Campaign*, p. 71.

30. "Conversation with N. B. Judd, . . . Feb. 28, 1876," in Burlingame, *An Oral History of Abraham Lincoln*, pp. 46–47. Judd's quote to his wife reproduced in "How Lincoln Was Nominated," *Chicago Tribune*, July 11, 1888.

31. All telegrams sent May 15–16, in LP.

32. Stampp, *The Imperiled Union*, pp. 143–46; Browning diary, May 16, 1860, p. 407; "The Chicago Convention," *Baltimore Sun*, May 17, 1860.

33. Delahay to Lincoln, May 16, 1860, LP; Edward Chase to Salmon P. Chase, May 21, 1860, in Niven, *The Salmon P. Chase Papers*, vol. 3, p. 29.

34. Butler to Lincoln, May 16, 1860, LP.

35. "Republican National Convention," *Aurora Beacon*, May 20, 1860.

36. Ibid.

37. Glyndon G. Van Deusen, *Thurlow Weed: Wizard of the Lobby* (Boston: Little Brown, 1947), p. 251.

38. M. H., "Telegraphic," *Cincinnati Daily Commercial*, May 18, 1860.

39. "Defeat of Seward," *Cincinnati Daily Commercial*, May 21, 1860; Van Deusen, *Thurlow Weed*, p. 251.

40. Butler to Lincoln and Delahay to Lincoln, May 17, 1860, LP.

41. Herndon, *Life of Lincoln*, p. 374.

42. McClure, *Lincoln and Men of War-Times* (Philadelphia: The Times Publishing Co., 1892), pp. 34–36; Stanton L. Davis, *Pennsylvania Politics 1860–1863* (Cleveland: Western Reserve University, 1935), p. 105; Baringer, *Lincoln's Rise to Power*, p. 277; Charles Gibson, "Edward Bates," Missouri Historical Society Collections, January 1900, p. 55 (quote in Pratt notes, Harry E. Pratt Papers, ALPL).

43. Luthin, *The First Lincoln Campaign*, p. 158.

44. Casey's quote in Erwin S. Bradley, *Simon Cameron: Lincoln's Secretary of War* (Philadelphia: University of Pennsylvania Press, 1966), p. 151. Swett quotes taken from Rufus Rockwell Wilson, *Intimate Memories*, p. 296, and Leonard Swett, "Lincoln and Weed," *Chicago Tribune*, July 14, 1878. Perhaps no single nomination issue has generated more disagreement among historians than whether or not cabinet positions were promised in return for delegate votes for Lincoln. Advocates and dissenters are too numerous to tally here, but using criteria that combine primary evidence, logic, and known outcomes, the alleged bargains for votes from Indiana and Ohio do not hold up to historical scrutiny. Pennsylvania, on the other hand, appears to have been persuaded to vote for Lincoln largely because they believed Judge Davis had made a promise to them. This conclusion is based upon the aforementioned Casey letter (as close to a "smoking gun" as can be found on this issue); the actual vote of the Pennsylvanians on the second ballot compared to that of the wavering New Jersey delegates, who also had agreed to go to Lincoln on Thursday night but without a bargain (see chapter 11); and Judge Davis's telegram to Lincoln in the very early aftermath warning him, "Write no letters and make no promises until you see me" (Davis to Lincoln, May 18, 1860, LP), a telltale piece of evidence suggesting that Davis had made at least one

convention promise of which Lincoln was unaware. Together, these sources and outcomes argue strongly—too strongly to be discounted—that the Pennsylvania deal was
made.

45. Davis to Lincoln, May 17, 1860, LP.
46. "Defeat of Seward," *Cincinnati Daily Commercial*, May 21, 1860.

ELEVEN: THE WIGWAM

1. Herndon, *Life of Lincoln*, p. 374.
2. "Address of Richard Price Morgan," in Angle, *Abraham Lincoln by Some Men Who Knew Him*, p. 68.
3. Because of suspect testimony after the fact and accounts that seem to conflict, there exists considerable controversy regarding the sequence of events that Lincoln engaged in that morning. I have generally adopted the analysis and subsequent chronology provided by J. C. Thompson, "Where Did Mr. Lincoln First Receive the News of His Nomination? Did Mr. Lincoln Play Hand Ball?" Manuscript 2 (Springfield, Ill.: Lincoln Foundation, 1925), pp. 3–15 (copy in ALPL).
4. Abner Ellis statement, January 23, 1866, *HI*, p. 174; Christopher Brown interviews, *HI*, pp. 437–38; Charles S. Zane statement, *HI*, p. 490. Zane claimed Lincoln entered the office "about nine oclock" that morning. Based on the sequence of previous and subsequent events, it appears to be half an hour later. The anecdote is not word for word, but a composite of two aforementioned accounts.
5. Christopher Brown interviews, *HI*, p. 438; Charles S. Zane statement, *HI*, p. 490.
6. Luthkin, *Lincoln's First Campaign*, p. 161.
7. This ticket story has been considered apocryphal and too unreliable to be universally accepted in the Lincoln literature. The original source is from a letter written by Henry C. Fell (son of Jesse Fell) to his sisters on February 10, 1909 (reproduced in Luthkin, *Lincoln's First Campaign*, p. 161. Although the source is a secondary one from fifty years after the fact, its accuracy should be reevaluated. It is inconceivable that the son of Jesse Fell made up the story, so the reliability lies with its originator, Jesse Fell (who must have relayed this story to his son). I have deemed this story feasible based on four premises: (1) Jesse Fell could have embellished it but would have had no reason to fabricate the entire account to his son; (2) Jesse Fell was in a position and had the skills to oversee the production of these tickets; (3) it is logical to conclude that members of the Republican State Central Committee would have taken advantage of their roles as the hosts to tweak the system in favor of the home crowd, particularly to offset what they feared were extra tickets carried by the Seward supporters; and (4) there apparently was a disproportionately large pro-Lincoln crowd in the building on Friday, which would have been the natural side effect of the additional tickets.
8. Cole, *The Era of the Civil War*, pp. 192–93; "Defeat of Seward," *Cincinnati Daily Commercial*, May 21, 1860; Luthin, *The First Lincoln Campaign*, pp. 160–61.
9. Farnsworth to Washburne, May 18, 1860, Washburne Papers, LOC; "Defeat of Seward," *Cincinnati Daily Commercial*, May 21, 1860.
10. Caleb Smith to David Davis, January 13, 1861, Davis Papers, ALPL. Interestingly, the same delegate would vehemently oppose a cabinet position for Caleb Smith in Lincoln's administration.

11. Ibid.; Swett to Drummond, May 27, 1860, in Oldroyd, *Lincoln's Campaign*, p. 72.

12. "Defeat of Seward," *Cincinnati Daily Commercial*, May 21, 1860; "Had to Prod Up Lincoln," *Chicago Tribune*, September 5, 1891; Edwin O. Gale, *Reminiscences of Early Chicago and Vicinity* (Chicago: Fleming H. Revell, 1902), p. 400; Currey, *Chicago: Its History and Its Builders*, p. 95.

13. "Defeat of Seward," *Cincinnati Daily Commercial*, May 21, 1860; "Had to Prod Up Lincoln," *Chicago Tribune*, September 5, 1891.

14. "Regular Report of the Proceedings," *New York Tribune*, May 19, 1860.

15. "Defeat of Seward," *Cincinnati Daily Commercial*, May 21, 1860; Swett to Drummond, May 27, 1860, in Oldroyd, *Lincoln's Campaign*, p. 72; "Had to Prod Up Lincoln," *Chicago Tribune*, September 5, 1891.

16. "Regular Report of the Proceedings," *New York Tribune*, May 19, 1860; "Republican National Convention," *Cincinnati Daily Commercial*, May 19, 1860; "Defeat of Seward," *Cincinnati Daily Commercial*, May 21, 1860.

17. The time is estimated. Ballot totals here and in subsequent paragraphs obtained from *Cincinnati Daily Commercial*, May 19, 1860, and *Aurora Beacon*, May 24, 1860.

18. Charles Zane statement, 1865–66, in *HI*, p. 491.

19. Joseph Medill account in Matilda Gresham, *Life of Walter Quinton Gresham, 1832–1895* (Chicago: Rand McNally, 1919), vol. 2, p. 566.

20. "Defeat of Seward," *Cincinnati Daily Commercial*, May 21, 1860.

21. Ibid.; Gresham, *Life of Walter Quinton Gresham*, p. 566.

22. "Defeat of Seward," *Cincinnati Daily Commercial*, May 21, 1860; "Had to Prod Up Lincoln," *Chicago Tribune*, September 5, 1891. Joseph Medill claims that by sitting next to Cartter during the balloting, he convinced him to switch those four votes to Lincoln in exchange for a cabinet position for Salmon P. Chase. (See MacMillan, "Recollections of Lincoln, Furnished by Joseph Medill," *Chicago Tribune*, April 21, 1895.) Medill's claim is often-cited, but is so suspect as to be discounted here, for it would have required Cartter to change four votes on his own, phantom ballots not linked to any specific delegate. In fact, the names of the four Ohioans who announced their switch to Cartter have been identified. See "A Chess Player's Vantage. How a Quick Perception Gave Votes to Abraham Lincoln," *New York Times*, May 29, 1887.

23. "Defeat of Seward," *Cincinnati Daily Commercial*, May 21, 1860; "Had to Prod Up Lincoln," *Chicago Tribune*, September 5, 1891; Gerry W. Hazelton, *Lincoln and the Convention of 1860* (Tarrytown, N.Y.: William Abbott, 1917), p. 96; "A Chess Player's Advantage," *New York Times*, May 29, 1887.

24. "Republican National Convention," *Cincinnati Daily Commercial*, May 19, 1860.

25. Quote from a letter from Jesse Fell to an unidentified senator, in J. H. Burnham, comp., *History of Bloomington and Normal, in McLean County, Illinois* (Bloomington, Ill.: J. H. Burnham, 1879), p. 106.

26. Fell to Lincoln, May 18, 1860, LP.

TWELVE: THE NOMINEE

1. "Where Did Lincoln First Receive the News of His Nomination?" pp. 8–11; Charles Zane statement, *HI*, p. 491.

2. Charles Zane Statement, *HI*, p. 491.

3. Ibid.; C. S. to the editor, May 19, 1860, *Aurora Beacon*, May 24, 1860.

4. C. S. to the editor, May 19, 1860, *Aurora Beacon*, May 24, 1860; John Hay to the editor, May 21, 1860, in Burlingame, *Lincoln's Journalist*, p. 1.

5. Burlingame, *Lincoln's Journalist,* pp. 2–3; C.S. to the editor, May 19, 1860, *Aurora Beacon*, May 24, 1860; "Nomination of Hon. A. Lincoln. Exciting Time in Springfield," *ISJ*, May 19, 1860.

6. Knapp to Lincoln, May 18, 1860, Delahay to Lincoln, May 18, 1860, Wentworth to Lincoln, May 18, 1860, and Davis to Lincoln, May 18, 1860, LP.

7. C. S. to the editor, May 19, 1860, *Aurora Beacon*, May 24, 1860.

8. Koerner, *Memoirs*, p. 94.

9. "How Old Abe Received the News," *CPT*, May 22, 1860; Paul M. Angle, *"Here I Have Lived": A History of Lincoln's Springfield* (Chicago: Abraham Lincoln Book Shop, 1971), pp. 238–39.

10. "How Old Abe Received the News," *CPT*, May 22, 1860.

11. List of buyers and number of rails in Oglesby Papers, ALPL.

12. Meeting of Republican State Central Committee," *CPT*, June 5, 1860; Mary Lincoln to Amos Tuck, June 4, 1860, in Thomas F. Schwartz and Anne V. Shaughnessy, "Unpublished Mary Lincoln Letters," http://www.historycooperative.org/journals/jala/11/schwartz.html.

13. Fehrenbacher and Fehrenbacher, *Recollected Words of Abraham Lincoln,* p. 76; John Hay diary, November 22, 1862, in Burlingame and Ettlinger, *Inside Lincoln's White House*, p. 116.

14. Henry to Lincoln, February 16, 1859, LP; Lincoln to Henry, July 4, 1860, *CW* 4: 82.

BIBLIOGRAPHY

MANUSCRIPT COLLECTIONS

Abraham Lincoln Presidential Library, Springfield, Illinois
David Davis Papers.
Ozias M. Hatch Papers.
Norman B. Judd Papers.
Lincoln Legal Papers.
Richard Oglesby Papers.
Harry E. Pratt Papers.
Orville Hickman Browning letter to Charles Gibson, February 8, 1860.
J. C. Thompson, "Where Did Mr. Lincoln First Receive the News of His Nomination? Did Mr. Lincoln Play Hand Ball?" Manuscript 2. Springfield, Ill.: Lincoln Foundation, 1925.

Library of Congress, Manuscript Division, Washington, D.C.
Jesse W. Fell Papers.
Abraham Lincoln Papers.
John McLean Papers.
Lyman Trumbull Papers.
Elihu B. Washburne Papers.
Thurlow Weed Papers.

New York Public Library, New York City
Horace Greeley Papers.

BOOKS

Angle, Paul M., ed. *Abraham Lincoln by Some Men Who Knew Him.* Freeport, N.Y.: Books for Libraries Press, 1969.

———. *"Here I Have Lived": A History of Lincoln's Springfield.* Chicago: Abraham Lincoln Book Shop, 1971.

Arnold, Isaac N. *The Life of Abraham Lincoln.* Chicago: Jansen, McClurg, 1885.

Ayres, Carol Dark. *Lincoln and Kansas: Partnership for Freedom.* Manhattan, Kans.: Sunflower University Press, 2001.

Baker, George, ed. *The Works of William H. Seward.* 4 vols. Boston: Houghton Mifflin, 1884.

Baringer, William E. *Lincoln's Rise to Power.* Boston: Little, Brown, 1937.

Basler, Roy P., ed. *The Collected Works of Abraham Lincoln.* 8 vols. New Bruswick, N.J.: Rutgers University Press, 1953–55.

Basler, Roy P., and Christian Basler, eds. *The Collected Works of Abraham Lincoln, 1832–1865.* 2 suppls. New Bruswick, N.J.: Rutgers University Press, 1990.

Biographical Sketches of the Leading Men of Chicago. Chicago: Wilson & St. Clair, 1868.

Bonham, Jeriah. *Fifty Years' Recollections with Observations and Reflections on Historical Events.* Peoria, Ill.: J. W. Franks & Sons, 1883.

Bradley, Erwin S. *Simon Cameron: Lincoln's Secretary of War.* Philadelphia: University of Pennsylvania Press, 1966.

Browne, Francis Fisher. *The Every-day Life of Abraham Lincoln: A Narrative and Descriptive Biography with Pen-Pictures and Personal Recollections by Those Who Knew Him.* Chicago: Browne & Howell, 1913.

Burlingame, Michael. *The Inner World of Abraham Lincoln.* Urbana and Chicago: University of Illinois Press, 1994.

———, ed. *Lincoln's Journalist: John Hay's Anonymous Writings for the Press, 1860–1864.* Carbondale: Southern Illinois University Press, 1998.

———, ed. *An Oral History of Abraham Lincoln: John G. Nicolay's Interviews and Essays.* Carbondale: Southern Illinois University Press, 1996.

Burlingame, Michael, and John R. Turner Ettlinger, eds. *Inside Lincoln's White House: The Complete Civil War Diary of John Hay.* Carbondale: Southern Illinois University Press, 1997.

Burnham, J. H., comp. *History of Bloomington and Normal, in McLean County, Illinois.* Bloomington, Ill.: J. H. Burnham, 1879.

Carnegie, Dale. *Lincoln the Unknown.* New York: Century Company, 1932.

Carpenter, Francis B. *Six Months at the White House with President Lincoln: The Story of a Picture.* New York: Hurd & Houghton, 1866.

Cole, Arthur Charles. *The Era of the Civil War.* Springfield: Illinois Centennial Commission, 1919.

Currey, J. Seymour. *Chicago: Its History and Builders.* 5 vols. Chicago: S. J. Clarke Publishing, 1912.

Davis, J. McCan. *How Abraham Lincoln Became President.* Springfield, Ill.: Press of the Henry O. Shepard Co., 1908.

Davis, Stanton L. *Pennsylvania Politics 1860–1863.* Cleveland: Western Reserve University, 1935.

Dittenhoefer, Abram J. *How We Elected Lincoln.* New York: Harper & Brothers, 1916.

Dodge, Grenville M. *Personal Recollections of President Abraham Lincoln, General Ulysses S. Grant and General William T. Sherman*. Council Bluffs; Iowa: Monarch Printing, 1914.

Donald, David Herbert. *Lincoln*. New York: Simon & Schuster, 1995.

———. *Lincoln's Herndon: A Biography*. New York: Alfred A. Knopf, 1948.

Fehrenbacher, Donald E. *Chicago Giant: A Biography of "Long John" Wentworth*. Madison: The American History Research Center, 1957.

Fehrenbacher, Donald E., and Virginia Fehrenbacher, comps. and eds. *Recollected Words of Abraham Lincoln*. Stanford, Calif.: Stanford University Press, 1996.

Gale, Edwin O. *Reminiscences of Early Chicago and Vicinity*. Chicago: Fleming H. Revell, 1902.

Gary, Ralph. *Following in Mr. Lincoln's Footsteps: A Historical Reference to Hundreds of Sites Visited by Abraham Lincoln*. New York: Carroll & Graf, 2001.

Gresham, Matilda. *Life of Walter Quinton Gresham, 1832–1895*. 2 vols. Chicago: Rand McNally, 1919.

Guelzo, Allen C. *Abraham Lincoln: Redeemer President*. Grand Rapids, Mich.: Eerdmans, 1999.

———. *Lincoln and Douglas: The Debates that Defined America*. New York: Simon & Schuster, 2008.

Hayes, Melvin L. *Mr. Lincoln Runs for President*. New York: The Citadel Press, 1960.

Hazelton, Gerry W. *Lincoln and the Convention of 1860*. Tarrytown, N.Y.: William Abbott, 1917.

Herndon, William H., and Jesse W. Weik. *Herndon's Life of Lincoln*. Reprints, New York: Da Capo Press, 1983.

Hertz, Emanuel. *Abraham Lincoln: A New Portrait*. 2 vols. New York: Horace Liveright, 1931.

———. *The Hidden Lincoln: From the Letters and Papers of William H. Herndon*. New York: Blue Ribbon Books, 1940.

———, ed. *Lincoln Talks: A Biography in Anecdote*. New York: Viking Press, 1939.

Holzer, Harold. *Lincoln at Cooper Union: The Speech That Made Abraham Lincoln President*. New York: Simon & Schuster, 2004.

Hudson, Frederic, Alfred McClung Lee, and Frank Luther Mott. *American Journalism, 1690–1940*. New York: Routledge, 2000.

Jaffa, Harry V., and Robert W. Johannsen, eds. *In The Name of the People: Speeches and Writings of Lincoln and Douglas in the Ohio Campaign of 1859*. Columbus: Ohio State University Press, 1959.

Kenny, Daniel J. *The American Newspaper Directory and the Record of the Press*. New York: Watson & Co., 1861.

King, Willard L. *Lincoln's Manager: David Davis*. Cambridge, Mass.: Harvard University Press, 1960.

Kinsley, Philip. The Chicago Tribune: *Its First Hundred Years*. 3 vols. New York: Alfred A. Knopf, 1943–46.

Kirkland, Carol. *Chicago Yesterdays: A Sheaf of Reminiscences*. Chicago: Daughaday & Co., 1919.

Kyle, Otto R. *Abraham Lincoln in Decatur*. New York: Vantage Press, 1957.

Lamon, Ward H. *The Life of Abraham Lincoln: From His Birth to His Inauguration as President*. Boston: James R. Osgood, 1872.

Luthin, Reinhard H. *The First Lincoln Campaign*. Cambridge, Mass.: Harvard University Press, 1944.

McClure, Alexander K. *Abraham Lincoln and Men of War-Times*. Philadelphia: Times Publishing, 1872.

McCormack, Thomas J., ed. *Memoirs of Gustave Koerner, 1809–1896*. 2 vols. Cedar Rapids, Iowa: Torch Press, 1909.

McPherson, James M. *Battle Cry of Freedom: The Civil War Era*. New York and Oxford: Oxford University Press, 1988.

———. *This Mighty Scourge: Perspectives on the Civil War*. Oxford and New York: Oxford University Press, 2007.

Meredith, Roy. *Mr. Lincoln's Camera Man, Mathew B. Brady*. New York: Charles Scribner's Sons, 1946.

Miers, Earl Schenck, ed. *Lincoln Day by Day: A Chronology, 1809–1865*. 3 vols. Washington, D.C.: Lincoln Sesquicentennial Commission, 1960.

Niven, John. *Salmon P. Chase: A Biography*. New York: Oxford University Press, 1995.

———, ed. *The Salmon P. Chase Papers*. 5 vols. Kent, Ohio: Kent State University Press, 1996–98.

Oldroyd, Osborn H., ed. *The Lincoln Memorial: Album-Immortelles*. New York: G. W. Carleton, 1883.

Ostendorf, Lloyd. *Mr. Lincoln Came to Dayton*. Dayton: Otterbein Press, 1959.

Oswald, Harold G., and Garrison Villard, eds. *Lincoln on the Eve of '61: A Journalist's Story by Henry Villard*. Wesport, Conn.: Greenwood Press, 1940.

Page, Edward L. *Abraham Lincoln in New Hampshire*. Boston: Houghton Mifflin, 1929.

Palmer, John M. *Personal Recollections of John M. Palmer, the Story of an Earnest Life*. Cincinnati: Clarke Press, 1901.

Pease, Theodore C., and James G. Randall, eds. *The Diary of Orville Hickman Browning*. 2 vols. Springfield: Illinois State Historical Society, 1925–33.

Plummer, Mark A. *Lincoln's Railsplitter: Governor Richard J. Oglesby*. Urbana and Chicago: University of Illinois Press, 2001.

Pratt, Harry E., comp. *Concerning Mr. Lincoln, in Which Abraham Lincoln Is Pictured As He Appeared to Letter Writers of His Time*. Springfield, Ill.: Abraham Lincoln Association, 1944.

Pred, Allan R. *Urban Growth and City Systems in the United States, 1840–1860*. 2nd ed. Cambridge, Mass.: Harvard University Press, 1973.

Putnam, George Haven. *Memories of My Youth, 1844–1865*. New York: Knickerbocker Press, 1914.

Rankin, Henry B. *Intimate Character Sketches of Abraham Lincoln*. New York: J. B. Lippincott, 1924.

Ray, Perley Orman. *The Convention That Nominated Lincoln*. Chicago: University of Chicago Press, 1916.

Rice, Allen Thorndike. *Reminiscences of Abraham Lincoln by Distinguished Men of His Time*. New York, *North American Review*, 1888.

Richardson, Albert D. *The Secret Service, the Field, the Dungeon, and the Escape*. Hartford, Conn.: American Publishing Company, 1865.

Ryan, Daniel J. *Lincoln and Ohio*. Columbus: Ohio State Archaeological and Historical Society, 1923.

Sage, Harold K. *Jesse W. Fell and the Lincoln Autobiography*. Bloomington, Ill.: Smith Printing, 1971.

Stampp, Kenneth M. *The Imperiled Union: Essays on the Background of the Civil War*. Oxford and New York: Oxford University Press, 1980.

Stevens, Walter B. *A Reporter's Lincoln*. Lincoln: University of Nebraska Press, 1998.

Tarbell, Ida M. *The Life of Abraham Lincoln*. 2 vols. New York: Macmillan, 1917.

Temple, Sunderine (Wilson), and Wayne C. Temple. *Illinois' Fifth Capitol: The House That Lincoln Built and Caused to Be Rebuilt (1837–1865)*. Springfield, Ill.: Phillips Brothers, 1988.

Thornbrough, Gail, Dorothy L. Riker, and Paula Corpuz, eds. *The Diary of Calvin Fletcher, 1817–1866*. 9 vols. Indianapolis: Indiana Historical Society, 1972–83.

Turner, Justin G., and Linda Levitt Turner. *Mary Todd Lincoln: Her Life and Letters*. New York: Alfred A. Knopf, 1972.

Van Deusen, Glyndon G. *Thurlow Weed: Wizard of the Lobby*. Boston: Little, Brown, 1947.

Villard, Henry. *Memoirs of Henry Villard, Journalist and Financier, 1835–1900*. 2 vols. Boston: Houghton Mifflin, 1904.

Ward, William Hayes, ed. *Abraham Lincoln: Tributes from His Associates*. New York: Thomas Y. Crowell, 1895.

Weik, Jesse W. *The Real Lincoln: A Portrait*. Boston: Houghton Mifflin, 1922.

Whitney, Henry C. *Life on the Circuit with Lincoln*. Boston: Estes & Lauriat, 1892.

Wills, Garry. *Negro President: Jefferson and Slave Power*. Boston: Mariner Books, 2005.

Wilson, Douglas L. *Honor's Voice: The Transformation of Abraham Lincoln*. New York: Vintage Books, 1999.

Wilson, Douglas L., and Rodney O. Davis, eds. *Herndon's Informants: Letters, Interviews, and Statements About Abraham Lincoln*. Urbana and Chicago: University of Illinois Press, 1998.

Wilson, Rufus Rockwell, ed. *Intimate Memories of Lincoln*. Elmira, N.Y.: Primavera Press, 1945.

———, ed. *Lincoln Among His Friends: A Sheaf of Intimate Memories*. Caldwell, Idaho: Caxton Printers, 1942.

ARTICLES AND PAMPHLETS

Currey, J. Seymour. *Abraham Lincoln's Visit to Evanston in 1860*. Evanston, Ill.: City National Bank, 1914.

Dickson, W. M. "Abraham Lincoln at Cincinnati." *Harper's New Monthly Magazine*, June 1884, pp. 62–66.

Douglas, Stephen A. "Popular Sovereignty in the Territories." *Harper's New Monthly Magazine*, September 1859, pp. 519–37.

Farley, Alan W. "When Lincoln Came to Kansas Territory." Address presented to Fort Leavenworth Historical Society, November 17, 1959.

Gibson, Charles. "Edward Bates." Missouri Historical Society Collections, January 1900, pp. 52–56.

Hickey, James T. "Oglesby's Fence Rail Dealings and the 1860 Decatur Convention." *Journal of the Illinois State Historical Society* 54, no. 1 (Spring 1961): pp. 5–10.

Hitt, Robert R. "An Unpublished Speech of Abraham Lincoln." *North American Review*, July 1893, pp. 120–24.

Lincoln Fellowship of Wisconsin. "Lincoln Visits Beloit and Janesville, Wisconsin." Madison: Lincoln Fellowship of Wisconsin, 1949.

Williams, Frank J. "A Candidate Speaks in Rhode Island: Abraham Lincoln Visits Providence and Woonsocket, 1860." *Rhode Island History* 51, no. 4 (November 1993): pp. 109–20.

NEWSPAPERS

Alton Daily Courier, 1859.

Appleton Motor, 1859.

Aurora Beacon, 1859–1860.

Baltimore Sun, 1860.

Bloomington Daily Pantagraph, 1858–60.

Carrollton Gazette, 1860.

Chicago Daily Democrat, 1859–60.

Chicago Herald, 1859.

Chicago Journal, 1859–60.

Chicago Press and Tribune, 1859–60.

Chicago Tribune, 1878–95.

Chicago Weekly Democrat, 1859–60.

Cincinnati Daily Commercial, 1859.

Cincinnati Daily Gazette, 1860.

Clinton Transcript, 1859.

Coshocton [Ohio] County Democrat, 1859.

Council Bluffs Bugle, 1859.

Council Bluffs Nonpareil, 1859.

Dawson's Fort Wayne Times, 1860.

Decatur Review, 1910.

Decatur Semi-Weekly Herald, 1903.

Decatur Sunday Review, 1915.

Erie Observer, 1860.

Harper's Weekly Illustrated Newspaper, 1860.

Hartford Daily Courant, 1860.

Illinois State Journal, 1859–60.

Illinois State Register, 1859–60, 1909.

Indianapolis Atlas, 1859.

Indianapolis Journal, 1859.

Iowa City Citizen, 1909.

Iowa City Press-Citizen, 1925.

Janesville [Wisc.] Gazette, 1879.

Janesville *[Wisc.] Weekly Gazette and Free Press*, 1859.

Kansas City Star, 1902.

Lacrosse [Wisc.] Republican, 1859.

Leavenworth Daily Times, 1859.

Leavenworth Weekly Herald, 1859.

Lincoln [Ill.] Herald, 1859.

[Middletown, N.Y.] Banner of Liberty, 1859.

Milwaukee Sentinel, 1859.

New York Herald, 1860.

New York Times, 1859–60.

New York Tribune, 1860.

Ohio State Journal, 1859.

Philadelphia Press, 1860.

[Platteville, Wisc.] Grant County Witness, 1859.

Portland Weekly Oregonian, 1859.

Prescott [Wisc.] Transcript, 1859.

Springfield Daily Evening Independent, 1859.

Washington Post, 1883.

Waukegan Weekly Gazette, 1860.

[Wellsborough, Pa.] Agitator, 1859.

Whitewater [Wisc.] Register, 1860.

AUDIOTAPE

Zarefsky, David. *Abraham Lincoln in His Own Words*. Great Courses, Teaching Company Limited Partnership, 1999.

WORLD WIDE WEB

Schwartz, Thomas F., and Anne V. Shaughnessy. "Unpublished Mary Lincoln Letters." http://www.historycooperative.org/journals/jala/11/schwartz.html.

INDEX